C000318632

THE LEARNING CURVE

Quality: Total Customer Service

SUNDAY TIMES BUSINESS SKILLS

Other titles in the series:

QUALITY: CHANGE THROUGH TEAMWORK
Rani Chaudhry-Lawton, Richard Lawton, Karen Murphy & Angela Terry
ISBN 0-7126-9833-7

This book is packed with case studies from companies of all sizes in both public and private sectors, plus analysis and practical ideas for bringing about change by the use of teams.

QUALITY: ACHIEVING EXCELLENCE
Edgar Wille
ISBN 0-7126-9863-9

Total quality management is about people and attitudes; achieving excellence through quality often requires a total transformation of the way we do business. An examination of the ideas of the quality gurus is accompanied by lively and original case studies and detailed analysis to give a blueprint for organisations wanting to achieve a total quality environment.

TIME MANAGEMENT
Martin Scott
ISBN 0-7126-9853-1

This book helps the reader to become more organised – both mentally and physically – and to overcome the feeling of overload, replacing it with a sense of control by developing a system of structure and overview.

EFFECTIVE MEETINGS
Phil Hodgson & Jane Hodgson
ISBN 0-7126-9873-6

Meetings are the lifeblood of an organisation, and are one of the most frequently used methods of 'getting things done'. Yet they are often unsatisfactory. The authors bring a new approach to making meetings more effective by helping the reader to become his or her own meetings specialist.

Each book provides a definitive, standalone summary of best management practice and is carefully co-ordinated to complement *The Sunday Times* 'Business Skills' video training package of the same name.

To place an order for the books, please telephone 0279 427203. Copies of the books can also be bought or ordered from all good bookshops.

Companies, institutions and other organisations wishing to make bulk purchases of any of the books should contact:

Direct Sales Manager, Century Business,
Random Century House, 20 Vauxhall Bridge Road, London SW1V 2SA
(FAX: 071-828 6681)

For information about the video packages and/or to place an order, please telephone 0403 42727.

Quality: Total Customer Service

by

Lynda King Taylor

C

CENTURY
BUSINESS

First published in the UK 1992
by Century Business
An imprint of Random House UK Ltd
20 Vauxhall Bridge Road, London SW1V 2SA

Random House Australia (Pty) Ltd
20 Alfred Street, Milsons Point
Sydney, NSW 2061, Australia

Random House New Zealand Ltd
18 Poland Road, Glenfield
Auckland 10, New Zealand

Random House South Africa (Pty) Ltd
PO Box 337, Bergvlei, South Africa

Reprinted 1992

Filmset by SX Composing Ltd, Rayleigh, Essex
Printed and bound in Great Britain by
Mackays of Chatham PLC, Kent

A catalogue record for this book is available from the British Library.

ISBN 0–7126–9843–6

Contents

Acknowledgements

I am so very grateful to all of those I worked alongside in the ten organisations illustrated in this book. Without them, there would be no book, and particular thanks are highlighted below. Apart from anything else, they all ensured that I enjoyed my time within their organisations, and, knowing my pressures, pulled out all stops to help me meet my deadlines. Thank you.

A book such as this does not happen without two vital supporters, those who key in my words, and my editor. Lucy Spencer, of the Computer Training Agency in Hatfield was the former, and she gave total customer service in her devotion to the project. Debby Gilby was also very helpful, and Sam and Marion gave their time when the deadlines were descending. My editor, Elizabeth Hennessy, knew from instinct when to motivate, and her team at Century Business are the most professional I have ever worked alongside. I am grateful to Sean Marriott for his copy editing skills. I would also like to thank Tony Buzan for personally teaching me mind power. His 'mind mapping' technique was the tool which enabled me to compose and complete a manuscript to a very tight deadline. I've become a devoted fan! To all of you, my many thanks.

There are others who support in different ways, family and friends who appreciate the stress of working to daunting deadlines and who are, quite simply, fantastic in their feedback. Too many to mention by name, this is to let you know how much I thank you all. Without your caring and kindnesses, there would be no book. I dedicate my book to you all, and especially to Crystal and Ashley.

Within the ten organisations illustrated, Lynda King Taylor would especially like to thank:

Texaco UK
. . . everyone whom I worked alongside within Texaco UK and who have helped enormously with this study, many of whom are mentioned in the text. Paul Ruggier, Peter Maneri and Peter Hughes were most helpful on organisation and managing major logistics. A further thank you goes to Barry Ashman for much support and direction. A special thank you is also due to all the managers, teams and service station staff for all their help.

Digital UK
. . . all those mentioned in the case study for their help and support while working at Digital. Mike Newell and David Jackson deserve thanks for their time and discussions.

I am very grateful to the Digital Equipment Company for allowing me access to documentation, and for being able to quote from its detailed research, in particular, its survey 'Service – The Role of Information Technology'. If readers would like more details on this survey, do contact David Jackson at Digital Equipment Company on Basingstoke 0256-843333.

I would particularly like to thank Ron Down – Customer Care Manager – and his team for managing the logistics and the many staff within Digital UK who have given such service excellence.

British Gas – South Eastern Region
. . . everyone who worked alongside me in British Gas, most of whom have been acknowledged in this case study. However, Ralph Ellis, operations director of British Gas – South Eastern gave me excellent service facilities during my time in the region, as did Colin Stevens, General Manager of British Gas – South Eastern, and all of his team at Crawley district. A thank you also to Peter Ashdown at British Gas's total quality project team and Bob Duncalf, Marketing Operations Manager, in London, who co-ordinated my activities, and were very helpful with the logistics.

The Metropolitan Police Service

. . . the Commissioner of the Metropolitan Police Service, Sir Peter Imbert QPM, for allowing me every access within the Service, in order to produce this study. I was given every encourgement to go wherever I wanted within The Metropolitan Police, to talk to anyone I wished to, at what ever level I chose.

I am most grateful to all those who gave me both their time and frank conversation during my work within The Metropolitan Police Service. The openness of the Service has been admirable, and one doubts if this would have been possible before The Metropolitan Police Service's PLUS programme! It certainly would not have been possible without the tremendous customer service afforded to me by the PLUS team. In particular I would like to thank Chief Inspector Tony Brooking, who organised all orchestration and managed the production pressures without one word of complaint.

I would also like to thank Assistant Commissioner Peter Winship for giving me his time during a most hectic schedule. Commander Des Flanders of 5 Area and Commander David Kendrick of 2 Area offered me much help when I was working within their Areas. I was most appreciative of Commander Flanders allowing me to attend his Area meeting and to Commander Kendrick for allowing me access to his team at City Road. Hendon Police College were enormously helpful with this study, giving me much time and support; nothing was too much trouble and I thank Commander John Grieve and his team.

I am also grateful to Dr David Hickman, who was the PLUS Component One Manager, and representative of all the trade unions on the PLUS programme. He was particularly informative, especially with issues that concerned civilian staff.

Finally, I would like to very much thank those at Divisional level who were especially helpful to this study. In particular, my appreciation to Chief Superintendent Gerry McBride and Detective Chief Inspector Heather Penna, who gave me much of their time within 8 Area at Paddington Green Division. Thank you also to Inspector Paul Ramsay, Sergeant Andy Norfolk; Detective Sergeant David Hills, of CID, was especially generous with his time. Inspector Paul

Holmes was a great help on the logistics. Paddington Green have every right to be proud of the many members of their team that I talked with and who constantly provide such a high standard of customer service. Thank you.

Sutcliffe Catering Group
. . . all of those at Sutcliffe Catering whom I worked alongside, particularly those mentioned in the case study. Special thanks also go to Carolyn Rynish of GCI Sterling who co-ordinated all of my work programme. Thanks go to the many Sutcliffe Catering Group staff who work with the clients and customers, and, in particular, those working and serving at Sutcliffe's client, British Airways, at London's Heathrow Airport. A special mention goes to Ian Mitchell, Sutcliffe's General Manager at London Heathrow, and Graeme Thomas, Senior Manager Restaurants and Clubs, British Airways who both gave me much of their time and enthusiasm during a particularly busy period of the year – Christmas! Don Davenport and Frank Whittaker have been enormously supportive and I am most grateful.

Hyatt Carlton Tower Hotel
. . . Michael Gray, General Manager at the Hyatt Carlton Tower and Vicky Brooke, Director of Human Resources for all their time, support and service. I would also like to thank Nicola Hancock, Director of Marketing Communications Europe, Africa and Middle East at Hyatt International Hotels. Nicky was extremely helpful in organising the logistics, and responding to my numerous queries directed to the USA with all speed. A special mention must go to all of the staff who work in the Hyatt Carlton Tower and who do so much to make customers *want* to return.

Portman Building Society
. . . John Gully, Head of Corporate Affairs, and his team in Bournemouth, Dorset, England, for all their help. Also, John Clarke, General Manager – Marketing and Corporate Affairs, and Pauline Clenshaw, Head of Training and Development gave much time and effort, and which is most appreciated.

A special thank you goes to those staff within the Society who give such customer service excellence. In particular, to those at the Portman Square Branch in central London who have consistently shown the 'high level of customer service' referred to in their Society's mission statement.

National Health Service – Hastings
. . . David Townsley, Acting Chief Executive, who allowed me every facility within Hastings. Special acknowledgements go to Dilly Millward. Dilly did much sterling work as Clinical Services Manager at St Mary's teaching hospital in central London before continuing her challenges within Hastings as their Director of Nursing and Quality Assurance. She was responsible for organising all of the logistics for my work within the health service and worked long hours alongside me to ensure our task was completed. I am most appreciative of such excellent customer service. I would also like to thank all of the staff who constantly strive, sometimes under very difficult conditions, to maintain high standards of quality and patient care for their customers, some of whom are mentioned in the study.

Dell Computer Corporation UK
. . . all those mentioned in the case study for their help and enthusiasm whilst I was at Dell UK. Ray Ursell, Head of Customer Services and Claire Allen, Human Resources Director, were most generous with their time. I would also like to thank both Sarah Howe and Michele Bayliss from GCI Sterling, who were most kind in organising the logistics, and always answering my calls, by return.

Simon Access
. . . very many people within the Simon Access Division and at Simon-Dudley, in particular Alan Tilley, Managing Director, Simon Access International, Malcolm Parkinson, Managing Director, Simon-Dudley, and to his team at the Dudley manufacturing plant, who kindly worked alongside me, especially during the Christmas period when they should have been enjoying the festivities!

I would like to thank the West Midlands Fire Brigade who are a major customer of Simon Access Division and Simon-Dudley who also gave their time to co-operate with this study. A thank you also to David Dowse of Royal Crescent PR in Cheltenham who was primarily responsible for managing all the logistics ranging from helicopter flights to multi-meetings.

A special thank you goes to John Barker, Managing Director of Simon Access Division, who ensured that everyone in his Division gave me such enthusiastic customer service.

Lynda King Taylor
London 1992

Foreword

First, what this book is not! It is not an academic treatise on the theory of quality or total customer service. There are no hard and fast textbook rules or quick fixes for introducing customer service programmes into an organisation. There are, however, ways of introducing change programmes that are wrong, or are doomed to failure. That is what this book concerns itself with, illustrating, as it does, the lessons learnt within ten very different organisations attempting to improve their quality service to customers and the general public.

In a *Sunday Times*/MORI poll undertaken in early 1992 – to accompany the launch of the video *Quality: Total Customer Service* to which this book is linked – more than 90 per cent of senior managers from some 200 UK companies indicated that customer service excellence was a clear priority in the boardroom. However, the method of achieving it was less clear. Only 58 per cent of the companies interviewed, with between 25 and 500 employees, had what they believe to be some sort of customer service progamme, and seven in ten of those – even higher (77 per cent) in larger companies – recognise it could be enhanced and upgraded. Even among those companies who felt their customer service programme to be very effective, some two-thirds, 66 per cent, said it could be 'much improved'. Only 55 per cent of the respondents claim that at least some of their staff receive training in customer service – even lower in manufacturing, at 48 per cent. And all this tragedy from UK companies who admit to some kind of progamme.

In another survey of executive opinion on customer service* sponsored by Digital – one of the case studies in this book – of almost 4,000 managers, 75 per cent of whom came from companies with over 5,000 people and a further 25 per cent from companies with over 2,000 people, less than 50 per cent of managers had attended any learning activity focused on customer service.

In the Digital-sponsored survey, 80 per cent of the UK sample believed that 'giving superior service to the customer is the key to competitive success'. Yet, only slightly more than half the sample had any regular reports and analysis prepared by their organisation on customer satisfaction. Less than 25 per cent had 'total commitment' to customer service; that is, systematically studying the competition, analysing them, buying their products or using their services, in order to discover what they do better. In the *Sunday Times*/MORI survey only one in five had any form of 'total commitment', and the bulk of their customer satisfaction measuring was being done informally and indiscriminately, rather than through the methodical approach so favoured by service excellence companies, such as questionnaires, customer clinics and market research.

The Digital survey covered executive opinion in the UK, Europe, USA and Japan. Interestingly, some 84 per cent of Japanese respondents felt that customer service was more important today than five years ago, and almost 90 per cent believed that service to the customer would become much more important over the next five years. This would be mainly due to service becoming a vital differentiator, competition getting fiercer, and customers becoming more demanding and wanting value for money. The research for this book indicates that the Japanese are bringing to bear on customer service the same intense, impassioned implementation that they have brought to products and their quality.

More than 700 executives were interviewed for the studies in this book, and their views on service organisations endorse the findings

* *Service – A survey of executive opinion in the UK* available from DIGITAL UK (tel 0256 843 333) conducted with joint research from Management Centre Europe and John Humble.

of the above surveys. In fact, our research on the same issues gave even more critical responses, and coupled with the *Sunday Times*/MORI findings of UK concerns, make for sad, if not shocking reading.

The task that all the executives interviewed in the above surveys believed they faced for the 1990s was to make total customer service a reality before either their competitors did, or their customers chose alternatives. The gap occurs when the survey findings reveal how poor companies are on implementation and how they feel they could improve their existing customer service.

Service today has become a vital element in the battle for the hearts, minds, money and (in the Metropolitan Police Service case study) support, of the customer and general public. In this book, total customer service is referred to in its widest sense. It reflects an organisation's mission and value statement, internally and externally: also its philosophy, people, policies, processes, procedures and personality, which provide the products and services to meet customers' needs and expectations. All case studies agree that the customer is the final arbiter and that service must always be measured from the customer's point of view.

Throughout the book, the practical experience of all the organisations is that customer service is perceived on three levels:

- The actual product or service.
- The way it is presented and served to the customer.
- The after-sales service and support.

The consistent feature of all the organisations presented in the book is service excellence being a balance between purpose, people and process.

Purpose is the mission statement, the values, the ingrained vision of the organisation. It is these beliefs which drive behaviour throughout the organisation.

Process is adapting the systems to suit the needs of the customer. It is also the support of all the people who work the system.

People are the staff who need to understand the value of the customers and general public they serve. To do this, they need to understand what business they are in and their role at work. They must be energised and empowered to make decisions and improve the system to better satisfy their customers.

There are other constants throughout the case studies that are worth noting:

- All interactions between customers and public provide opportunities to serve them, satisfy them and, indeed, delight them. To simply 'satisfy' is to settle for mediocrity. All the organisations *listen*; to staff, customers, competitors and public. They learn the truth and act on it.
- It is considered important that customers get 'responsive' behaviour from all staff. This means active listening, being open to suggestions rather than purely 'operative' actions such as following systems. For all organisations this has necessitated a move from a reactive management style to a proactive culture, with all the implications for changes in staff attitudes and behaviour. This is why the organisations in his book are totally committed to training; without service professionalism you cannot get service excellence.
- Listening and communication were considered by all case studies to be the key to service excellence with much hands-on, visible management. Management by walkabout became the norm.
- All the organisations realise that getting service to the customers and public – and maintaining it – is not a lip-service gimmick, or PR exercise. Organisations become flatter, teams get built, trust supersedes checking and control. It takes the entire organisation to be geared up for superior service. Therefore, if bureaucracy gets in the way of good customer service it must be eliminated.
- Measurement drives service performance, and all organisations placed great importance on this at the most senior level, usually in the boardroom. Customer questionnaires, user groups, forums and clinics become a way of life, as do personal visits between the organisation and its customers, freephone facilities, assessments and market research by outsiders. There will also be complaint and comment card analysis and regular team briefings

to discuss whether customers' needs are being anticipated, met, exceeded, and to measure customer satisfaction. Customer comments and complaints are considered challenges to improve service and thus enhance the customer's perception of the organisation.

- It is understood that a reputation for providing good service is the ultimate goal in giving a company a competitive edge and true partnership with those it serves.
- All the organisations in this book ultimately realised that it was individuals in the market-place who paid their wages and allowed them to operate or survive at all. They truly understood the value of satisfied customers. By constantly reviewing, and continually improving customer service, they not only identified and met customers' needs and expectations, but often exceeded them.

The challenge for UK companies must be to bridge that earlier mentioned gap: more than 90 per cent of respondents believing that customer service is a boardroom priority; more than 80 per cent saying it is the key to success, the competitive edge and survival partnership for the 1990s; yet genuine implementation of a customer service ethos being half that figure in UK organisations, and less than 25 per cent having 'total commitment' to customer service.

Total customer service may be boardroom-driven, but everything depends on the attitudes and behaviour of all the people in an organisation. Moving from being a product, procedure or process-orientated environment to a customer and service-centred culture is a profound philosophy and committed change for all concerned. This is especially true if all are to take ownership of customer service.

All the organisations in this book have had to remake themselves and this cannot occur without suffering. Service excellence for all of the studies is a continuing journey, not a destination, as the reader will discover when travelling through their corporate experience. Survival is not of course compulsory, failure is terminal. For the organisations in this book total customer service in the 1990s is not an option; there is quite simply no alternative.

Lynda King Taylor
London 1992

1. *Texaco in the United Kingdom*

Introduction

Texaco has a rich and diverse history, with roots going back to two main ancestors; the Texaco Petroleum Products Company, established in Britain in 1916, and Trinidad Leaseholds, formed in 1913. These two companies developed their UK businesses separately until they agreed to a merger in 1947. It was not until 1967, however, that Texaco's name was raised at service stations throughout Britain.

Texaco in the UK is now a fully integrated oil company. The scope of its activities encompasses exploration and production of crude oil in the North Sea, then the marketing of products through both a retail service station network and an authorised distributor network, as well as dealing directly with large industrial users. The UK operations also include: Pembroke Refinery, Llanelli Chemical Plant, Swindon Customer Service Centre, Manchester Lubricants Blending Plant; AFS and GRS (the company's joint venture aviation fuelling services, marine fuel and international trading operations) as well as depots and storage terminals sited around the UK.

Today, Texaco is a major oil company playing a full role within the UK. It is the fourth largest retailer in Britain and is among the top ten North Sea operators. Pembroke Refinery has been acclaimed as the United Kingdom's top refinery.

The Texaco livery uses the colours red, black and white and features the star logo. This corporate image identifies Texaco with the 'spirit of the star', a company committed to service excellence.

Today, there are around 1,300 Texaco service stations throughout the UK and these continue to be its public face. It is at Texaco's service stations that the public see a company striving to maintain the standards of service and quality that should be synonymous with the Texaco star.

Texaco's customer order and delivery service is centrally organised at a new Quality and Customer Care Division in Swindon. This case study discusses how Texaco is striving to improve its edge over its competitors through improved customer excellence via its customer service division at Swindon and also via its service stations throughout the UK.

TEXACO UK – TOTAL CUSTOMER SERVICE

'I guess I learn most from listening to the people I serve.'

Sales assistant, *Texaco service station, Central London.*

This remark serves well to introduce this case study. It reminds us that customer service must be measured from the customer's point of view, and that the only honest way to understand how to go about identifying customers' expectations is actually to listen to what they have to say.

Nowhere is this more important than in a market-place which is delivering a non-differentiated product; such as a transatlantic airline seat on a 747 or an executive bedroom in any international hotel. The oil business is one such industry, operating in an environment of increasing competitiveness and delivering a non-differentiated product – the litre of petrol. The only real difference between the various brands of oil and petrol is, quite simply, the way they are offered.

It is all too easy for the oil business to rely on the fact that we, the customers, are relatively indiscriminate in our choice of petrol. So much so, that in many forecourts self-service has given way to no service at all. The major pitfall at the point of sale is forgetting, all too easily, that the customer does have choice. When there is little to distinguish between similar products, what differentiates is the offering – customers choose because of the 'total experience'. To achieve this, one must listen to the customers, intently and regularly, and learn from them. To succeed in differentiating, an organisation has to 'hear' the customer.

Some would say that this sounds simple. However, as any seasoned observer of industry would comment, if it is this simple one wonders why everyone is not doing it. According to Glenn Tilton, Texaco's Chairman in the UK, the opening up of the lines of communication internally within an organisation to actually listen to the customer is a major boardroom challenge:

> *'Hierarchies throw up walls to preclude listening. This results in an organisation perceiving any customer criticism as inherently negative, with staff at all levels becoming defensive and arguing the point. What we have to do is move the boardroom closer to the customer, enabling all employees to have better market dialogue with their customers. You must involve all employees exactly as stated in the "vision" statement.' (See Figure 1.1.)*

Texaco's management believe the wrong way to achieve improved customer service would be to take a point of view in the boardroom and then tell that, or even sell that, to the rest of the organisation. Texaco believes that, in adopting this type of approach, you may sell 'service concepts' to the organisation, but it is highly unlikely that you will ever sell 'service' to your customer. If an organisation such as Texaco wants to put the spotlight on customer service then, according to Glenn Tilton: 'You must value your customer. You must survey everyone in the chain; that is, from the origin of the product through its distribution, to petrol being sold on the forecourts, and to the consumers buying it.'

In other words, a major effort must be directed towards discovering what all internal and external customer perceptions are of Texaco as a firm, and what these customers actually want. Armed with such evidence, you can then go to your staff, not with a board-

Figure 1.1 Texaco's Vision Statement

TEXACO TOTAL QUALITY PROCESS

OUR VISION:
To involve all employees in improving all activities on a continuous basis, to meet or exceed the expectations of customers.

OUR MISSION:
To create a continuous improvement process which unites Texaco in its commitment to a quality culture and focuses our efforts to meet or exceed customers' expectations by:

- Inspired leadership
- Employee participation
- Teamwork

room demand but, as Glenn Tilton expresses, 'with a much more compelling mission – we have got to do something together because this is what the customer wants'.

As any case study in this book will illustrate, achieving customer service must be boardroom driven, but the generator must be the organisation's relationship with its customers.

HOW CLOSE IS TEXACO TO ITS CUSTOMERS?

This is a most important management fundamental; being close to your customers means anticipating their wants, and then satisfying their needs. Many companies interviewed in the *Sunday Times*/MORI poll survey* and in the research for this book certainly talked about listening to their customers, but did not actually do it. The companies that did not listen, had not put across to their staff the simple business premise that all corporate success rests on making a sale which, at that moment, consummates the relationship between company and customer.

That commitment has to be understood by everyone in the organisation – not just those at the point of sale. The intensity of that simple message must pervade all aspects of the business if an organisation can truly call itself close to the customer. If this does not happen, then executive management, not the employees, have failed the organisation.

During my time with Texaco I talked to a wide range of employees, dipping into many parts of the business far removed from the point of sale. What intrigued me was that, although many organisations merely talk about being 'close to the customer', the majority of Texaco employees I talked with totally understood the importance of being customer-orientated. This attitude permeated all aspects of the business, and not just those areas having direct dealings with customers. The simple message that the customer, through their sales transactions, ultimately pays employees' wages was understood in all departments right through to the sales assistant in Central London who gave this case study its opening.

This consistent presence of service obsession was summed up on a Texaco forecourt when I asked an assistant what it was he sold, to which he responded, 'service'. This comment indicated to me an endorsement of what I have witnessed in those organisations that are truly close to the customer. That is, provision of service had become a reflex action rather than an afterthought. Perhaps this is what Glenn Tilton meant when he was suggesting that customer service was not about being 'driven by the boardroom' but rather about being 'driven by Texaco's relationship with its customers'.

Is 100 per cent of this type of service, and indeed service obsession, possible? 'Probably not,' according to Barry Ashman, Texaco's Manager for Retail in Europe, 'but that is what you have got to aim for'. Barry Ashman admits that if you do not aim for 100 per cent

* MORI poll completed for the *Sunday Times* on Customer Service in relation to this book and the *Sunday Times* video on Quality: Total Customer Service, 2.2.92.

and get things right first time, every time, and on time, then you are tolerating failure. Of course, in any large organisation, there will be mistakes and there will be things that go wrong, with service standards on occasions being lowered. That is why the emphasis on winning employees' hearts and minds is so crucial in any organisation which is focusing on the customer.

The customer services division of Texaco

The customer services side of Texaco is a major part of its UK operation and serves all Texaco's customers, both internal and external. Based in Swindon, this division has a simple objective – to use service to make Texaco the best in the industry. Texaco Swindon has a dual role – it not only provides a wide spectrum of services to all Texaco's customers, but also gleans information from them to enable Texaco's management to be responsive to changes in the market-place.

At Swindon there are sales and customer accounting groups who are responsible for invoicing retailers, distributors and commercial customers for products. They also handle the accounting for millions of gallons of oil and petrol handled each week by Texaco in the UK. Other staff deal with Texaco's internal customers, supervising the movement of Texaco product through the distribution system; by pipeline and ship from Texaco's refineries, or from outside suppliers, to terminals and ultimately to the customer. The Swindon team take telephone orders until 11 a.m. for delivery the next day, making Texaco probably the only major oil company to offer a 24-hour service. Each day, in fact, an average of 500 orders, 600 deliveries and 200 enquiries are handled by the fuels and distribution side of the customer services team (see Figure 1.2). It is at Swindon that the customer services group has to oversee the performance of maintenance contracts at all of the Texaco service stations (around 1,300 in the UK). It is their job to provide these Texaco retailers with maintenance and servicing of pumps, point-of-sale equipment, credit card terminals, lighting, security systems and other forecourt hardware.

Figure 1.2 Texaco's customer services division's basic delivery service

- Order until 11 a.m. Day 1 for delivery Day 2
- Orders accepted 0700 to 1900 Monday to Friday
0700 to 0900 Saturday
- Orders delivered within recorded delivery hours on requested day
- Contact customer if unable to deliver
- ETA available from 1500 on day prior to delivery
- Enquiry service available

  0700 to 1900 Monday to Friday
0700 to 1400 Saturday

Other internal customers would be the 600 road tankers who draw product from Texaco's terminals. Each of these must conform to the strictest of safety standards, with around 1,000 inspections conducted annually by Texaco's road transport engineers. These engineers report to Swindon on whether or not they are satisfied that a tanker meets Texaco's requirements. There are also continual spot checks during the year which ensure that all vehicles are maintained to the highest standard, including the entire company car fleet. Over 600 company cars are managed from Texaco Swindon which has responsibility for acquiring, running and insuring the entire company car fleet.

There is also a customer liaison team which deals with all types of customer; ranging from single service stations, to major motor manufacturers and local authorities with perhaps hundreds of locations. Texaco Swindon handles some 20,000 transactions every month, with around 2,000 customers a month calling the Texaco Hotline, also based at Swindon. This is a customer service line for assistance and advice on the products and services offered by Texaco.

Figure 1.3 Texaco Swindon's mission statement

CUSTOMER SERVICES GROUP MISSION

- Handle all Customer contacts in a friendly, efficient and professional manner, ensuring all enquiries and complaints are resolved to the Customer's satisfaction, in a timely manner.
- Accurately record all Customer details into the Customer Service system. Provide positive feedback by meaningful reports, making recommendations, to the relevant personnel, to communicate the changing demands of the Customer.
- Negotiate maintenance contracts and monitor their performance to ensure the 'best service' is being provided to our Customers.
- Treat every Customer as 'special', to build respect for, and loyalty to, Texaco.

This free service (motorists, or indeed any Texaco customer, can call Texaco's free line on (0800 333 111) is considered a vital part of the gleaning of information, obtained from customers themselves, to enable Texaco to provide an improved service. According to Peter Hughes, the Manager of Texaco Swindon:

> *'Our operation is totally focused on the customer – both internal and external. Our mission statement is geared towards treating every customer as special to retain our customer loyalty (see Figure 1.3). Customer service is one of the few ways for us to differentiate ourselves within the petroleum industry.'*

To achieve this, Peter Hughes highlights major ingredients vital to achieving excellence in customer service.

He endorses the need for a strong strategic commitment from the boardroom, but one which is directly focused on the customer's needs. For this to be realised, and for Texaco to make changes to the way it operates and gives customer excellence, it must listen to the feedback that it gets from customers. This feedback – from surveys, from customer panels and the 'Mystery Motorist' campaign (detailed on p.10) – all helps to cement customer service.

Peter Hughes insists that you have to identify what is important to customers, both inside the organisation as well as externally:

> *'For example, our motorists visiting a service station as well as those who serve them. Once you listen to the customer then you can begin to change the culture to one which is geared to giving that customer the best possible service.'*

IDENTIFYING TEXACO CUSTOMERS' NEEDS

The responsibility for monitoring and reporting back to Texaco on the level of customer service throughout Texaco's retail network belongs to Richard Squires. He is based at Swindon, and is the manager responsible for Texaco's customer-related quality programmes. Texaco's service stations remain the public face of the company and it has therefore been an important part of Texaco's customer services programmes to ensure that they supply what the customer wants. According to Richard Squires this is, naturally, an ongoing process:

> *'Through surveys, regular customer panel meetings, and the Mystery Motorist campaign we are able to obtain regular feedback on areas where we are doing well with our service stations and where improvements are necessary. There is also the national freephone customer services line which enables any customer, at any Texaco service station anywhere in the UK, to speak to our customer services team for free.'*

Some 2,000 customers a month call the customer service line for assistance and advice on the products and services offered by the company, and all of their calls are monitored to provide Texaco with accurate information as to what the customer wants. According to Richard Squires:

'Extensive qualitative and quantitative analysis is required on a perpetual basis if you wish to make a real contribution to improving relations with your customers. You can then take this information to the point of sale, which may be at the service station itself, or to the appropriate department within Texaco, in order that changes can be made.'

The Mystery Motorist campaign is a case in point. Every year Mystery Motorists visit every Texaco service station in the UK, to measure how successful Texaco has been in meeting motorists' requirements. Texaco appoint market researchers to perform this task. Teams of research assistants, posing as motorists, visit Texaco's 1,300 service stations three times a year. Their terms of remit are quite simply to measure the key quality service factors that motorists regard as essential when visiting a service station. These are factors that determine whether or not motorists use one service station or another. Texaco research has indicated that there are a considerable number of attributes which influence customer choice of service station. The Mystery Motorists are dispatched to discover whether all of these types of key quality attributes are being achieved.

- Ease of forecourt access and minimum congestion.
- Whether one has to queue at the tills.
- Good toilet facilities, particularly for women, mothers and babies.
- Site and forecourt both clean and well presented.
- Staff who are friendly, courteous, willing and knowledgeable.
- Forecourts that are well lit.
- A well-stocked shop, offering a comprehensive range of facilities.
- Payment method choices.
- Clear pump signage.

The results from the Mystery Motorist surveys have enabled Richard Squires and his team to draw up customer care indices for every one of Texaco's retail sites. Major competitors' sites – such as Shell, Mobil, Esso and BP – are also visited, allowing performance comparisons to be made against Texaco's national service stations' picture. The Mystery Motorist survey is both extensive and exhaustive, representing the first stage in the process of identifying what customers want at the point of sale. It allows Texaco management and the retailer to have a benchmark, against which they can not only be measured with their competitors but also with other similar types of service station within the Texaco network.

According to Richard Squires, anything that can be measured can be improved. It is this information which Texaco now give to all their regional and area managers in order that they can discuss the findings with their retailers to build on areas of customer strengths, and remedy areas of customer weakness.

Continual monitoring of customer service

The formula for linking customer loyalty to the Texaco brand begins to take shape (see Figure 1.4). Richard Squires highlights that Texaco will (and indeed does) make changes to the way it operates as a result of the feedback that it receives from customers. He also admits that there are areas where there is general scope for improvement at Texaco service stations; highlighting issues such as clarity of pricing for shop merchandise, and improved customer service by the sales assistants themselves.

For myself, I would add to the Texaco list, toilet cleanliness and improved 'spring cleaning' of forecourt grime. My own survey, amongst women drivers, reveals they are more likely to use a service station that is not only clean, with a high standard of toilet cleanliness, but also one which is well lit, particularly during the longer winter evenings. A cursory sample of local Texaco stations in my own area identified one in three as having one or more exterior lights not working, and this was during November. However, it is just this

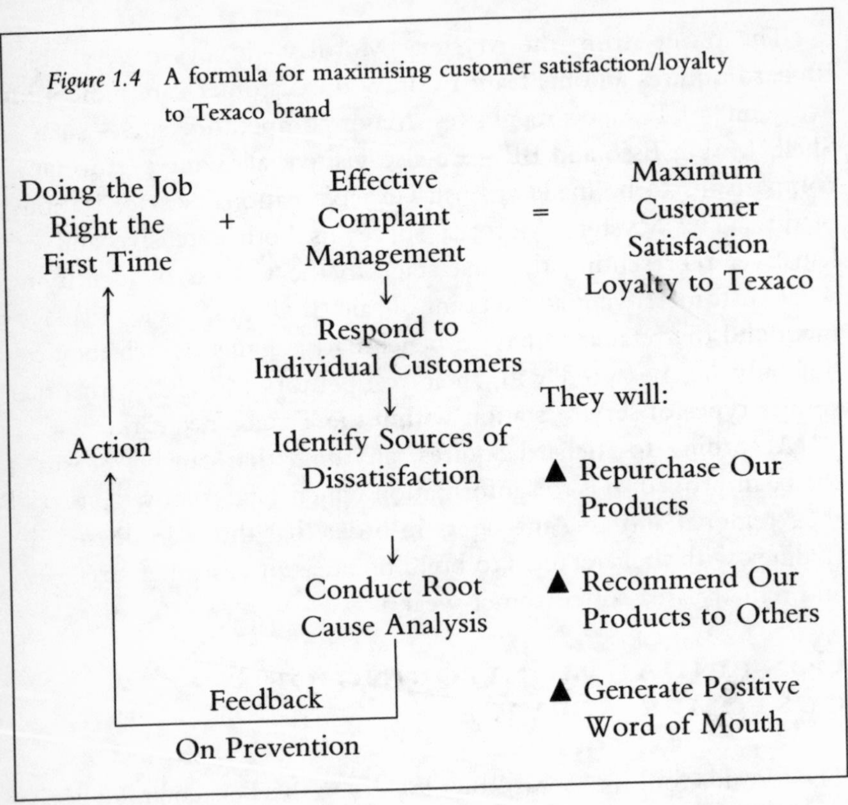

Figure 1.4 A formula for maximising customer satisfaction/loyalty to Texaco brand

type of customer feedback that Texaco want, and encourage, both through the mystery motorist campaign and the Texaco freephone helpline service. A problem, such as the one I have mentioned of poor forecourt lighting, would immediately be fed back to the area managers from Texaco Swindon's customer services base. It could then be taken onboard at a further stage of the customer service monitoring process – the customer panel forums.

These forums are regarded as an important channel of communication between Texaco and its customers. Again, in service excellence companies this two-way process of review is constant (see for example, the Simon Access study, Chaper 10), a fact that Peter Hughes is ready to acknowledge:

'We are back to listening again – at these forums we quite simply have a

listening brief. Of course, the ultimate customer is the motorist, but major customers of Texaco are our retailers and Texaco site and service stations. There is an enormous amount of retailing experience out there which we need to harness in a constructive way if we are to develop the whole Texaco service station network, and have that customer edge over our competitors.'

Similarly, Richard Squires recognises the need for effective communication:

'Research has shown that we have to communicate better with all of our customers, internally and externally, and the best way to do this is face-to-face. We bring groups of our retailers, distributors and commercial customers together, not only to air their views about Texaco products and services, but also to discuss problems that they encounter on the site, some of which are thorny.'

It is at these meetings that one really returns to the beginning of this case study, when Glenn Tilton emphasised the importance of a company attempting to achieve excellence in customer service by being close to their customer and actually hearing what the customers say. At these customer panel forums, for example, many of the customers have harsh things to say about Texaco; ranging from service station rent reviews, to grievances on pump repair, maintenance contracts, the need for improved fuel deliveries and better training for retailers and their staff. It is absolutely vital, therefore, that Texaco should tackle such issues and do something about them. Richard Squires, who organises these forums, explains:

'It is up to our customers, i.e. our retailers, to judge how effective Texaco is in providing solutions to many of the major issues raised in these forums. They do this, either through the customer panel meetings, their local field management or, quite possibly, the customer service department here at Swindon.'

ACTING, AND NOT JUST TALKING CUSTOMER SERVICE

There is no doubt that Texaco has begun to tackle some of the thorny issues that Richard Squires referred to. For example, when a retail panel reported dissatisfaction that fuel deliveries were being made by tankers not in the Texaco livery, the company responded by stipulating that only liveried tankers should deliver to Texaco service stations. On the issue of pump maintenance contracts, a new post has been created in the customer service group to oversee the performance of maintenance contracts at service stations. This aims to provide the Texaco retailers with a visible improvement in the speed and efficiency with which maintenance and servicing is carried out to the pumps, point-of-sale equipment, credit card terminals, and other forecourt hardware.

Many of the complaints emanating from the customer panel forums relating to pump maintenance contracts were mainly due to such contracts being fragmented, with different Texaco departments dealing with a variety of aspects. In 1992 all maintenance contracts have become centralised at Texaco Swindon. Under the administration of Colin Gibson, the new Manager for Contracts and Services, priority will now be given to addressing the problems of pump maintenance contracts. All retailers who experience problems or delays in service will be asked to call the freephone customer service line, where a customer care assistant will deal with them direct.

Another area of criticism levelled against Texaco related to fuel deliveries. At Swindon, the manager in charge of fuel services is Malcolm Seedhouse. He and his staff are well aware of the vital role they have to play in getting the product to the motorist. Their mission statement is displayed and understood (see Figure 1.5) and they appreciate that good service has to be fast and flexible. As previously mentioned, more than 500 orders, 600 deliveries and 200 enquiries are handled every day, most of them regarding delivery times. Given the feedback from the customer panel forums the Fuel Services Group at Swindon was reorganised on a regional basis with separate teams handling different parts of the UK.

Figure 1.5 Fuels and distribution mission statement

Ensure all customer fuel orders and order enquiries are answered in a prompt and courteous manner. All orders are input into the order entry system accurately. All delivery schedules are completed within laid down time restraints taking into account economics and customer requirements. Interface with supply locations and contractor on all matters relating to deliveries and action any problems that evolve during the day to day operation of delivering to Texaco customers.

According to Malcolm Seedhouse, under the old system some staff would deal with orders and others would deal with enquiries. Now things are somewhat different:

> *'Everyone deals with both orders and enquiries, in order that customers have a single point of contact when they ring Texaco. We have discovered that when the callers have a freephone line with only one number to ring this has helped build a better customer relationship. However, it is essential that the customer care assistant who takes the call must have a detailed knowledge of both the product – in order they can give a sensible and credible answer – and the particular part of the country where a fuel service or delivery has to be made. A team member now has responsibility for orders, scheduling and enquiries all within the one job description. The benefit of this is that they have a stronger sense of ownership of the work, the customer, the problem and the solution.'*

Excellence companies are renowned for building jobs 'up' – creating job enrichment which adds to a person's self-worth and motivation.

Malcolm Seedhouse and his team appreciate that service can still be improved; for example, better utilisation of the large 38-tonne tankers. This could mean a service station need only receive four or five deliveries in place of six smaller ones. There is also a need for improved investigation of forecourt obstructions which can hold up the tankers and cause knock-on delays to subsequent deliveries. Could there also be increased use of night-time deliveries which minimise disruption to the site during busy daytime hours and more accurately timed deliveries? These are the type of work and customer service issues that the team will look at.

FEEDBACK TO STAFF

It is important when giving good customer service that it is not only the customers who receive the feedback about what is going on, and why, but also the staff themselves. Staff have to be trained to become obsessed with service and at Swindon the formula, mentioned earlier (see Figure 1.4) for maximising customer satisfaction and loyalty to the Texaco brand is well understood by everyone you talk with. Noticeboards display constant monthly review figures, showing how well staff groups are performing in their respective areas of customer management. Again, this type of individual and team feed-back is a constant in service excellence organisations.

Take the information regarding the 2,000 customers a month calling the freephone customer service line at Texaco Swindon. The manager in charge of this aspect of customer services is Tony d'Angibau. The Texaco freephone service was installed to allow anyone to have free telephone access to Texaco. Previously, calls for enquiries, orders and complaints would be fragmented throughout the entire Texaco organisation. Customers would contact a local department, divisional office, service station, site or head office. Calls are now much more centralised. All types of customers, be they motorists, contractors, dealers, retailers, or managed site operators can talk to Texaco at any time they want.

However, it is imperative that all of this data is logged and used as management and customer information. Tony d'Angibau will do this on a monthly basis, by category, and then feed the information back to his staff and discuss it face-to-face (see Figure 1.6). According to Tony d'Angibau:

'The diversity of requests and comments from telephone callers has given us an enormous insight into what our customers expect from us at Texaco. The key to success must be the speed with which we provide the customer with a satisfactory answer to an enquiry.'

To achieve this means working very closely with Texaco's information technology departments, and other parts of the Texaco organisation. In this way, the customer care assistants are provided with the type of easy access to current Texaco information which enables them to give quick communication responses to telephone callers. (This is a strong need also highlighted in the Digital case study, Chapter 2).

If you talk to Vanessa Lee, the supervisor in charge of customer services, you will realise how vital it is for the customer services team to be closely linked to other departments within the Texaco organisation:

'Customer service assistants deal with calls on all manner of topics; from product specifications to environmental issues, from the new Texaco child road safety campaign to changes in the market-place. For example, during the Gulf crisis there were many enquiries from people who wanted to understand what was happening, and how it affected the Texaco oil business.'

This obviously means the team members must have a great deal of information and training in order to resolve customer enquiries satisfactorily. All members of the customer services teams have undergone actual on-site training to provide them with first-hand experience of customer contact at service stations. When it comes to handling complaints, Vanessa believes that, although some customers actually enjoy whingeing:

'The majority of customers who are complaining will feel guilty about doing so. Part of the job of the customer service assistant is to support them in making that complaint, overcome their embarrassment, and realise that is what we are here for – to help.'

Figure 1.6 Customer services group monthly review

BREAKDOWN OF LOGGED CALLS BY CATEGORY

Category	**May**	**June**	**July**	**Aug**	**Sept**	**Oct**
Staff	32	39	41	30	38	54
Injury	1	4	1	3	1	2
Contamination	12	12	36	26	17	45
Equipment	30	32	43	22	29	27
Promotions	68	118	156	80	56	81
Environment	19	22	25	24	14	16
Product	43	31	53	45	35	74
Contract FDEM	28	30	68	37	41	42
Sub Total	233	288	423	267	231	341
Campaign	43	96	33	12	13	1
General Enquiry	268	252	1075	607	598	468
T T T	14	38	10	13	13	3
Total	**558**	**674**	**1541**	**899**	**855**	**813**

Personally, having asked my colleagues to try out this free Texaco telephone service, and having done so myself, I can only say that Tony d'Angibau has every right to be proud of his team. I was a random telephone caller on no fewer than 30 occasions over a six-week period and found it a most impressive customer services arena, with an average delay in answering calls of eight seconds (British Gas take note!).

This offers an illustration of why service has to be obsessive in all departments and not just those dealing directly with customers. In Tony and Vanessa's customer service section, they rely totally on information and responses being forwarded from other departments quickly and efficiently in order to meet their own targets. These are to ensure that the customer has some management response within 48 hours; an impressive achievement when many of the calls are technical in nature or require more than one department's input.

Another aspect of life at Texaco in Swindon which impresses me, and leads me to believe that this is a company striving towards the achievement of customer service excellence, is that there is a great deal of team talking, as well as customer listening. Many of the case studies in this book will illustrate the point that feedback to the staff, regarding what is actually happening with the customer, must be available on a regular basis. Not just through posting information on noticeboards, but rather through direct face-to-face briefings. All the managers do this at Swindon, led by Peter Hughes and his example. Again, this kind of 'think tank' approach to customer service is an inextricable link between staff and customers. Staff talk together regularly in groups about customers' wants and expectations. Equally, customers can come together in the forums and customer panels alongside staff to talk about their expectations of Texaco, its products and services.

Of course, this takes time. Also massive management effort and energy, reinforced by constant visible reminders right down the line. Constant reinforcement of the customer service mission through feedback and training is, in fact, a consistent theme throughout service excellent organisations.

CONTINUAL REINFORCEMENT OF THE CUSTOMER SERVICE MESSAGE THROUGH CUSTOMER TRAINING

In order for Texaco to be sure it is in close contact with the customer, it must measure both internal and external customer satisfaction on a daily, weekly, monthly, quarterly and annual basis. It also has to reinforce its 'close to the customer' service beliefs with intensive training for all of its staff. This has been a major objective of Barry Limb's department. He is the Manager of Training in Sales and Marketing, and has seen his 1990 training budget of £150,000 escalate to almost £2 million in 1992. Training all the 8,000 people who work full and part-time at Texaco service stations is not only a huge and expensive task, but also an essential one if improved customer service at its public face is to give Texaco the competitive edge.

In this study I do not wish to detail the management training endeavours to facilitate change within the Texaco organisation as this is well documented in other studies. It is, however, worthwhile discussing the comprehensive training campaign in Texaco which introduces retailers and their staff to the latest in customer service techniques. This has the ultimate objective of making motorists aware of the exceptional way they should be treated at Texaco service stations and sites.

Barry Limb explains that it was another demand from the customer panel meetings, mentioned earlier, which indicated the need for Texaco to invest in a massive training programme for service station staff. He endorses the point made earlier that, in the oil industry, the means for differentiating Texaco from its competitors are very limited indeed. It is therefore vital that the service stations should stand out for the standard of service that they offer: 'Any training has to have two major inputs; why delivery of service must be improved, and how this can be achieved.' Texaco's field management, retailers and all sales assistants attend various training workshops where they not only exchange ideas about customer care, but also improve their own interpersonal skills.

The training programme for the Texaco service station network began with a total of 100 regional managers, field co-ordinators and area managers attending a course that lasted two days. During this time they learned advanced training techniques and details of the course material that was to be taught to the sales assistants throughout Texaco. It was important that all the field co-ordinators and area managers were well versed in every aspect of customer care and service. In this way they could gain an overview of the material that the 8,000 people who work at Texaco service stations would be learning. It would also enable them to discuss ways of supporting their staff once they had been through the training initiative and returned to their workplace.

The next stage was to conduct a series of 34 two-day workshops for all the service station principals, which were held in hotels as far afield as Perth and Plymouth. An important part of the Texaco training philosophy has been to have area managers very much involved in the actual training of all the site and service station staff. It was keenly felt at Texaco that this would help strengthen the lines of communication between area management and local staff; ultimately allowing sales assistants to be nearer to the line managers, and thus become part of a strong team. Similar programmes were also implemented on the distribution side, with depot managers, distribution principals and their staff also being introduced to both the concept of customer service and the personal skills needed to achieve improved customer excellence.

Training manager Barry Limb saw the entire process as a response to fundamental organisational needs:

> *'Retailers had indicated that, in their opinion, they had nowhere near enough training to be able to make a major impact on improving customer service. It was imperative that we learned from our customers – our retailers – what training we needed in order to produce a credible programme of customer care throughout the entire Texaco service station network. Certain areas were highlighted as being of vital importance; for example, interpersonal skills, dealing with particular customer problems, product knowledge and actual customer service. It was also important that the training should be as participative as possible for the*

audience and, most important, it should be fun! We really wanted service station staff to leave the course believing in customer service; also much better versed in customer service techniques, and appreciating that their personal skills had been enhanced.'

The aims of all the seminars have been quite simple:

- Emphasising the main message – customer service – and the Texaco vision.
- Explaining why any company should bother about customer service; specifically, why Texaco thinks that customer service is vital.
- Establishing the importance of sales assistants in the customer service initiative.
- Assessing what sales assistants actually do at work and how this can be improved.
- Learning how to identify strengths and build on them.
- Learning how to identify areas with deficiencies in performance and recognising what improvements can be made.

It was important for everyone to appreciate that effective customer service was about Texaco profit – differentiation leads to customer retention. This is true of this type of training in other excellence studies – to recognise that good service is not the result of luck or accident but rather it is the manifestation of a well managed organisation. According to Tony Price, General Manager of Sales and Marketing at Texaco:

'It is vitally important that all staff appreciate how we can set ourselves apart from our competitors. The customer service training initiative has been crucial, because it was designed to give the customer what he or she wants, and that is real service; something that is often lacking in Britain today.'

Tony Price and the Texaco management explain to all seminar delegates how customer care is about making the whole purchasing experience better for Texaco customers, so they will want to keep coming back. This is good for everyone; good for the customer, good for the sales assistant and for Texaco. As Tony Price sees it:

> *'If our staff can promote a more friendly interaction with the customer I think they will find the job more interesting, more satisfying and perhaps less lonely. However, this does not imply that it has always been done badly in the past; it has not. Nevertheless, it can be done better and we can help make it easier, because I know that working at a service station is not the easiest of jobs, no two days are ever the same.'*

What Texaco do in these training sessions is to focus on the delegates' common experiences and their common problems at the workplace. By sharing them they find ways of developing and overcoming their difficulties. Neil Lambert, Manager of Texaco's Retail Sales Division, explains:

> *'Every time a member of the motoring public visits a Texaco site, regardless of whether it is a Star service station, a company owned site or an independent dealer site, everything they see is a reflection of Texaco. This process starts even before the customer's car enters the forecourt, and continues throughout the whole period of their time on the site. But, within that process, the actual point of contact between the motorist and the sales assistant, or any member of staff who is working on the site, is absolutely vital. In other words it is the people on-site who create the predominant impression and who have, if you like, the critical and sometimes only direct interface with the customer. It is their response, their attitude, their service and attention which will determine whether a motorist leaves the site with a good, bad or neutral perception. By creating a positive impression every time with all our customers, Texaco can start to beat the competition and start winning motorists for all our sites.'*

At the beginning of this case study, Glenn Tilton stressed the importance of, so-to-speak, bringing the boardroom to the forecourt. Not dictating from the boardroom what executive management want but instead enabling line staff at the point of sale to appreciate what customers want, achieving their support in providing their requirements.

This philosophy is very much part of the Texaco training programme throughout their retail service station network. For example, delegates are asked to consider a variety of issues, such as:

- What makes a customer turn to your service station?
- Is it the colour?
- The design?
- The easy access to the forecourt?
- Your reputation?
- Familiarity?
- Location?
- The absence of queues?
- Price of petrol?
- Free gift tokens?

Put another way, if the main product, petrol, is pretty much the same wherever they buy it, what makes your service station different? By answering questions like this, the service station principals and staff are able to discuss all the feedback Texaco gleans from the customer through the various information tools mentioned earlier. During these seminars delegates learn what Texaco calls their 'customer service equation':

1. Know your job.
2. Know your customer.
3. Know yourself.

As Barry Limb explains: 'It is important that all delegates at these seminars appreciate what customer service is all about.'

What I trust will become a dominant theme throughout the case studies in this book is that customer service is not just about being nice to people, or the 'have a nice day' syndrome which is so often displayed when politeness appears to be an effort, and the greeting is not really meant. As all the case studies illustrate, customer service should be a way of life throughout an organisation. It is a way of doing things which not only improves ones own interpersonal skill, but also the overall business skill of the organisation. As far as Texaco are concerned, customer service is as much about knowing yourself (the individual giving the service) as it is about knowing your job and your customer.

A major part, therefore, of the retail service station network training programmes in Texaco is to emphasise to all the delegates what exactly 'service' means to the customers who come into contact with Texaco. For example, appreciating the results of the Mystery Motorist campaign is essential to enable staff to do their job better. The training programme has a great deal of role playing within it that can demonstrate to delegates the difference between dealing with customers' problems and getting caught out by them.

It is possible to change, from being a sales assistant who gets easily irritated by customers, into a sales assistant who sees the difficulties presented by a customer as a challenge rather than a chore. The delegates are also asked to examine their own personal attitude towards their job and their behaviour at work. For example, they can compare a poor attitude with a positive one.

Sales assistant No. 1 talking about their job

'What do I do? My job? Well sometimes I serve behind this glass thing, I stack shelves, I take money, I sweep and I clean, I get lonely, I get bored, I don't make as much money as I would like, I work shifts and that is about it I think – it's a job.'

Sales assistant No. 2 talking about their job

'What is my job? I am a service station sales assistant. What do I do? What don't I do! I run the place, and it is quite a responsibility. I am in charge of the till, I look out for things like customers smoking on the forecourt, I promote goods, I keep the shop looking tidy and well stocked, I make sure that the equipment and forecourt are kept clean and well maintained, I sign for deliveries, I make sure they are put where they belong

out of the way, I do a lot of things really. It is my job to make sure the customers get what they want and go away happy. I get a number of difficult customers who do "have a go", but I see my job as trying to win them over. I also get a lot of nice customers who have a chat and always have a nice word to say. No two days are ever the same.

'Sometimes I walk in here and I think, "what is going to happen in here today?" but that is the fun of it. Sometimes it is very hard work, but I would rather be rushed off my feet than going daft with nothing to do but pace around the place. When I think about the real challenge of my job . . . I believe no one likes buying petrol, I suppose I see my challenge as making each customer enjoy coming here. As for the skills and attitudes I need in my job, well, responsibility would be top of my list, then there is a neat appearance, confidence, ability to keep calm, work alone for long periods, reliability, a sense of humour, flexibility, accuracy, selling skills, a good memory, efficiency, and you have got to be able to give a good smile!'

Ironically enough, when I visited a number of Texaco service stations in the London area, on spec, I did meet these two very different types of sales assistant. That is why coming into the classroom and sharing experiences is so important. Texaco has learned that sales assistants of the No. 1 type above may not necessarily be a lost cause if they are supported in a learning environment, and are allowed to grow alongside those sales assistants who have the attitudes of sales assistant No. 2.

Delegates, therefore, appreciate that there are different ways of looking at one's job, and of doing it. They are also asked to appreciate that customers, too, have different needs. Although buying a litre of petrol is considered a chore, customers still have a choice and can always go down the road to a competitor's site. It is therefore instilled in the delegates that a customer only becomes a customer when he or she chooses to stop at their particular service station. The challenge is to make sure that customers stop at Texaco, then keep on stopping at Texaco. The delegates gradually begin to appreciate that, in any business, choice is in the hands of the consumer.

If a customer chooses not to use Texaco products, then Texaco employees are out of a job. During the seminar, delegates will also discuss customer profiles and, in the training sessions, sales assistants will gain experience in dealing with different types of customer. For example, the 'Sunday driver' versus the 'Ferrari driver', versus the 'exhausted mum with two kids driver' or the 'corporate driver'. Four very different types of customer, with a variety of needs, all of whom require different types of customer care and service.

Other skills training is given in body language and appearance, for example. Delegates are taught to appreciate the maxim that you 'never get a second chance to make a first impression'. They have to begin to look critically at themselves in order to improve their self awareness and their behaviour towards the customer. The training sessions are based around examining values, looking at the way staff approach their jobs and whether the present way of doing things actually gets better results for customers. The seminar will also cover detailed areas of product knowledge and various sales techniques. At a later date all the delegates will return to the classroom to share the experiences they have encountered back at the workplace, and to discuss the type of customers they have met and their problems.

In the shared learning experience they begin to appreciate that the Texaco business is all about service station staff who know their products, who can handle difficult customer situations and win the customer over. They are also taught the difference between *reactive* and *proactive* selling. Reactive selling is all about responding to a situation in which the customer has a demand, and supplying it; proactive selling, on the other hand, is all about developing a situation where what the sales assistant eventually supplies is jointly influenced by themselves and the customer. They begin to learn that a sales assistant cannot simply push goods on to a customer who does not want them. They are, however, in a position to raise a customer's awareness of what the service station has to offer in total.

Product knowledge is a fundamental part of the seminars. Texaco realise it is essential that service station staff should have a comprehensive knowledge of all their various products – for example, the different types of oil sold (customers get irritated when they do not receive answers).

Finally, the workshops cover the interpersonal skills needed to deal with difficult customers. Troubleshooting case studies are developed which cover various aspects of problems on the forecourt: from customers driving off without paying, to car wash damage; from petty pilfering to more serious robberies and hold-ups; from dealing with customers who insist on smoking, to dealing with a customer using a cheque without a banker's card. These are all familiar problems to sales assistants, and the Texaco training environment has to transform these sales assistants into professional problem solvers. Many of those attending the seminars genuinely felt that, following the seminars, they were no longer 'ground down' by problems. They could now view such problems as learning experiences, helping them to get better at their jobs.

Winning at customer service

What is perhaps most impressive about the Texaco training initiative is its simplicity. First there is the simple message: Texaco = total customer service. As Barry Ashman, Texaco's Manager for Retail in Europe, told me: 'If you keep the philosophy simple, people will start talking about the philosophy, and then they may well start living it. Even if they do not get all of the words of the mission statement and philosophy right.'

I have, nevertheless, talked to a great many employees in Texaco who still do not think that the Texaco approach to customer service means, at present, that much to them. It is, however, interesting that those who went on the training programmes in 1991 are now taking on the Texaco way with much more commitment. The mission statement now has more meaning and relevance to them at their point of sale.

It is interesting that all the companies and organisations discussed in this book view themselves as having a strong sense of 'corporacy'. This seems to represent the concept of getting people throughout the organisation to think of themselves as part of an extended family, no matter what size the organisation.

Another striking characteristic of the Texaco seminars was the company wanting these training programmes to be conducted by the manager within the same chain of command structure. By doing so, they actually threw away the chain of command. Of course, the command hierarchy in Texaco still exists when it comes to important areas of decision-making. However, getting the team-based training programmes evolving, using both regional and area management with their own local teams, allowed a much more spirited exchange of information to occur. It also enabled senior management within Texaco to be in more 'informed' contact with employees at the lowest level in the organisation. Informality was the norm, and this formed the foundation for 'visible' management.

Again, in really excellent organisations 'management by walkabout' is a way of life. (This is particularly endorsed in the Sutcliffe Catering study at chapter 5.) This 'visibility' has been an important cultural change in Texaco, given its history of being more an authoritarian organisation than an entrepreneurial one. Some management called the old Texaco fairly cold and autocratic. Now it is moving towards a more friendly and informal organisation. It is certainly true that companies which achieve excellence in customer service have much more visible and informal management than other poorer organisations which do well to achieve mere mediocrity.

Wandering around, standing up and being counted, listening, and engendering informality do not come easy to all managers. This can be seen in other case studies where management by walkabout can be construed as checking up on employees; intrusive or condescending management behaviour. However, judging by the feedback that I received from many delegates on the Texaco training programmes, the way the seminars were conducted became a stepping stone to cultural change.

Another characteristic that has been consistent from the feedback I received regarded how delegates were treated. They felt they were treated as important, with respect, and with a feeling that they were 'all in it together' – a partnership geared towards achieving Texaco's objectives of total customer service. This made them feel good and, as individuals, the delegates came to realise they were a major source of Texaco's productivity and profit gains.

Respect for the individual is a common characteristic in service excellent companies and, although it may be a simple concept, one suspects that unless it is ingrained within an organisation one can never achieve total customer excellence. As Glenn Tilton puts it:

> *'Since Texaco's UK beginnings, 75 years ago, there has been one key factor that has enabled our company to survive and prosper – its people. In the decades that have followed, we have learned that it is not always possible to beat the competition merely by the quality of our production platforms, refineries or service stations. What makes the difference is the quality of the individuals at work within Texaco. Times have changed, but people will always be at the heart of a successful customer service company.'*

It would be foolish to suggest that Texaco do get it right first time, every time, on time. Nevertheless, when I entered a Texaco service station, as I did recently near Southampton, a sales assistant told me: 'Of course you get bloody-minded customers, and yes, they can be an absolute pain in the butt, but they are my bread and butter and I am only here because of them.' Hearing that, I believe the message is getting through, and Texaco really are striving towards excellence in total customer service.

2. Digital Equipment Company UK

INTRODUCTION

Digital Equipment Company is the wholly-owned subsidiary of the Digital Equipment Corporation, the world's leading manufacturer of networked computer systems and associated peripheral equipment. Digital is the leader in systems integration with its networks, communications, services and software products. Basically, Digital in the UK is involved in four businesses.

1. It offers commodity products that are standard in the industry and include personal computers (PCs), UNIX workstations and servers, and a wide range of peripheral products. It is also a leader in the Advanced Computing Environment (ACE) initiative to ensure common standards across these systems.
2. It offers VAX systems that meet all common standards and are capable of outperforming other systems via their unique abilities. These are rapidly becoming directly price competitive with UNIX machines.
3. It offers extensive systems integration, tying together the complete range of products into simple or complex systems to provide complete solutions for their customers' requirements. Digital also integrates software and hardware from other manufacturers. Systems integration is an important area of growth in the business, because Digital customers usually want to buy a complete system that is designed to fulfil a specific function.

4. It offers a wide range of services in order to meet customer requirements comprehensively and effectively. For example, Digital's service organisation designs and installs networks, integrates systems, runs complete information shops, supports standard PC software, runs networks of PCs and provides all the services that the customer wants or needs on its own, or multi vendor equipment. This profitable growth area of business provides the key to Digital's success.

Digital is one of the largest computer manufacturers in the world, operating in some 82 countries. Its business activities cover research and development, manufacturing, sales and support, and services ranging from repair to management consultancy. In the UK, Digital employs around 7,000 people throughout the country.

Digital has had to change, today it does not just sell computers. More than 40 per cent of Digital's revenue comes from services – activities which include planning, designing, implementing and managing complete systems for its customers. The service required of Digital these days is no longer one of supply. It has to be a partner in business with its customers – sharing risks and resources with those customers and providing solutions to their business problems. As the market-place has changed, so has Digital, and its organisation has had to change with it. This case study discusses the redirection of the organisational structure at Digital in order to achieve improved customer service excellence in a highly competitive environment.

DIGITAL UK – TOTAL CUSTOMER SERVICE

'The challenge we all face in redirecting organisation structure for service excellence is to release initiative. Achieving constant service excellence is all about creating flexible organisations. Organisations which can cope with change and which allow for personal initiative and enterprise to flourish.'

Geoff Shingles, *Managing Director, Digital Equipment Company UK.*

According to Kenneth Olsen, President of the Worldwide Digital Equipment Corporation, these are challenging times for Digital, and all the computer industry: 'At no time in Digital's history have the productivity, the enthusiasm, the thrill of new products and new ways to help the customer been so strong.' If I were to highlight an outstanding characteristic that I discovered when I was involved with Digital, it would be the number of times that each person I talked with mentioned the customer. Everyone discusses the customer or, more often, 'our customer'. On entering their UK head office at Worton Grange in Reading, a suspended electronic display reminds staff and visitors how many customers have telephoned Digital during the course of that day to place orders. At 9.00 a.m. the neon display had notched nearly 90 calls; by 10.00 a.m. that had more than trebled. The entire organisation appears to be built around the customer.

On reading the company's annual report, one is naturally pleased that emphasis is placed on the contribution made by employees. It is, however, the number of times that the customer is referred to – in comparison with the annual reports distributed by many of Digital's competitors – that is most impressive. One feels that this is an organisation putting the customer first; not just in their organisational structure, but in their thinking and their behaviour. It is summed up by a Digital salesman, Jeremy Deaner, when he says: 'We are not just in the business of keeping the customers happy – we want to *delight* them. Long-term survival of Digital depends on delighting the customer and dealing with a customer is an opportunity to delight them.'

John Barrett, Digital UK's Deputy Chairman admits that this was not always the case. According to him it was not that long ago that Digital's idea of 'service' meant, 'supply it'. Digital engineered, manufactured, distributed, and sold. As the market-place grew there appeared on the scene a swarm of suppliers. Competition became fierce, and service grew from mere supply to supporting with product choice and after-sales maintenance. As the computer industry moved into the 1990s its technology became the very foundation for all aspects of business. The concept of service has progressed to specifically attending the individual needs of customers and the complexities of the commercial climate. John Barrett explains:

> *'As the computer industry moved from being a seller's market into a buyer's market, the customer was spoilt for choice of supplier. At Digital we realised that customers would choose the supplier who gave the best service. However, it is very important to find out just what your customers want and, in this regard, we have to listen to what our customers are saying. They did not just want a supplier of computer equipment; our customers wanted solutions to their business problems. I believe that listening to our customers has been a key enabler in making Digital run faster in the market-place.'*

CUSTOMER SERVICE AND INFORMATION TECHNOLOGY

It is not only the market-place that has changed in the computing industry, it is also the customer. The customer has become a much more sophisticated and knowledgeable individual, with high expectations. They rightly demand high standards of service and, in the information technology industry, take superior quality for granted. In a faster-moving world they want faster response times and highly specified, customised products and services at a value for money, mass market price. Businesses now look to information technology to help integrate their growing organisations and services which are increasingly spreading out to their customers. The power of information technology lies at the heart of most businesses. This is illustrated in all of the case studies in this book, as businesses are increasingly reliant on the skills and knowledge of their staff to enable them to deliver the levels of competence and capability demanded by their customers.

Information technology has a major role to play in helping organisations to match their structure to that of their customer's needs. Information technology must therefore also have a customer focus. In fact, it has made a significant contribution to customer service for organisations in all sectors; some, of course, more than others. All successful business excellent companies in this book focus on the known and anticipated customer needs; this has certainly been true of Digital.

A consistent theme throughout these case studies is the need for an organisation to discover exactly what customers feel about it and its product at any given moment; identifying where customers feel that it can be produced, performed or purveyed better. Digital believes that information technology systems have got to be capable of supporting whatever organisational structure is appropriate to meet the constantly changing customer needs and wants in a competitive market-place. Therefore the role of information technology in achieving customer service excellence must be identified.

Digital sponsored a major survey, in association with John Humble, to look at senior management attitudes and practices around service, and to examine the contribution of information technology to service excellence.

Digital's survey findings, (see Appendix 2.1, at the end of this chapter) gave Digital vital information about the market-place:

- More than 70 per cent of the respondents said that information technology had played a positive role in helping their organisation achieve its customer service goals.
- Some 30 per cent of respondents presently used information technology to help them track customer satisfaction. Within three years this number will have grown by almost half.
- One finding predicted a doubling in the use of information technology to achieve customer service goals within the next three years.
- To improve service, electronic data links with customers and suppliers are growing rapidly.
- Disturbingly, more than 70 per cent of respondents did not feel that they were effective in absorbing customer information into their organisations.
- Disruption, cost, incompatible systems and lack of training were considered the biggest headaches facing organisations which introduced computer systems to improve customer service.

- Information technology alone was not considered enough. One in three respondents also had to reorganise to improve service to customers. A third of Digital's respondents said that information technology had facilitated these reorganisations.

The survey findings allowed Digital to better identify its customers' needs and expectations. The findings also allowed Digital to restructure its own organisation to both supply, and exceed, its customer's (in this case the information technology user's) existing and future requirements.

The survey, entitled 'Service – the Role of Information Technology', provided Digital with general insight into the promise and capability of information technology to deliver customer service excellence. Digital also collected a number of examples of how leading UK companies are using information technology within a wider framework of change to deliver significant service improvements. David Jackson, a business consultant at Digital primarily involved with the report, drew examples from a variety of industries which illustrated the best way that information technology can be used to deliver service (see Appendix 2.2). Nevertheless, as David rightly points out:

> *'Information technology alone will not bring success. Only when it is directed towards an organisation's defined and articulated purpose – serving the customer – will major improvements be realised. The design must encompass new forms of work and organisation as well as ruthless removal of bureaucracy and red tape.'*

In fact, Digital offers an excellent action plan and corporate checklist to help customers identify those areas where information technology can help deliver service excellence. (See Appendix 2.3.)

When I was in the customer services division of Texaco (see chapter 1) I felt I was in an information technology wonderland. Without information technology, Texaco could quite simply not deliver the style or quality of customer service it was hoping to achieve at the point of sale; nor could it measure effectively its level of customer satisfaction. Texaco is not, however, in the information technology business. Its core business is oil. Therefore, when selecting information technology to improve its service excellence to customers, Texaco would go with that problem direct to the information technology supplier.

Texaco would expect that supplier to provide a solution to its business problem; not just to supply the information technology, but to plan, design, implement and manage a complete system, to be a partner. The company would want its information technology system to be customer-focused; the supplier would be required to match this capability by developing networks which interact with each other directly, in the way that people do. The service the supplier provides goes beyond information collection. It facilitates the flow of information throughout the organisation and optimises the use of information and resources locally, nationally and internationally. This flexibility enhances customer service.

Information technology must work in harmony with the organisation structure. Texaco's customer service division at Swindon is a good example of this – it has to have a relationship with other departments, and parts of the Texaco organisation, which are equally geared to a mission statement of service excellence. In other words, the organisational structure has to back the business, rather than hold the business back, when it comes to customer service.

Digital, therefore, does not just supply the customer with a partial solution to the problem of achieving improved customer service. It has realised that what its customers look for is a total solution – help not only with the systems solutions to improve a user's customer service, but also support in helping re-engineer a management structure which strengthens customer service.

THE CLIMATE FOR CUSTOMER SERVICE

Another problem consistently highlighted in the case studies in this book is that as market-places and customers change, becoming more diverse and demanding, organisations become even larger to accommodate these trends. As these organisations grow, (for example, the

Metropolitan Police case study, Chapter 4) they tend to become introverted, focusing their attention on their own internal structure rather than the customers they should be servicing. The very people that these organisations seek to serve become forgotten as responsibilities become apportioned within job descriptions, task roles, functions, or departments and divisions within the enterprise. The end result is an organisation built of completely separate compartments which do not even communicate with one another. A consequence of this is the compulsion to have restricted and inflexible management control systems, often centrally-based, with tight reins and austere limitations to authority.

If you observe service excellent organisations, a consistent characteristic is one of flexibility, a spirit of entrepreneurism and a team-based environment that encourages staff initiative. The organisation itself, in its structure and systems, has to be innovative and inspirational. How can an organisation respond to customers' demands and make resources swiftly available to meet constantly changing customer culture, if its structure and style is insipid, inscrutable, and insensate?

A recurring theme in this book is that no matter how large the organisation, or its scale of operation, the enterprise, its beliefs and its behaviour should be constantly focused on the customer. It is not just the fact that the customer is paying, rather that the customer is first; the boss's boss is the customer.

To be a truly service excellent enterprise, being aware that your market-place is changing and that your customers now have different needs and wants is simply not sufficient. You must get the organisation to change with it. In the Metropolitan Police study (see chapter 4), it is easy to see that the bigger the organisation, the more difficult it is to change, and therefore the more service excellence and support is at risk.

I have been in organisations which are dynamic and diligent enough to release the creative energies of their people, but ultimately they are not giving the service that their customers want. Superficially, the company may appear to be organised to meet customers' needs, but on closer inspection it is apparent that the customers, in fact, come second to the control and reporting needs of the company. When control takes precedence over the customer then the organisation cannot retain the flexibility required to meet ever-changing customer demands. Digital recognised this problem within its own organisation.

MAKING CUSTOMER SERVICE HAPPEN AT DIGITAL

Digital appreciated that it had to redirect its own organisational structure if it was to offer service excellence to its customers, and help supply them with business solutions that, through information technology, would give them a new competitive edge. It was essential for Digital to build a customer-focused organisation and its approach is based on a relatively simple, but powerful, idea.

John Barrett explains a familiar organisational concept that basically gets everyone in the organisation focused in the same direction; they call it the 'inverted triangle':

> *'If you are going to provide what your customers want, you must have an organisation that can listen, and stay close to the customer. This means that the top of the organisation is the part of Digital that is closest to our customer. This indicates to everyone that the customer is given the highest priority. This is also the broadest part of the organisation and the management structure below this, in effect, supports the front line. This is our customer-focused organisation.' (See Figure 2.1.)*

Ron Down, Digital's Customer Care Manager highlights how this concept of the 'inverted triangle' forces Digital to effectively flatten the management hierarchy for greater efficiency. 'It also encourages the idea that, even if you do not work directly for the customer, you work for someone who does.' He explains that there are three major elements that must work together to achieve this:

- Purpose.
- People.
- Process.

Figure 2.1 Mission statement

BUILDING A CUSTOMER FOCUSED ORGANISATION

To win the hearts and minds of customers (to say nothing of their purses) demands concerned action on three fronts: Purpose, People and Process.

Purpose – A customer focused organisation clearly states its intentions to the customer. The vision alone is not enough. It has to be clearly communicated and constantly re-inforced. Saying one thing and doing the opposite is a sure road to failure. Top management must lead by example. Customer thinking must be clearly visible in their words, their decisions and their actions.

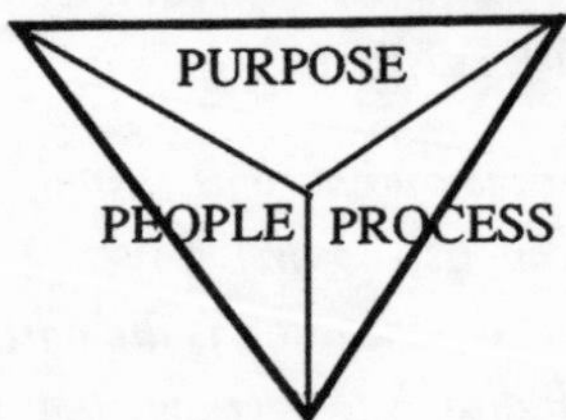

People – When a customer meets an employee, they meet the organisation. Each and every person must understand how they impact the customer. They must be trained, organised and rewarded to suit the needs of the customer.

Process – Friendly co-operative staff, following an inspired vision often find cumbersome, functionally based business processes and information systems a major obstacle. Being 'easy to do business with' is high on the list of many buying decision makers. Steps have to be taken to remove the red tape and provide staff with all the information and support they need to serve the customer.

The elements of the 'inverted triangle' are explained by Geoff Shingles:

> *'Our purpose springs from a deep understanding of ourselves and Digital; on which our guiding philosophy, values and beliefs are based. This is what underpins the whole oganisation and gives it direction.*
>
> *'The attitudes and behaviour of our people need to be brought into line with our purpose through training, rewards and recognition. Because customers are central to our purpose we group our people around the customer, with skill and resources immediately available.*
>
> *'Our processes and systems – the object here is quick response – make life easy for our customers. Systems should reduce complexity and release our people to serve the customer, as well as providing management reporting information. They must allow the distributed skills and resources of the company to communicate; and of course they must help us to fulfil our purpose.'*

Ron Down explains that Digital, having a heritage of being an equipment company and now moving towards a service image, has had to journey through a transformation; in other words, the change from being product-orientated to becoming service-centred:

> *'The three elements of purpose, people, and process must fit together but you have to constantly check that they are always in alignment because, in a constantly changing customer climate and dynamic market-place, any single change can upset the balance between these key elements.'*

This is endorsed by John Barrett who explains:

> *'Digital's aim is to organise ourselves in whichever way is necessary to address our customers' needs, demands and, indeed, opportunities. A healthy organisation can only stay healthy by carrying out this constant review as a matter of discipline. It is recurring in all of our business. Quality and customer service is an integral part of all of our activities and that fact remains constant. Quality and customer service are attributes of everything we do and of the way we do it. We define quality and*

customer service to show that it is an integral part of Digital's strategy. Although corporate strategy develops and evolves with time, these basic principles remain at the heart of our activities.'

These principles are:

- Quality and customer service is creating value for the customer.
- Total quality and service is doing that by the most efficient means.
- Total quality and customer service management is mobilising the whole organisation to do these things.

The important thing about philosophies, visions, service excellence, being customer-focused and so on, is that they are not actions on the boardroom hit list. There has to be a strong, supported and sustained approach to continuous improvement. In Digital, the route map was laid out as follows:

- Fundamental internal and external research to discover, and understand, what Digital customers really want and value.
- Sensing, and listening to, what customers and workforce feel about Digital's performance measured against the factors identified in the various research findings.
- Evaluating all this information and then taking action on it.
- Continuously improving on the 'inverted triangle' in order to enhance Digital's quality and customer service excellence.
- To achieve service excellence, each person in the organisation needs to be capable of fast response and useful contribution. This depends on having the right information and knowledge in the right hands, in the right place, at the right time.

To achieve major organisational change, and an understanding of its purpose, there has to be an attitude change through education experience. One part of the job role of Mike Newell, Digital's UK Quality Manager, is to get it through to all employees that everyone in the organisation has a customer. He has to make people appreciate why this major organisational change, moving from the 'classic triangle' to the 'inverted triangle', is so essential to Digital's own customer service excellence and ultimate survival. 'Employees will talk about it, but you must have evidence of active pursuit,' says Mike Newell. This requires much enlightened thinking throughout the company's entire education process and seminars. It also requires much counselling and coaching for those who find the change either too daunting or too dramatic.

Mike Newell doubts whether you can have a quality and service environment without a few qualms:

> *'When you are reorganising it is a very fragile experience, especially if everyone knows that you are redirecting your organisational structure, for whatever reason. The boardroom know that you are trying to achieve quality and service excellence, but the qualms are felt by the staff and indeed the customers. It is very tempting at this stage to give up but you have to stick with it, keep your nerve while keeping your antennae up. That is why the vision, the belief, and the high level management attention is so essential; without that it just would not work.'*

For Mike Newell, this has meant developing a whole new way of thinking within the workforce; through education, understanding and learning. As with other case studies the energy devoted to education is enormous. Middle and upper level managers throughout Digital attend seminars which cover a variety of topics, including; customer/supplier relations, organising for quality and service, quality and service leadership, and creating business excellence.

This learning enables participants to develop a plan for implementing service improvements in their part of the organisation. (In fact this action-learning approach is consistent throughout all the case studies.) For this type of training to be successful participants need to be committed to developing specific plans for service improvement in their work area, then sticking to them. It is emphasised in these seminars – which last some three days – that in order for Digital to achieve a strong customer focus and service process, everyone must ensure that their part of the organisation is structured

Figure 2.2 An example of Digital training course objectives

CREATING BUSINESS EXCELLENCE THROUGH QUALITY AND SERVICE IMPROVEMENT

This course for management provides an overview of customer service and quality topics, including customer-supplier relations, process improvement, cost of quality and service, organising for quality and service leadership.

Upon completion of the course you will be able to:

1. Discuss how a total quality and customer service management approach can be used to attain an organisational vision of business excellence.

2. Integrate quality and service goals into the strategic and operational plans and business goals of your organisation.

3. Identify tools and processes to develop and sustain business excellence.

4. Sustain your business excellence efforts by applying leadership principals to identify resources, train and motivate your staff.

5. Discuss how to develop the cross-functional and customer-supplier relationships that are a part of business excellence.

6. State your role and responsibilities as a model of leadership excellence.

7. Develop business excellence strategies and tactics for your own organisation.

8. Identify available resources which will support your business excellence efforts.

for quality and service improvement. They must therefore ensure that their staff are empowered for that improvement.

Much of the training is geared to giving managers the skills necessary to lead their staff towards business excellence. (See Figure 2.2.) Emphasis is placed on the customer, and this is where all the feedback from the internal and external market research is so valuable. Again, a constant theme throughout these case studies is that the organisation is not improving customer service simply because the boardroom want it, but rather because the market-place and customers are demanding it.

As a result, many of the modules of the training programme at Digital discover exactly why the customers are changing, what they are demanding, and how Digital is going to manage those needs. Managers also debate how the company's processes can be designed and improved, to ensure quality services and products. Other parts of the programme discuss the organisation, staff and management development needed to achieve business excellence.

Continuous improvement is an essential component in a service excellent company, as it is always driven by the customer eye. Continual market-place surveys, both internally and externally, work group discussions, and the training sessions all serve to reinforce this message at Digital.

Coming closer to the customer

All this training has been essential to help support the changing organisational structure towards the 'inverted triangle'. One such structural change is Digital's approach to organising for customer needs through an 'account group'. This is based upon every customer having a team of people within Digital who are dedicated to that customer's service. However, according to Geoff Shingles, it is more than that: 'Each team needs to provide a unique set of complementary skills and resources. These skills and resources will change from time to time, but will always be tailored specifically for each customer.' However, Geoff Shingles admits that this is not enough on its own to achieve service excellence; you have to take this 'organisation by customer' one stage further, using what Digital calls the 'entrepreneur model'. As Geoff points out:

> *'It is no accident that the word entrepreneur is synonymous with the spirit of initiative, freedom and energy. The entrepreneur model means that each customer account becomes a business unit in its own right. Each account manager becomes a business manager with full responsibility for customer satisfaction and profitability. Their job is to apply company resources to customer needs, profitably. As one of our employees said, "working for Digital is the closest you can come to running your own business while still being part of a large organisation".'*

Of course, this can be daunting for those people who are now in a position of much more accountability than they ever were previously. This is another reason why the education process is a priority, as it is this management structure that is supporting the front line of the account group. Customers help too; sharing the organisational structure with the customers creates an affinity with them, their needs and their wants.

The change in environment within Digital is encouraged by having an open dialogue with customers through service and quality forums. These forums have their focus on the quality of Digital's products and business service. (See their early constitution which is, naturally, constantly updated. Figure 2.3.) For example, a regular forum occurs between Digital and one of its major clients, British Telecom. British Telecom discusses with Digital how they perceive its services and products; the business constant is to drive continuous quality and customer service improvement through a formal and partnered organisational approach. This type of customer clinic exists in most service excellent companies and is illustrated in different formats in this book (for example, the Fire Brigade User Group in the Simon Access study; see chapter 10).

The British Telecom/Digital quality and service forum offers a shared viewpoint on quality and service between customer and supplier. It fosters a closer relationship, facilitates a shared quality and service vision, encourages a common vocabulary, and enables a

Figure 2.3 British Telecom/Digital Quality/Service Forum

TERMS OF REFERENCE

1. To provide a corporate-wide meeting point for users of Digital equipment with an interest in Quality/Service related topics of mutual concern.

2. To act as a focal point for the above subjects and interface between British Telecom and Digital to solve Quality/Service issues and disseminate their resolution.

3. To act as a Working Group of the British Telecom/Digital Technical Board to resolve issues identified by them as constituting Quality/Service issues and formally reporting progress and resolution to the Technical Board.

4. To interface with other Working Groups established by the British Telecom/Digital Technical Board e.g.:

   British Telecom/Digital Procurement User Group.
   British Telecom/Digital Technical User Group.

   Resolve issues identified by the Working Group as constituting Quality/Service issues and formally reporting progress and resolution to the relevant Working Group and the Technical Board.

5. To increase awareness within British Telecom and Digital of both Companies' commitment to Quality/Service Improvement by publication of the minutes of the Quality/Service Forum meetings, which will include Action points and their resolution, to all interested parties in both Companies. The main method for this will be by British Telecom/Digital INFOLINK.

6. To jointly fund a Quality/Service Improvement Team comprised of members of the Quality/Service Forum of their appointees.

   The purpose of this Quality/Service Improvement Team is to act as a focus for identifying and monitoring Quality/Service Improvement opportunities within the processes which operate in and between both Companies. Thus the resolution of operational problems are carried out as completely as possible by existing management procedures. The Quality/Service Improvement team will therefore only address those issues which offer a Quality/ Services Improvement opportunity which are not covered by the normal interfaces or are identified as not having been resolved by them.

mutual learning experience to take place. Effectively, it allows Digital to listen to its customer and allows British Telecom to build a strong relationship with its supplier. This type of forum naturally helps Digital achieve continuous improvement of the three key elements of its 'inverted triangle'.

The whole focus of Digital in the 1990s is its capability through dedicated teams to come closer to its customers, wherever those customers are in business throughout the world. Digital has the systems and processes to achieve this; over 50,000 computers linked together in the world's largest commercial network. Within that network Digital has the freedom to organise its processes and people to meet whatever needs its customers may have.

The manager responsible for the world-wide business with Unilever, for example, stays in touch with a distributed team of 120 people across 15 time zones by utilising electronic mail and electronic conferencing. All the information needed to service the customer is shared; what is more, Digital can communicate directly with the customer by electronic mail. In this way, the full capability of the Digital people throughout the world is made available to the customer.

This is also true of its customer support centres. Here, again, technology and a world-wide organisation combine to provide service excellence. Technical specialists are on the end of a telephone to help the customer 24 hours a day. Their single objective is to solve problems quickly. All calls are logged and routed by computer to the appropriate specialist. These specialists have access to the same database of all known problems and solutions, and this avoids constantly 're-inventing the wheel'. Quite simply, this means that if engineers in Australia come up with a new idea, they can make it instantly available to their counterparts anywhere in the world.

The whole ethos of Digital staff working in a team-based environment, with responsibility spread throughout the team, can also be witnessed in its manufacturing plant at Digital Ayr, in Scotland. Since 1980, Digital Scotland's plant has grown from 25 employees operating in an assembly and test environment, to a 1,500-strong workforce operating within a vertically-integrated manufacturing plant (or, as Digital prefer to call it, 'a business solutions environment').

Today, Digital Ayr is a showpiece of manufacturing, having moved away from a sequential manufacturing process to a totally integrated holistic approach. It has created an environment in which, as in the rest of Digital, the customer is at the top of the organisation chart, and in which marketing and sales work hand-in-hand with manufacturing.

This team approach gives Digital greater flexibility, as has been the case with British Telecom, one of its major customers. British Telecom approached Digital Ayr knowing what it wanted from a new national database system, but not knowing what that new system should be.*

According to the Digital Ayr site manager:

> *'People are the most valuable asset any organisation has, but they need to be encouraged to work together as a team. They have to understand that one function does not operate in isolation from another, and they must use their collective strengths to maximum advantage. We reorganised our plant in such a way that the elements – people across a range of disciplines, technology and capital investment – were all complementary. Above all it was an environment in which people were the master.'*

In effect, at Digital Ayr the manufacturing process has evolved into an environment of innovation with a high degree of autonomy and entrepreneurship down the line. (This is also a consistent theme in many of the excellence case studies in this book.) The inspiring asset of an innovative company is that the atmosphere is not impersonal like that of a large corporation, but rather it is a collection of close-knit individuals motivated by a customer-focused corporate philosophy.

People need to have a sense of self value. The traditional assembly line process, for example, never engendered a sense of self

* This customer service project is discussed in more depth in the *Sunday Times* video accompaniment to this book on Quality: Total Customer Service.

value because people only ever saw one small part of the product. Because they never saw the wider aspects of the business it was difficult for such individuals, say assembly operators, to relate to the corporate vision. What Digital has done has been to give people a sense of ownership, responsibility and empowerment to make management decisions. Managers have had to learn to stand back, instead of imposing their solutions to problems on the workforce. People have been encouraged to solve problems directly related to their work, allowing them the satisfaction of manufacturing a product from front to back.

According to Dave Lawrence, Managing Director of Digital Scotland:

> *'The results have been a real revelation, in that the ability to rise to this reorganisation and customer focus challenge exceeded all our expectations. Staff were innovative in problem solving and set themselves tougher goals than any traditional manager. Give the people the right tools to do a job and they will generally succeed. Give people the incentive to learn and develop their skills, and the investment in training and education benefits everyone. Customers benefit from a significant improvement in quality, reliability and delivery performance, the workforce benefit from a higher level of job satisfaction, and Digital Ayr benefits from a staff turnover of less than one per cent.'*

As the Digital Ayr workforce began to understand business enterprise they were also given responsibility for their own quality, within Digital's total quality and customer service approach. This approach also extends to managing relationships with suppliers. Suppliers have to be a natural extension of Digital's own manufacturing resources and they must be as committed to excellence as Digital Ayr, being completely in tune with their business objectives. This marriage of joint excellence objectives between manufacturer and supplier can be witnessed in a great many excellence type organisations. The organisational restructuring and commitment to customer focus has, for Digital Ayr, had a number of tangible results:

- First and foremost, Digital Ayr believes it has a committed, motivated, fully trained workforce who regard change as an opportunity, not a threat.
- Increased manufacturing output; in the space of four years it rose from $205 million to $1.7 billion.
- Within two years there has been a 60 per cent increase in shipments.
- An improvement in inventory turns of 67 per cent.
- A reduction in ending inventory of 10 per cent.
- An improvement in inventory ageing of 15 per cent.
- An overall space saving of 20 per cent.

Management can now concentrate more on the strategic issues of leading Digital Ayr into the next ten years, from a position of strength that was certainly not apparent a few years ago. John Hodge, Low End Systems Manufacturing Manager at Ayr, explains:

> *'The support for our situation here in Ayr can be shown in our quality, customer service, and productivity improvements. Over the last few years we have shown a significant and continuing improvement in many areas: our orders are shipped regularly, on time, to weekly schedules; we have grown output with no additional stress added; raw materials inventories have remained flat, whilst we have tripled the output. Today our people are trained, qualified and better ready for the challenges of tomorrow.'*

Digital Scotland is also well placed to service the European market with complementary activities like product design, European order administration and manufacturing operations from silicon processing through to solution support. Colin Finlayson, European Business Centre Manager says:

> *'We recognise that you cannot continue to do things the way that you have always done them. The computer industry is moving so fast that we have to service our customers faster and more efficiently in order to make the money that the company needs to make to be successful. So we have*

concentrated very much on changing processes to look for speed and efficiency. For example, during the last couple of years we have reduced our order turnaround time from over 20 days to more like five or six, and we have now the potential to reduce this to 24 hours.'

REMAINING CUSTOMER-FOCUSED

No organisation involved in manufacturing can afford to stand still; the benefits Digital derived from reacting positively to market change and customer expectations raised a whole new set of issues. The winners in this competitive environment, the organisations that have reached the top, are those which can move quickly enough to grasp opportunities. Digital feels that the unprecedented human investment in change, of the kind displayed in this study, is the key to current and future business survival and growth.

Digital can, however, go one stage further in its dedication to servicing its customers. According to Geoff Shingles:

'Through the application of artificial intelligence we are able, at Digital, to monitor our customers' computer systems remotely and sense upcoming problems. This allows us to fix problems before they even happen. For Digital, service excellence is also about anticipating needs and providing service that our customer does not yet realise he or she wants!'

When leaving the Digital building, with people still at work well past the going-home time, one realises that so much of excellence in service and performance has to do with ordinary individuals at work being motivated by simple values. Simple values, yet compelling ones (see the mission statement in Figure 2.1, p. 39).

Jeremy Deaner is right to suggest that the long-term survival of Digital depends on delighting the customer. However, this can only happen in an organisation which is in the 'people' business. It is, as Geoff Shingles said in the opening comment to this study: 'All about creating flexible organisations.' An organisation where the majority of the workforce develop commitment through effective training, personal identification with Digital's success and, most important, the commitment that exists between individual employees, their boss and their customer.

By redirecting their organisational structure, goals and values, Digital management has, in effect, been telling its workforce that those at the frontier know the business and the customer best. It is they who deserve all management support; hence the 'inverted triangle'. The challenge for Digital over the next decade will be to continually remind everyone in the organisation that this is the case, and reinforce the message.

A service excellent organisation relies heavily on an individual's creativity or a team's initiative for its innovation. The importance of treating individuals well, and maximising them to their fullest potential, has long been the management style of Japanese companies. In a way the individual becomes greater than any other part of the organisation. I think that is what Digital are trying to achieve. As John Stuart Mill (1806-1873) said: 'The great creative individual . . . is capable of more wisdom and virtue than collective man ever can be.'

Appendix 2.1 IT Survey

SECTION ONE: SURVEY FINDINGS

WHAT IS IT?

In this report, the term Information Technology (IT) is used to represent a range of technologies to capture, store, process and transmit information. The core technologies are computers and telecommunication networks.

1. IT's impact on service

Information Technology has made a significant contribution to customer service for organisations in all sectors - though for some more than others.

Have developments in IT in your company in the last three years made a positive or negative contribution to the quality of customer service?

What do you think the contribution of IT will be in the next three years?

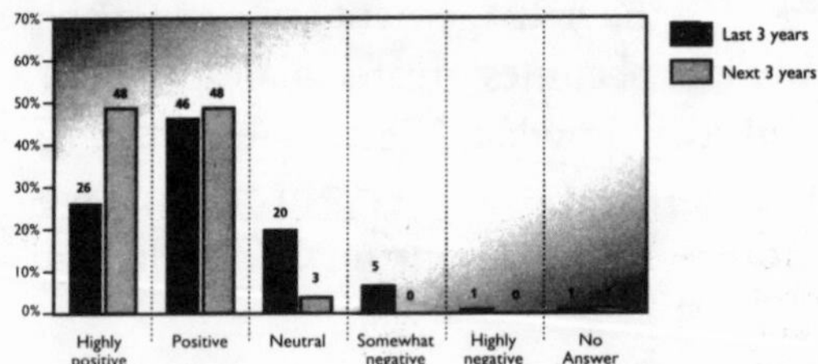

Small companies (fewer than 100 employees) are most enthusiastic about IT's advantages, perhaps because it can put them on an equal footing with larger companies with relatively smaller investments.

What of those who answered neutral? Does this represent mixed experiences, reluctance tempered with a sense of duty or eagerness tinged with frustration? Whatever the reason, the undecided become converts within three years when almost all see only positive results.

IT has to be applied to areas the business has chosen to focus on. In our next question, we asked if this important link is in place.

Does your IT strategy statement include an explicit reference to quality and/or customer service?

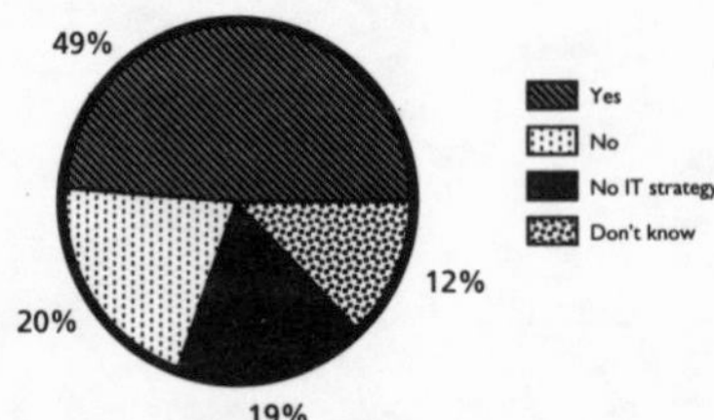

If service is a clear business priority, then this must be reflected in IT investments. Too often, organisations do not link business and IT strategies, a failing which is a proven track to lower returns.

One in three companies have re-organised in the last three years to improve service to customers. But is IT a barrier or facilitator of change?

In which, if any of these ways has IT helped you to improve customer service? (Multiple replies allowed)

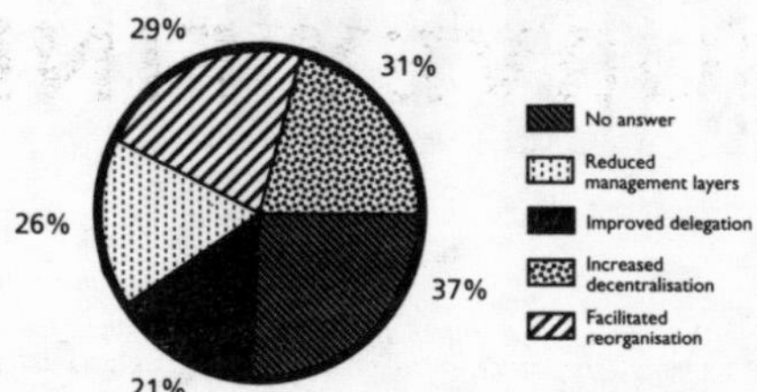

It would seem the jury is still out. Approximately one-third clearly do not believe IT helps organisational change. The remainder have benefited, with de-centralisation coming out as favourite. Empowering staff (often a driver for and result of de-centralisation and reduced management layers) is recognised as key in creating a customer focused culture. IT delivers the right information to the right people at the right place and the right time and can be readily 're-plumbed' as organisations change.

If it can be measured, it can be moved. The measurement of service performance is customer satisfaction. Our survey shows that the use of IT to measure customer satisfaction is still in its adolescence.

Does your company use computer systems for measuring customer satisfaction? Do you expect to introduce it in the next three years?

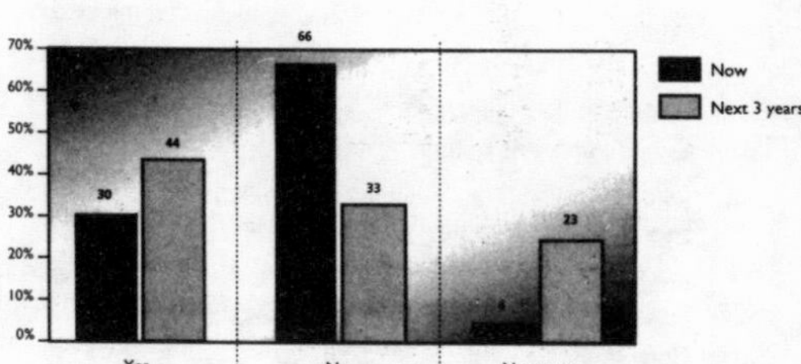

Use of tools is one thing, but how effective are they? We asked the question.

To what extent does/would each of these tools give your company a competitive edge? (0=not at all, 5=very great)

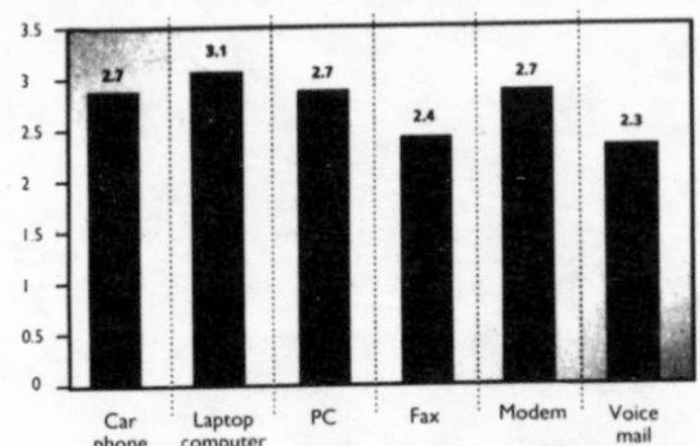

With the exception of the laptop computer, none of the tools ranked very highly. Is this because they are being used to simply automate what is already done rather than a tool to find a different way of doing things? Or is it that no advantage can accrue when everyone is doing the same thing? Looking at the growth in the use of these tools, perhaps we should be talking about competitive necessity rather than advantage. Laptop computers are set for the most rapid and continuing penetration. Companies are clearly aware of the competitive advantage of being able to provide detailed product support, quotations and availability on the spot - particularly when product and service portfolios are becoming increasingly complex.

3. The Problems

Finally, we asked what problems people faced when implementing service orientated information systems.

To what extent has your company experienced any of the problems listed when introducing or increasing its use of IT in the customer service arena?

	Not at all %	To some extent %	To a serious extent %	No answer %
Disruption during changes	12	58	16	14
Incompatibility of systems	15	53	19	13
Cost over-runs	15	46	24	15
Lack of attention to training	17	50	17	16
Inaccuracy of information	17	51	15	16
Lack of skilled IT staff	21	46	18	15
Unreliability	20	55	9	15
Information overload	22	48	13	16
Poor cost effectiveness	28	45	10	17
Middle mgt antagonism	39	36	9	16
Demotivation of those affected	39	37	5	19
Loss of efficiency	40	35	5	20
Loss of flexibility in response to customers	45	31	6	18
Depersonalisation	51	26	5	19
Threats to confidentiality	50	28	3	19

Why include links with suppliers in a survey about customer service? It is difficult to give good service if you don't get good service. As the saying goes, you are only as strong as your weakest link. Providing good service implies effective management of the total supply chain. The relatively high number of links with customers suggest a significant investment in service orientated IT. An alternative interpretation is that large customers are forcing their suppliers into these investments.

The figures do however confirm the rapid growth of electronic trading. Developments of computer and communications technology are providing an infrastructure where an increasing quantity of business will be transacted electronically. For many, service leadership will only be achievable through leadership in the electronic market-place.

Over the past five years, a number of new tools have emerged which help front-line staff, notably sales and service to stay in close touch with customers.

Which, if any, of these tools does your company provide to its salesmen or field staff? And which do you expect to be provided in the next three years?

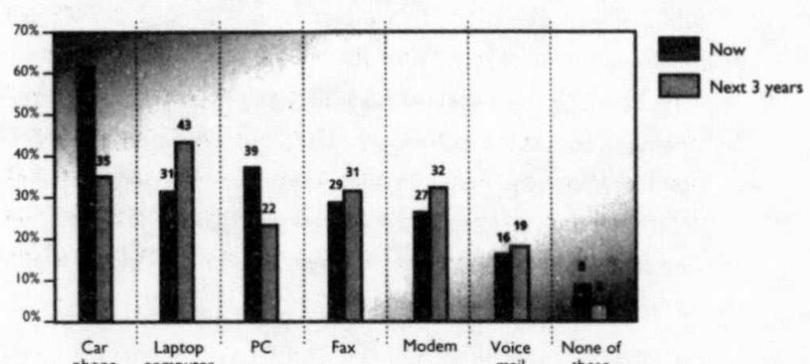

Clearly The Chancellor will have mixed feelings. His new tax on carphones will raise more money, but will he have more interrupted restaurant meals? Almost all mobile front-line staff will soon have some form of communication tool. Larger companies are more likely to equip their field staff with car phones and voice mail whilst smaller companies favour equipment which will allow their field staff to do more of their own back-up work. The growth in laptop computers suggests an increase in tele-working (no permanent office base) and fuels the growth of the electronic market-place. An increasing number of companies are turning to portable computers to provide support to salesmen selling increasingly complex products and services.

Computers are ideally suited to the analysis of the large quantities of data involved in most customer satisfaction monitoring schemes. But analysis is only part of the story, without action, measurement is a wasted activity.

We end this section with a look at how effectively information about the customer is used.

Do you believe that information from the field is adequately absorbed into your management information system?

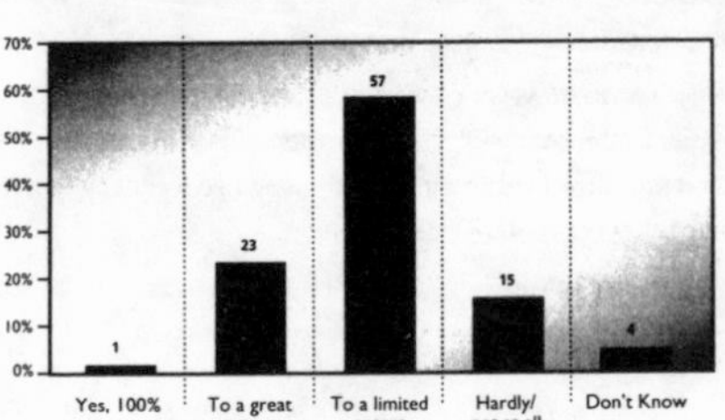

It is alarming that 72% believe information from the field, the market-place, is only to a small extent being absorbed by their organisations. How can the customer be well served if their messages are not heard? When the customer airs a view, gives a suggestion or makes a verbal complaint to a member of staff, they are addressing the whole organisation. They assume - not unfairly - that the information will be shared. Research by American consultants TARP show that top level managers only receive between 0.5% and 2% of all complaints.

Interestingly, our survey shows that small companies suffer much less from information starvation, reinforcing the saying that 'small is beautiful'.

2. IT & the customer interface

Service is experienced at the interface between buyer and supplier. What role does IT have to play in this interface? That was the subject of our next set of questions.

Have you in the last three years introduced or increased electronic links with customers or suppliers? Do you expect to do so in the next three years?

	Last 3 years	Next 3 years
With customers	%	%
Paperless transactions/ invoicing	35	47
Integrated electronic mail	25	37
Delivery systems (eg JiT)	15	29
Production information	16	26
Automatic call-off systems	15	26
Product catalogue info	12	27
Other	12	10
With suppliers		
Paperless transactions/ invoicing	27	43
Delivery systems (eg JiT)	15	29
Production information	14	25
Product catalogue info	9	18
Other	3	5
None/No answer	27	19

Change management, incompatible systems and budget over-runs are problems associated with most IT investments. More surprising, and disturbing is the 37% who felt that introducing systems to improve service had actually reduced the flexibility of response to customers. Computerised red tape is the worse form of bureaucracy. The key is to design work and systems to suit the customers, or at least the people who directly serve the customers.

Systems incompatibility is a two part problem. The move towards 'open systems' - computers that can talk to each other will ease the technical problem. A greater problem is the need to re-direct fundamental designs away from functionally based systems and towards systems which match the way a customer inter-acts with the organisation.

Appendix 2.2 IT Survey (cont.)

SECTION THREE: **SERVICE IN ACTION**

The Digital survey provides general insights into the ability and promise of IT to deliver service excellence. But as the saying goes "Actions speak louder than words". In this section of the report, we have collected a number of examples of how leading companies are currently using information technology within a wider framework of change to deliver significant service improvements.

These examples, drawn from a variety of industries, illustrate the best way to use IT. Information technology alone will not bring success. Only when it is directed towards an organisation's defined and articulated purpose - serving the customer - will major improvements in service be realised. The design must encompass new forms of work and organisations as well as a ruthless removal of bureaucracy and red tape.

ROYAL AUTOMOBILE CLUB "COMPUTER ASSISTED RESCUE SERVICE"

Highlights

- Since 1985 the RAC has undergone radical changes including a major IT investment programme.
- The RAC have achieved a unique blend of system features, benefits and IT skills that has brought them substantial competitive edge and enabled them to refocus their business.
- The Computer Aided Recovery System has enabled the RAC to fundamentally improve performance and control of its business.
- Information captured at an operational level has facilitated sophisticated business analysis and improved efficiency.
- An increased number of members are enjoying an improved service provided to them more efficiently.

The Company

The Royal Automobile Club is the second largest motoring organisation in the UK. The largest, the Automobile Association (AA) reigned supreme until 1985. It had six million members compared to the RAC's two million. Since then the transformation has been astonishing. The RAC now has 5.2 million members compared to the AA's 7.5 million. Although still some way behind, the RAC is catching up fast.

The catalyst for this change was the appointment of Arthur Large as chief executive in 1985.

In 1985 the RAC was known very much as a gentleman's club, with an institutionalised management structure. Managers were known as superintendent, inspector, chief superintendent and sergeant. Staff saluted their superiors while wearing white gloves and military style uniforms.

Large joined from British Leyland where he had worked closely with Michael Edwards. He took a more focused view of the purpose of the RAC. His view was that:

> "What the motorist wanted most was for his motoring organisation to answer the phone quickly, to get to him quickly and to re-mobilise him"

He saw this mission of running the RAC as an efficient and profitable business to be clouded by tradition and beset by embedded practices. His objective was to transform the RAC into a business minded organisation.

The problem

In 1988, the volume of calls from motorists exceeded the capacity of the RAC's paper based system. The RAC had little management information coming back from the system and no effective way of controlling the business or of monitoring its performance.

The RAC divided the country up into 17 autonomous regions each with its own control room. Members had a card with 34 different emergency phone numbers. Only if they called the right number would they get through to the control area that could help.

A number of advisory committees dedicated to changing the whole direction of the company were formed. Recruiting new members, making a profit and becoming a high-tech company were set as the new goals. Corporate objectives and targets were issued to everyone and updated annually. Staff were encouraged to adopt a more informal and friendly style more atune to a modern company.

During Large's tenure at the RAC unnecessary levels of management were axed. The marketing and sales departments spawned selling teams to sell bulk memberships to car manufacturers, securing deals that would be the basis for phenomenal growth. The personnel department was charged with sorting out internal communication, and management and technical staff brought into reality the idea of a computerised rescue service based on a fully automated and nationally integrated network. The CARS system (Computer Assisted Rescue Service) emerged.

The solution

The CARS system allows calls to be handled anywhere in the country. It combines a central computer-based "command and control centre" supported by 17 regional centres with direct two way communication to the patrolmen via mobile data terminals.

Wherever the breakdown occurs, the motorist now calls a single freephone number. The motorist's information is recorded directly into CARS, identification of membership, members location and an analysis of the fault are performed and the data relayed to the mobile data terminal in the patrolman's car.

It is these mobile data terminals that have revolutionised the organisation. Management information is now flowing directly from the sharp end of the business to managers providing them with timely and accurate information. From being an antiquated organisation the RAC is now probably better organised in their field of operation than any other commercial organisation.

The RAC's Service Managers now have the ability to manage. This in turn has enabled budgetary control to be devolved to the Regional Service Managers who now have control over service costs, the operation of vans and patrolmen and how well these and agent resources are used.

HERBERT SMITH

Highlights

- Word Processing, considered by many as a lowly office tool, improves the quality of finished work but changes the way work is carried out.
- Information is critical to professional services. The quality and speed of availability of information are key determinants in winning and keeping business. Improvements have a direct impact on business results.
- Creating a customer relationship database will further improve customer focus and improve productivity

The Firm

Herbert Smith is one of the UK's leading law firms. Over 1,000 staff world-wide (including 350 lawye and 94 partners) provide a broad range of legal services to major national and multinational companies. The company were actively involved in the privatisation of Gas, Water and Electricity companies. In addition to its London base, Herbert Smith have offices in Brussels, Hong Kong, New York and Pari

The Problem

Customers in this business are won and kept through the quality of the professional advice and servi matched with competitive fee rates.

In providing legal services, fee earners have to research vast quantities of rapidly changing informatio from a diverse range of sources. The quality of this information has a direct impact on the quality of service. A further problem facing Herbert Smith was to ensure that key learnings which arose during case/assignment were captured and shared throughout the organisation.

The Solution

To solve these problems, Herbert Smith followed a four pronged strategy.

Word processing was introduced to speed up the production and improve the quality of the docume which form the basis of much of the work done for clients. The checking and amendment of these documents by the variety of parties involved in most legal assignments is simplified. Exchange of flop disks removes the need for re-keying vast quantities of data.

To improve access to the latest information, Herbert Smith have introduced TRIP, an on-line legal info mation system. Available to all professional staff, TRIP provides a single source for the majority of inf mation a fee-earner might need. In addition to Law Reports and precedents, the database captures work by the lawyers which may be of value to others in the firm. This includes Model Conditions of Contract, Model Contract Clauses, drafted non-standard documents, advice from counsel and proce ings from conferences. A quality check ensures the accuracy and relevance of the information befor is entered into the database. Information on other professional contacts (counsel, overseas lawyers, surveyors, engineers, interpreters, accountants etc) is also available. This facility has significantly improved productivity in the firm as re-inventing the wheel is no longer necessary.

Digital's office automation tool All-in-One is used for electronic messaging and word processing. Electronic messaging allows instant access to all members of the firm, or a particular group. For exa ple all members of the team of lawyers engaged on a particular transaction use this to save time an paper. All-in-One is also used by many professional staff to do their own basic word processing.

The final thread of Herbert Smith's solution is a client management system - AMIS. AMIS (Accounting Management and Information System) records the expenses incurred for a particular assignment thus ensuring the client is properly charged for the work done. Over time, this has built into a database of client activities which is now used to identify potential conflicts of interest when discussing new business. This ability to quickly identify any potential conflicts enhances the firm's responsiveness to new business opportunities. AMIS is also a valuable tool for managing the business.

The Future

Plans are already underway to extend AMIS into a complete customer relationship management tool. Data about the customers officers and activities will further improve fee-earners productivity

Key Learnings

Involving users is always critical. When professional staff are involved, this is doubly important. The systems Herbert Smith have introduced have changed the way people work. This is only truly effective if the users have been involved in the design work.

Training is also critical, particularly to the speed and extent of individual user take-up. Basic training, showing people how to access and use TRIP is given to all staff, including all new members of staff. Advanced training is available on demand.

YORKSHIRE WATER SERVICES

Highlights

- Privatisation and a new regulatory framework has changed the shape of the business with price and investment decisions being heavily influenced by service performance.
- The registration and subsequent processing of all contacts with customers was critical to achieving service quality standards.
- Linking the initial contact with work scheduling and tracking provided a workflow orientated approach which has changed the way people work.

The Company

Yorkshire Water provides water supply and sewerage services to a population of around 4.5 million people in Yorkshire and part of Humberside. It builds and operates engineering works that collect and treat water, maintains the water distribution system, controls flows into sewers and alleviates flooding from rivers. The company employs 4,000 people, will invest more than £600 million in the next five years and supplies around 300 million gallons of water each day.

The main objectives of the Company are:

To offer a quality of service that is acceptable, having regard to costs and effects on the environment and to remedy recognised deficiencies over a reasonable period.

To achieve these service objectives at the least cost and with steadily improving efficiency, making the best possible use of manpower and assets.

The Problem

YW deals with upwards of 120,000 customer contacts each year and carries out a similar number of jobs as a result. With the paper based system it was impossible to track these jobs at the 40 Depots across Yorkshire and Humberside. Progress and quality of service information was dispersed making reporting back to the customer and the company impossible at other than the local level. To provide company information, Depot Managers produced summaries - a time consuming and inconsistent activity. The result was that decisions were being made with incomplete or inaccurate base data. Financial penalties have been imposed by the Office of Water (OFWAT) where service standards are not met.

The Solution

Following a period of study, a system for monitoring all customer contacts and the resultant jobs was implemented company wide. Development work began in September 1986 and the first module - Customer Contact - was implemented on schedule in June 1987. It has achieved all its objectives and now plays a major role in the operation of the Company. 1,000 members of staff now use the system as an integral part of their daily work.

From the customers viewpoint, the benefits are:

- Simplified registration of contact (service request, complaint) with immediate routing of the job t the appropriate depot. This reduces the time between registration of the job and its completion.
- Instant feedback on the progress of their job.
- Improved responses to questions about supply interruptions or other problems. All jobs which impact customers are registered on the system allowing Customer Contact Centres to give immediate answers to customers.
- Certainty of action is assured. The system tracks outstanding jobs producing action reports again pre-set service quality standards.

Yorkshire Water have experienced additional benefits:

- The ability to maintain (and prove) that the required service standards will improve the performa of the Company as measured by OFWAT. This has a favourable impact on the constraints around price control and investment imposed by the regulator.
- The availability of sound operational management information enables problems to be identified and corrective action taken quicker.
- Improved business performance measures and statistics facilitates improved long term business planning.

The Next Steps

Yorkshire Water is currently driving through a "Quality Initiative" to improve the standards of service its customers. The system provides performance inputs to the Quality Initiative and will be modified t maintain the required standards. Further improvements will give customers advance warnings of planned supply 'shutoffs' and request feedback on the services provided. Customer billing is currentl separate from this operational management system. Plans are in place to integrate these two activiti and thus provide a single point of contact for the customer.

The Major Lessons

The introduction of OMS was a driving force in changing the way people work. It is the vehicle used by staff to drive their work - it is the first place they turn to. This level of acceptance would not have been possible without extensive training - a major feature of the continuous process of implementation. The system also makes the relationship between jobs and the customer much clearer, thereby contributing to the building of a customer focused organisation.

Whilst the benefits of such a system to customers are usually self evident, benefits to the users are not always as obvious. They see only a small part of the total picture and are often concerned only with entering data. There is a constant need for education of users as to the benefits to the company as a whole.

Yorkshire Water anticipate further changes to the organisation over time. This has been considered in the system design which was built to accommodate such changes. Without this consideration, the future flexibility of the organisation is constrained.

Benefits.

The RAC's £30million investment in IT and buildings is beginning to pay off in increased membership, market share and profits. After an initial loss two years ago when the bulk of the investment was made, it generated a £7million pound profit in 1990 on a turnover of £155million whilst the AA made a £4.1million profit from a turnover of £231million.

In parallel to their investment in IT the RAC launched a programme to provide motoring services both to company fleet operators and, through agreements with manufacturers on the sale of new cars. This Motorman programme has been pivotal in developing the business of the RAC. The CARS system has proved key to winning many of the new contracts.

The increase in the quality, quantity and availability of management information, has not only improved operational efficiency but enabled the organisation to be streamlined. It now has six levels of management compared to the AA's eight.

Summary of Benefits

- Management information is readily available
- Organisation flexibility is achieved
- Resource allocation is optimised whilst service levels are maximised
- Cost control is now easily managed
- Reduction in administrative cost
- Enables location of members to be easily found, secures service efficiency

The next steps

The further development of technology and RAC's business run hand-in-hand.

Under consideration are in-car communications devices which will alert the Command and Control centre of the need for assistance without the member having to find a telephone, and future devices for advanced fault diagnosis.

P&O EUROPEAN FERRIES

Highlights

- Reduced check in time from 45 to 30 minutes
- Significant improvements from re-structuring work enabled by IT
- Improved service and reduced costs are not conflicting objectives

The Company

P&O European Ferries is the UK's largest car ferry operator, transporting 3.2 million vehicles and over 12 million passengers each year. To cater for this traffic, it operates 23 ships and up to 70 sailings each day. In 1990, the company revenues were £420 millions.

The Problem

The Channel Tunnel, due to open in 1992, has intensified competition in the cross channel ferry business as operators seek to improve service and efficiency.

In the peak holiday season, thousands of passengers pass through P&O's Dover and Calais docks. The sheer volume of passengers checking in, coupled with passenger requests for changes and departure information meant a check in time of at least 45 minutes was needed. Further delays could occur as the check-in details were translated into a loading plan and manifest. Plans to increase passenger volumes would exacerbate these problems.

Management information was difficult and slow to produce, often requiring the re-keying of large quantities of data. This limited management's ability to respond to changing market conditions.

The Solution

A single improved check-in reduced the check-in period, thereby improving customer satisfaction and reduced costs. This was achieved by issuing a credit card style ticket, with the reservation information magnetically encoded. Details about daily reservations are passed from the central reservation system to the local port handling system. On arrival at the check-in desk, the check-in clerk reads the ticket and if correct, simply confirms the booking. If required, changes to the reservation can now be made at the check-in gate rather than having to go to a separate sales office.

One of the most common causes of delayed sailings was the availability of the ships manifest. The ship's Captain cannot sail without a complete and accurate list of passengers and cargo. This delay has been removed as the manifest is now produced electronically based on the check-in data. This again has reduced the time needed to get passengers through the port and onto the ship.

Management information has also been improved as information is passed from the ports to a central management information system at the end of each day. This up-to-date performance data enables management to identify more easily booking performance and adjust sales and offers accordingly.

The Benefits

The required check-in time has been reduced from 45 to 30 minutes with further reductions planned. Sitting around waiting to board the ship is a most frustrating time and any reduction significantly enhances customer satisfaction.

Costs have been substantially reduced through the removal of a whole facility - the separate sales centre at the port and the automation of the production of the manifest. Removing the need for re-keying the booking information to create the management information has further reduced costs.

Management has better information for decision making. It is more accurate and, more importantly, is available more quickly; critical in selling a service with a completely fixed shelf life.

The Future

P&O European Ferries are currently further integrating their port handling and reservation systems with a real time link. The result of this will be even greater flexibility at the port to offer alternative services.

Key Learnings

Selling new ways of working to the people involved is essential if the introduction is to be smooth and effective. Training is only part of the task. Explaining the need for the changes and how they fit in the company's overall plans for future growth is equally important.

Planning a major change to work is critical. Without such planning, many forseeable problems arise.

Service improvements and cost reduction are not contradictary objectives. If the process is carefully examined and creativity is applied at the design stage, improved service can be delivered at lower cost. Both objectives however are unlikely to be met if attempts are made to automate the existing process.

IT must be used to support the business. P&O European Ferries are very clear about what it takes to succeed in the business of crossing the channel. Clear goals are essential if IT is to be harnessed to the benefit of the business.

Appendix 2.3 IT Survey (cont.)

SECTION FOUR: ACTION PLAN

Information is useful only if it results in action. Our hope is that the survey findings and case studies will prompt you into doing something to further improve your service. The problem, is where to start.

To help, we have developed two action checklists.

The Personal Action Plan highlights actions you can take.

The Corporate Action Checklist asks a number of key questions to help you identify where IT can help improve your service performance. This is best completed as a team exercise by a group of senior managers.

PERSONAL ACTION PLAN

Here are five things you personally can do to improve service to customers. Remember, improving quality is about doing everything a little better all the time. Do not dismiss your own contribution.

- When creating, assessing or approving IT investments, consider how they impact customer satisfaction?
- Pick your best competitor and ask them for some information about a product/service. How do they respond? Now test your own organisation.
- Take a simple transaction, fulfilling an order or answering a query. How many steps are needed to complete the transaction? Is all the information available and accurate? How can this process be simplified and improved?
- Ask your customers what they think of your administrative/ transaction systems? Ask them how they can be made more friendly.
- Do you always provide the correct information, on-time to your customers, including internal ones? What changes are needed to ensure you always supply information right first time?

HERE ARE TEN WAYS INFORMATION TECHNOLOGY CAN HELP

- Liberate people
- Create an integrated view of the customer
- Improve speed of response
- Create new products/services
- Increase personalisation
- Re-structure and improve workflow
- Improve quality by building in checking
- Reduce costs, time and errors
- Facilitate de-centralisation and empowerment
- Avoid duplication

CORPORATE ACTION CHECKLIST

This checklist is designed to help you identify those areas where IT can help deliver service excellence. Whilst true excellence will need concerted effort over all activities, identifying those areas which can make the greatest initial contribution is the key to getting started. If you are in any doubt about what makes the most difference, ask your customers!

ACTIVITY	ACTION
Is there a clearly defined and well communicated strategy for customers? Does the IT strategy reflect this customer focus?	
When considering IT investments, do you assess their impact on customer satisfaction?	
Is customer satisfaction a key driver when establishing IT projects?	
Have staff got all the information they need to serve the customer? Can they answer a query or satisfy a complaint quickly?	
Can IT improve teamwork by bringing geographically dispersed people together in 'virtual teams' to solve customer problems?	
Can IT be used to automate all or part of a transaction and free staff to build that all important relationship?	
Can you improve the quality of help and support you give by providing 'expert systems' to help your sales and service force? Can such systems be provided directly to the customer?	
Can IT enhance your product or service?	
How many points of contact does your customer have to make to complete a transaction? Can this be reduced?	
Do you have electronic links with customers?	
Do you use IT to provide new delivery channels? eg ATMs, Electronic Catalogues, Computer Reservation Systems?	
Do you provide an 0800 number to capture customer comments and complaints?	
Do you use IT to track work is completed on time and to the satisfaction of the customer?	
How 'customer friendly' are your systems? Are you an organisation which is easy to do business with or do your systems represent a barrier and source of frustration to your customers?	
Do you have valuable information which you could make available to customers directly?	

3. British Gas – South Eastern Region

Introduction

In the UK, British Gas have more than 17.5 million customers, over two million shareholders and some 80,000 employees. British Gas supplies over 40 per cent of the energy needs of British homes, factories and offices. There are three distinct businesses within British Gas. The first of these is the UK gas supply, where British Gas manages the transportation and distribution of gas, a major installation and contracting service and some 650 showrooms throughout the country. In the second, British Gas is involved world-wide in exploration for, and production of, gas and oil. In the third, British Gas is creating a global gas business, seeking new opportunities and markets for its expertise.

The principle business of British Gas is the purchase, transmission and sale of natural gas to domestic, industrial and commercial customers in Great Britain. This gas business comprises a headquarters and 12 regions. Headquarters is responsible for formulating policies, for co-ordination, and for the direct management of centralised operations such as gas purchasing, bulk transmission of gas and gas transportation services. The regions are largely concerned with the management of the gas business locally, including customer-related activities, distribution and sale of gas, retailing, installation and servicing of gas appliances, meter reading and the collection of accounts and maintenance of emergency services.

British Gas also attaches great importance to the activities which support its gas marketing effort. In particular, appliance trading and customer service play a key role in supporting the domestic gas market. British Gas records figures such as a turnover of more than £9,000 million, profits after tax in the region of £900 million, with earnings per share over 20p.

Against a background of such a highly successful core gas business, readers may be surprised to hear that during the 1990s, British Gas embarked on a sweeping package of organisational changes. Why play around with such an obvious formula for success? The reason was that British Gas was entering one of the most demanding periods in its history, with the twin forces of regulation and competition having an increasing impact on the gas business in the UK. According to British Gas Chairman, Robert Evans:

> *'We are responding to these challenges and reshaping the organisation to take advantage of the many opportunities that lie ahead. This reshaping takes the form of the Regional Organisational Review (ROR) which is designed to equip the gas business to meet the new competitive pressures in the 1990s and beyond.'*

A major development of significance to the gas business has been the emergence, and growth, of competition in the UK contract gas market. Independent suppliers are likely to secure a substantial share, and the impact of this industrial and commercial competition will be felt most in the regions. With the emergence of real competition, it will be the regions that will face the biggest challenge of winning new industrial and commercial sales against those competitors. The ROR has therefore been introduced to ensure that the gas business can meet all of these competitive demands.

The first major phase of the ROR occurred in 1991 and involved the appointment of district general managers within each region, to take control of each of the 91 districts covering the whole of the UK. Each district contains, on average, around 200,000 customers, and each general manager is now being assessed not only on the district's financial performance, but also on the standards of service excellence provided for customers.

Figure 3.1 British Gas – South-Eastern Region

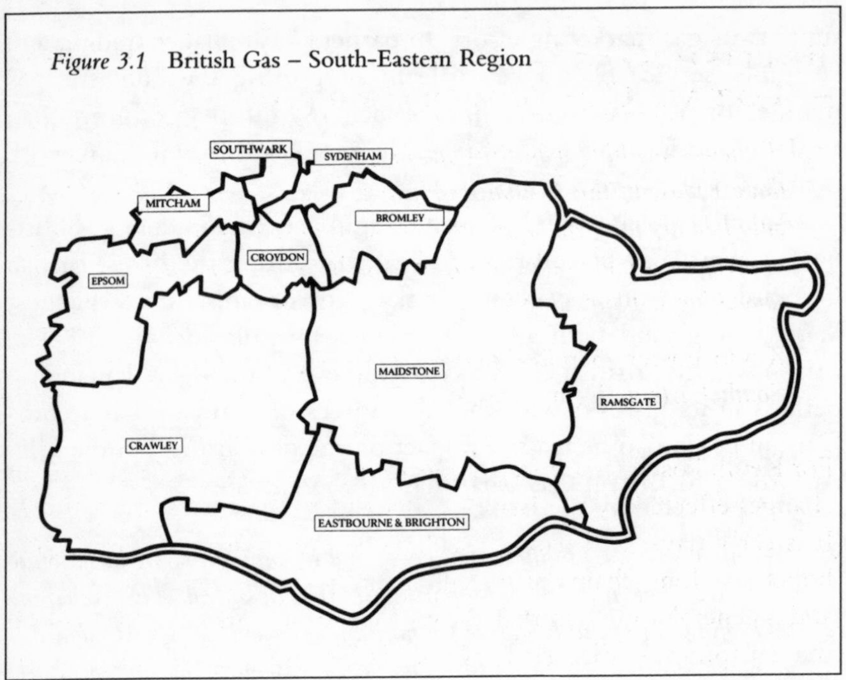

This case study discusses how the ROR has taken effect within British Gas – South Eastern Region (see Figure 3.1). It concentrates on the leadership required in the region in order to provide an integrated responsibility for customers, local responsibility for operations, and focusing on service excellence in order that British Gas can prosper in the competitive business environment of the 1990s.

British Gas – South Eastern Region – Total Customer Service

> *'I knew something was different, maybe it was starting to go right. But there I was, in this customer's kitchen, and she was telling me that not only had her problem been sorted out quickly, but neither she nor the service engineer had needed to speak to a British Gas manager; I thought, something is happening!'*
>
> Kevin Foster, *Service Engineer, Crawley district, British Gas – South Eastern Region.*

For Kevin Foster, a service engineer with Crawley district, the major changes effected by the British Gas ROR have not yet been noticed. It is early days, and habits that have led to poor communication – hopelessly long chains of management, systems that built in delays, and a general approach that shows that some staff have lost sight of the customer – die hard. Kevin is probably like many of the employees who make up the 7,000 workforce of British Gas – South Eastern. For them, it will take time, not to mention effort, energy and enthusiasm, for the British Gas industry to transform from what many perceived to be an autocratic and archaic organisation to one which is much more autonomous and entrepreneurial.

Another service engineer told me that the chairman had got it wrong; British Gas did not have its beginnings at the start of the nineteenth century. This would be bad enough, as it would require almost 200 years of public sector mentality to be shifted. No, British Gas would have to change seven centuries of management attitude because the first burning of natural gas actually was observed by Marco Polo at Balue in 1872! A manager was slightly optimistic; he recalls that Johannes van Helmont actually coined the word 'gas' in 1610 (although 'gas' is from the Greek 'chaos'!).

'Random chaos' is what Ralph Ellis, the Operations Director (West) of British Gas – South Eastern called his industry's history.

> *'We had a bad level of customer complaints, we never sold enough, we never made our targets, and we made islands of quality in areas that*

customers got most het up about; it was dreadful, all very amateurish. In some parts of our business we are first class, for example, we have a safety record that is second to none. However, we were certainly not a customer-focused organisation; neither internally nor externally.'

David Wells, the Regional Chairman of British Gas – South Eastern believes that the ROR was essential.

'Our internal support operations did not always feed our front line staff as well as they ought to have, and our support systems were often imperfect. Most of our employees in British Gas – South Eastern do not go out of their way to do a bad job, indeed most of our employees do a good job. But how many of us actually looked at the way we did our job from the outside; from the customer's point of view? With the emergence of real competition, we must meet, and beat, their challenge over the next few years. The gas business is the main core of the company. It accounted for 75 per cent of British Gas's operating profits during our last financial year, and this will remain so for the foreseeable future. Therefore, it has been vital that British Gas has made changes within its own organisation not only to help maintain its prosperity in the competitive environment of the 1990s but also to gear itself to meet the challenges of rising gas demand and high customer expectations.'

It was not only the impact of industrial and commercial competition which forced British Gas to change its organisational structure, but also changes to its tariff formula. This formula controls prices for domestic and smaller industrial or commercial customers and, in a review undertaking by Ofgas, the British Government's gas industry watchdog, tough new ceilings on prices were announced in a sector accounting for around 65 per cent of the British Gas group's turnover. For five years, from April 1992, increases in the non-gas part of the tariff price are limited to five per cent less than the increase in the Retail Price Index (RPI). The previous limit, under which British Gas has operated since its privatisation in 1986, was two per cent less than the RPI.

The formula also includes a new approach to the cost of gas bought by the company, and a requirement to publish and monitor service standards. In 1991, gas prices were 14 per cent lower in real terms than when the company was privatised in 1986. The new formula, however, places an even greater emphasis on efficiency and responsiveness.

Value for money is one of the reasons for the popularity of gas. During 1991, for example, more than a quarter of a million new domestic customers gained the benefits of the fuel and, despite higher interest rates in the UK during 1991, half a million new central heating systems were sold in Britain (three out of four gas customer homes are now centrally heated). However, as David Wells states: 'Service to the customer is as important as making the gas available, and British Gas needs all of its strengths and professionalism to maintain a lead over customer service competitors.' David Wells indicates that over 40,000 gas installers are now registered with the Council of Registered Gas Installers (CORGI) and, says Wells, 'They are all determined to take business from British Gas'.

Ofgas has imposed strict requirements on British Gas to publish and monitor its service standards, and the company's performance will, in the 1990s, be even more in the public eye. Ralph Ellis explains that British Gas has been committed to improving its standards of service for many years. British Gas has several special services; for example, to elderly or disabled customers. However, as Ralph Ellis acknowledges, service excellence has to be more than just targeting specific customers and their special needs.

> *'Excellence is about improving through doing 1,000 things one per cent better. Service excellence is about removing our outdated systems, policies and procedures which, in many instances, prevent employees from doing their jobs as well as they can for their customers. The mission statement, called our Direction Statement, sums up what we are trying to achieve, however alien it is to British Gas's culture.' (See Figure 3.2.)*

The gas industry has traditionally been a manufacturing/production type of culture rather than a service-centred one. David Wells admits

Figure 3.2 British Gas – South Eastern Region direction statement

STRIVING FOR EXCELLENCE
DIRECTION STATEMENT

STATEMENT OF INTENT

To be excellent in all we do, for our customers, employees, shareholders and the community.

OUR PRINCIPAL AIMS ARE

- To provide an excellent service.
- To improve profitability.
- To be an excellent employer.
- To play an active part in the community.

ACTION FOR EXCELLENCE

A successful business must have satisfied customers. We will treat them as we would wish to be treated ourselves. They require an excellent service and our work must therefore be undertaken with our customers as the key focus, providing better products and services than our competitors. We will measure the quality of our service and look for continual improvements.

We will place the strongest emphasis on safety, both in the workplace and in the supply and distribution of gas.

To achieve excellence requires that we value each other. This means an open approach, listening to each other, praising success and learning from mistakes, whether we are in the front line or providing back-up support. Time will be taken to keep everyone in the picture, encourage new ideas and develop individuals and teams. We will devolve responsibility and authority so that key tasks can be clearly targeted and progress monitored. We will avoid waste and take care to obtain value for money in everything we do. We will deal with suppliers and contractors as partners. We will judge their products and services on quality and value.

Excellence will improve the financial performance of the company, for the benefit of employees and shareholders.

We will strive to have a 'good name' in the community. We will give particular attention to the young and to older and disabled customers. We will show a real commitment to the protection of the environment.

that it is a powerful challenge to change the attitudes that pervade this type of culture:

> *'We call it striving for excellence, and at the present time there is no denying that it is a lot of strive and not so much excellence. Realising this, it was vital that in redirecting the organisation to one of customer focus, we had to have the visible and totally committed support of the senior regional management.'*

STRIVING FOR EXCELLENCE

The regional management committee (see regional organisational chart Figure 3.3) retired to a retreat for some five days to discuss the 'Striving for Excellence' initiative. As a team, they appreciated that without their example, energy, enthusiasm and empowerment the new organisational structure and its goals would never succeed. David Wells and his team were not advocating an absolute adherence and allegiance to the human relations school of management, nor

Figure 3.3 British Gas – South Eastern regional organisation

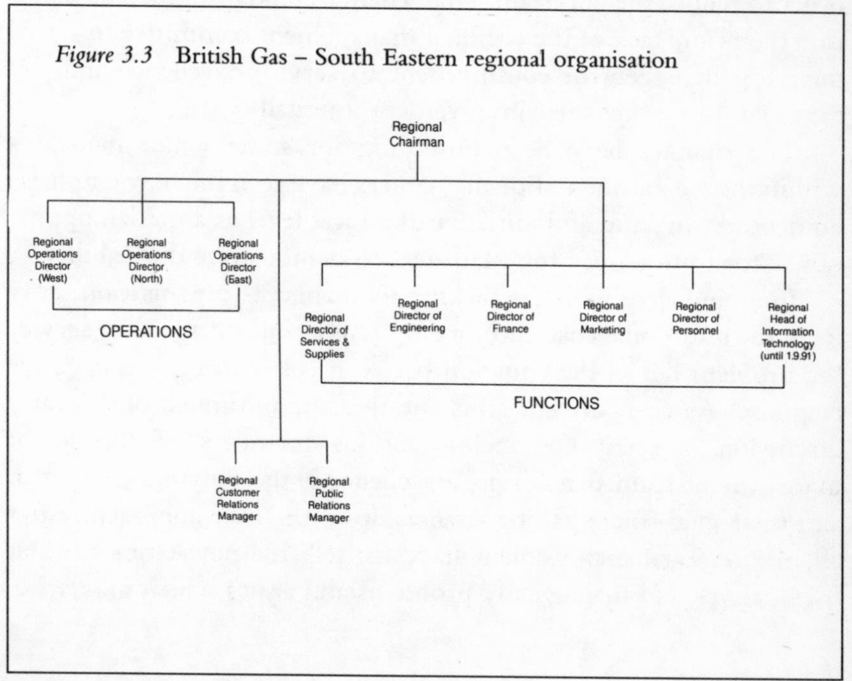

were they prepared to dispense with the domination of rationalism that some may say had stifled the gas industry. There was no doubt in the regional management committee's mind that British Gas had for too long relied on strict planning and bottom-line management results in a heavily procedured, cost-conscious and controlled environment. They needed to journey towards a more open management style, one which was more hands-on and value-driven from the regional and, as important, district level.

The company's regional structure had been altered to make local management even more responsive to customers' needs. David Wells, along with his regional management committee, firmly believed that for this to occur, the local district management had to be set an example by the regional board, which would commend their commitment to change.

The ROR had been primarily introduced to help ensure that the gas business could meet all of the new demands that it was facing in the 1990s, particularly in the area of customer service and increased competition. The new organisation had been put in place quickly in order to reduce the uncertainty that change could bring. It was therefore the prime task of the regional management committee to signal their top management commitment to service excellence and, by example, to market their involvement internally.

The changes have been unsettling for some senior managers within the gas business. Equally, others have seen the new emphasis on decision-making and initiative at a local level as a golden opportunity for tomorrow's top managers to demonstrate their ability.

In an industry which is seeking to change its organisation away from the traditional cost-cutting emphasis to one of customer service the problem lies in the equation between cost-cutting and negative response. As costs are cut so is enthusiasm, and much of the early discussion is spent convincing various members of the senior management team that service excellence is the only way forward, and their vital role is taking ownership of the new approach. After all, the regional management have to 'sell' the new ethos to their own groups and manage any problems and issues which may arise.

Basically then, these major workshops with senior management are really discussing the direction of the business. 'How is British Gas doing now, where should we be going in the future, and how should we achieve our goals and objectives?' The end purpose is to have a corporate global response to the mission and direction statement in order that all senior managers feel they have ownership of this. Locked away in an environment far from the place of work – in this instance a country hotel – senior management were able to debate their qualms and questions, such as:

- How do we help a new culture work with some old systems still in place; should we as British Gas – South Eastern Region scrap some of the old systems?
- How do we manage the conflict between cost benefits and the provision of customer service?
- How do we stop the final direction or mission statement being perceived as a one-off project and therefore worthy only of lip service by the middle management?
- How should we manage the staff problems that will arise with the new culture?
- How will we get better face-to-face communication in an industry that has long had a barrier between its industrial staff and others?
- How do we deal with a flatter structure, brought about by the new organisation review, apparently getting in the way of possible promotion?
- What service are we providing to our internal customers, to allow them to supply our external customers?
- How do we manage in a way that ensures all individuals *want* to do a good job?
- How do we get consistency across the region and throughout the districts?
- How do we keep our nerve when things go wrong?
- How do we 'live' quality and service, and how do we get people to 'own' the standards?

Figure 3.4 Internal/external customers – review of working group deliberations

KEY ISSUES

1. Concept of Partnership.
2. To develop an agreement process giving rise to the contents of an agreed contract.
3. Ability to deliver – timescales; and
   – resources, both human and cost.

CONFLICTS TO BE RESOLVED

1. Functional targets as against customer expectations.
2. Managing the transition for 'Yes, But' to 'Yes, Fine'.

IDEA FOR ACTION

Each item at the workshop to meet and agree a service agreement (interpreted as a common understanding for the way ahead to achieve a service charter). This process to be facilitated by Striving for Excellence Steering [SFE] Group.

DISCUSSION HEADINGS

Concept of Partnership

Ensuring that managers are committed to SFE internal customer concept.
Need to develop strong supplier/customer partnerships.
Introduce trust into the relationship.
Changing attitudes from reactive to proactive.
Concept of bringing suppliers 'on board'.
Achieve a mutual understanding.
Seeing the other person's point of view.
Internal customers –
(1) talk to other Departments about issues; and
(2) meeting/talking to District staff.

Figure 3.5 Striving For Excellence blockages

ISSUES

- Team Building
- Quality Circles
- Training in TQM
- Setting tangible targets

CONFLICTS

- Need to resolve 'Start Method' (All do own thing?)

ACTIONS

- All do it!

IDEAS FOR ACTION

1. Ask staff what they view as a blockage – (Me).
2. Build my team – identify a process – (Me).
3. Regional Management Committee [RMC] to generate greater openness at all levels.
4. RMC to be more visible.
5. RMC to remove instructions and replace with guidelines/ controls – safety needs to be conserved (Them).
6. In the last resort identified blockages which are not resolved should go to RMC (Me).
7. Set up Quality Circles (Me).
8. Managers to walk the floor at least once a week (Me).
9. Managers to take action on blockages when identified (Me).
10. RMC to tell us to get on with it (Them).
11. Quality starts with me and I will get on with it (Me).
12. RMC must pedal SFE for 2 years.
13. DGMs/Regional Management to get on with it.
14. Identify training in TQM (Me)
15. Define what Quality means in my department (Me).
16. Set tangible Quality Targets (Me).
17. Promote Quality and Service.
18. To share quality ideas and mistakes (Us).
19. Consult specialist consultants who have achieved B55750.
20. Stop playing games (Us).

It is not surprising that the regional management committee were in conclave for some five days and nights while reviewing such issues. In the weeks that followed, the feedback from their syndicate groups and brainstorming sessions was distributed to each member in a document entitled 'Setting Sail'. Working groups' deliberations were highlighted for action. (See examples at Figure 3.4 and Figure 3.5.) The disposition and spirit that cascaded from the 'Setting Sail' cabinet forum led to further senior management workshops named 'Welcome Aboard'. It is worth indicating at this point that British Gas – South Eastern decided not to launch their 'Striving for Excellence' philosophy with the razzamatazz and *son et lumiere* production that has accompanied some other organisations' customer service programmes.

Ralph Ellis feels that British Gas – South Eastern had one, and only one, chance of journeying through the change:

> *'Given our history, we are an industry that has very cynical employees and rather than have fanfares the approach was, if you like, more subversive. It was essential that all senior and middle managers deliberated on all aspects of the "direction statement" in order that they could truly gain ownership. Eventually we have to get the message through to all 7,000 employees in British Gas – South Eastern, and this will never be done successfully unless all those employees witness managers actually doing rather than talking.'*

As David Wells puts it: 'The management teams must sign on to gain ownership and that is why it is vital that the feedback from senior management seminars is transferred quickly and professionally into action.' This approach is certainly a consistent theme in all service excellent companies. Senior managers are often seen as either being authoritarian or democratic. At British Gas – South Eastern, however, they discovered that they can be neither and both at the same time! David Wells admits that the cascade approach of introducing change is very worrying for a chairman. While treating people as adults – inducing practical innovation, entrepreneurship and ideas from all managers – carrying out an open door style of management also means being tough.

A consistent characteristic of the leaders in service excellent companies is, therefore, that they have a caring side *and* a tough side. In British Gas – South Eastern, this has been exemplified through the participative induction of all the innovative issues from the senior management seminars, coupled with rigorous action plans to ensure things happened.

The various senior management seminars at British Gas – South Eastern were not in the business of producing paper plans, they were in the business of producing business solutions. Major action projects were set up at senior level in order to indicate to the workforce in the districts how seriously senior management took the 'Striving for Excellence' initiative. Five major projects were initiated, covering areas as diverse as:

- Improved payment procedures for suppliers.
- Improved recruitment practices within British Gas – South Eastern Region.
- A review of 'three star' service contracts.
- A review of all internal communication procedures, ranging from improving the internal telephone directories and noticeboards, to better face-to-face communication through team briefing.
- Improving the clothing for all those personnel required to wear uniforms.

Many companies I have talked to would never have conceived of sending away their top managers together for one solid week; nor to further intense assemblies during the succeeding months in order to review what had actually happened.

Figure 3.6 British Gas – South Eastern district organisation

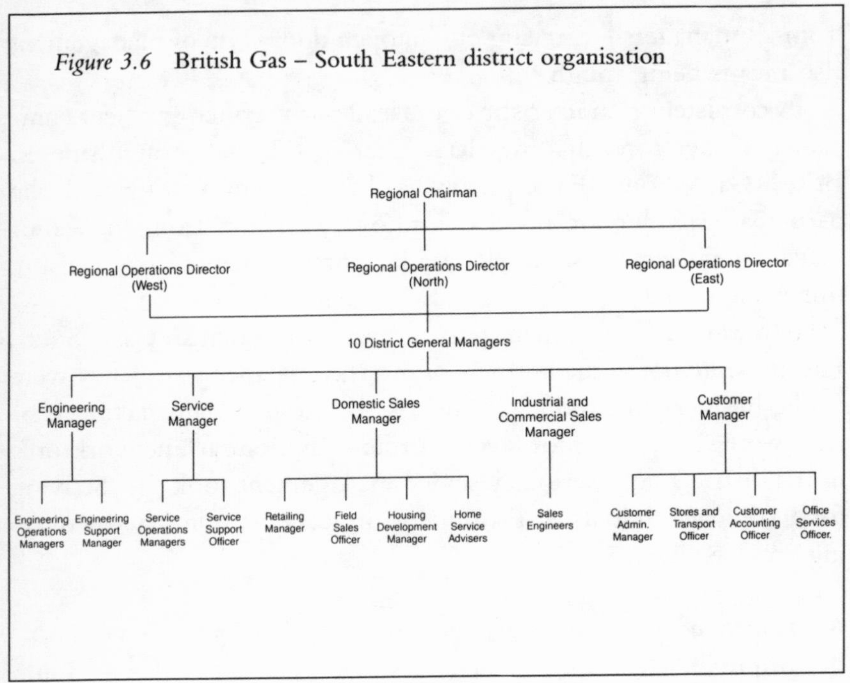

CUSTOMER EXCELLENCE DOWN THE LINE

In the district organisation (see Figure 3.6) the same process continued. Colin Stevens, the general manager for British Gas – South Eastern, Crawley district was responsible for sharing the vision with all his district team. Colin Stevens was responsible for steering the 'Striving for Excellence' ethos through the district. (See Appendix 3.1, at the end of this chapter.) Project teams have evolved to discuss and review major themes which have resulted from the senior management workshops.

For example, Colin Stevens was part of the senior management team on the clothing project and explains their approach thus:

'Originally in British Gas – South Eastern there was no co-ordinated policy on clothing. Traditionally, regional headquarters organised uniforms and industrial clothing without reference to the users. You can imagine, service engineers got trousers that did not fit, or jackets that fell

apart, because no one ever asked them what type of uniform was needed for them to do their job better. Now that has changed. We have a project group here at district level which deals with it – a clothing group which comprises those people responsible for buying the clothing and those using it.'

Colin Stevens is trying to have some of the initiatives that came out of the senior management workshops converted into action plans at the front end of the operation; that part of the business that actively deals with British Gas customers. As he explains:

'With our customer management we have set ourselves a number of key principles and objectives which include:

- *Placing the reasonable expectations of customers above the systems and procedures.*
- *Treating the customers as we would wish to be treated in their situation.*

However, we all recognise that the people most important to the achievement of high customer satisfaction are the boundary staff who meet and speak with the customers.'

In order to achieve this, Colin Stevens realises that he must devolve authority more towards line level. To achieve this will require much education and understanding by people who have never before been empowered to make decisions.

Laurie Robinson is the Customer Manager at British Gas – South Eastern, Crawley district, and his role is that of an educator and facilitator of change programmes for the first line staff. Robinson discovered that, although management were keen to delegate empowerment to line level and allow those dealing with the customers to use their best judgement in all situations, it was clear that their best judgements were all very different.

'We needed to have a more consistent approach to meeting and exceeding customer expectations. We have, therefore, focused on an open learning

technique where you bring the work groups together to solve fairly typical customer situations, at the end of which each member of staff is asked to indicate what they would do to help that particular customer. (See Appendix 3.2.)

'We remind the participants that the objectives of this exercise are to support each other, and to learn. There will, of course, be no retribution for minority opinions or for being wrong. It is important in these training sessions that the customer assistants remember the ultimate beneficiary of all of this learning and work study will be the customers, who will hopefully receive a more consistent level of service and satisfaction.'

Gaining champions for customer service

The philosophy at Crawley district is quite simple and, again, a recurring theme in excellence companies. The simpler your philosophy, the easier it is for those interacting directly with the customer to understand what the organisation is trying to achieve and help meet those objectives. At Crawley the philosophy is as follows:

- Getting customer service right first time.
- Supporting each other.
- Learning from our mistakes.
- Exceeding customers' expectations.

Other initiatives happening at Crawley district are directly related to the major projects which originated from the senior boardroom discussions and debate to agree the British Gas – South Eastern 'Striving for Excellence' direction statement. Keith Linzner, the Customer Administration Manager at British Gas – South Eastern, Crawley district, is working on making British Gas's internal documents more erudite and specifically orientated to the audience:

'If you are going to empower the troops to make decisions, they must know more about the business they are in. This means opening up com-

munications on issues that actually affect them at work. For example, customers may phone us with concerns about gas work going on in the streets, safety issues, or environmental matters, as well as enquiries about their meters, accounts or orders. It is vital that we give an immediate response to our customers if we are to stay ahead of our competitors. To enable these customer assistants to give immediate feedback we need to share information with them. This is regularly done through team meetings, but it means a lot of knowledge, information and business data must be opened up to them, in a way they can relate to and that is easily understood. This is all part of developing and supporting inter-personal service and quality skills; how to deliver what your customer expects.'

Some of the learning situations are general and will discuss, for example, the approach which should be adopted with customers who telephone Crawley district. (See Appendix 3.3.) It is vital that customers get 'responsive' behaviour from British Gas – South Eastern; that is, active listening, rather than defensive or purely operative action based on following the system. This is the cascading of autonomy and customer service down the line.

Other issues are much more specific. Laurie Robinson, for example, is reviewing the stores operations at the depots within Crawley district; again this has been done in conjunction with the people who actually use the store, for example the service engineers. The storekeepers have traditionally never considered their stockroom as a shop; one which serves the service engineers, who serve the customers. The important point to make is that ownership of this problem has been devolved to those people who work in the stores, and those who use them. It is another example of a service organisation striving for excellence through devolving autonomy to the area that directly interfaces with the customer. No one, however, would deny that it does take time. It is especially difficult in an environment clouded with cynicism. That is why it has been so vital for David Wells to find his 'champions' at all levels in the organisation.

In excellence companies 'executive' champions abound. They are the people who have the gift of steering problems into challenges, and mistakes into opportunities. They redirect the organisation's formal tendency from negation, towards achievement.

Excellence companies also have the 'statesman' champion who, in effect, provides the role model for championing; every case study in this book has them at the top of the organisation. They are the kind of leaders who make the more junior people in the organisation take risks, and make them want to be entrepreneurs because they know that the organisation will support them. That is why it has been so vital in the training sessions at Crawley district to remind all delegates that with empowerment there will be no retribution for making wrong decisions, and why the open learning experience and the action plans are a fundamental part of achieving customer satisfaction. It is important for staff to learn to delight the customer, to simply satisfy is to opt for mediocrity.

Embarking on any major customer service programme is a two-way street along which communication will not always be easy; or, in a more entrepreneurial environment, controllable. If you succeed, the rewards will be high; by getting it right, first time and on time, the staff at all levels will support the initiatives with a sense of ownership, care and commitment. However, to get it wrong will cultivate cynicism, making it extremely difficult to try again. Any current levels of service excellence will be compromised as a consequence.

What all the service excellent companies in this book illustrate is that; when entrepreneurism and innovation are pushed down the line, and work groups are allowed to work out problems for themselves, they then work more effectively on these solutions than on any that would have been imposed upon them by senior management. The on-going service excellence commitment has always come about as a reaction to clear perceptions of what customers' needs and wants are, not just 'informed' internal views of what the boardroom perceives their needs and wants to be. There are a wealth of compliments when you talk of British Gas – South Eastern; nevertheless, there are still major shortfalls in levels of service and the company is the first to admit it.

Only time will tell if British Gas – South Eastern has got it right. As far as service engineer, Kevin Foster, is concerned, 'something is different'. He has got a 'good feeling' about the changes going on in British Gas – South Eastern, but remains cautious. The changes have not affected him too much as yet, but he has noticed a difference in the way that he is becoming much more involved in matters which affect his job and the service he ultimately gives to the customer (for example, with the changes to the storeroom). I suspect, however, that Kevin Foster will be a 'product' champion for David Wells and his team. A product champion is the one at the product and service level with the customer who effectively sponsors, at the interface, the entrepreneurial spirit generated from the top. Champions need their support systems too, however, and in excellence companies you will find that those who get the most from their champions are those who provide the strongest support networks.

Meeting Kevin Foster, over sandwiches with Colin Stevens and other members of the management team, I reflected that he was a 'product' champion who did have his sponsor. That is good, for without 'champions' striving for excellence, there is likely to be more external 'strive' than everlasting excellence.

Appendix 3.1

British Gas – South Eastern Crawley District

STRIVING FOR EXCELLENCE

1. Quality and Service Programme

A Quality and Service Programme is to be introduced into all Regions of British Gas.

The quality and service process has been proven and it enables companies who achieve it to stay ahead of the competition.

Companies which have succeeded with quality and service programmes include Marks and Spencer, Mercedes-Benz and British Airways.

2. What is Quality and Service?

IT IS ABOUT:

creating an environment and changing attitudes so that every employee wants to improve the quality and service of his/her performance.

questioning procedures and systems.

replacing "rules with principles, guidelines and judgement.

all our routine activities.

all of us working as a team.

encouraging employees to make decisions as if they were customers.

prevention, not reaction.

getting things right first time.

IT MUST:

involve everyone.

never stop.

recognise internal customers as well as external customers.

IT WILL:

help to ensure that customers get an excellent service.

help the Company retain existing business.

help the Company grow, hereby benefitting employees and shareholders.

3. Cost of Quality and Service

improved quality does not increase cost – it reduces it.

in service industries, 40% of turnover is wasted by not "getting it right first time".

by not "getting it right first time" costs are increased by:

- wasting materials
- breaking promises
- causing customer complaints
- reducing customer satisfaction

errors and defects are not free.

4. Customers

Everyone has customers.

Internal customers must be treated in the same way as external customers.

Everything done effects customers in the end.

Customers don't depend on us – we depend upon them.

Customers are the reason for our work, not an interruption (e.g. customers phone calls must be considered as top priority).

Customers pay our wages.

Customers are our business, not outsiders.

It is our job to fulfil our customers' needs.

It costs five times as much to get a new customer than to keep an old one.

Only 4% of customers who are dissatisfied complain – the rest take their business elsewhere.

On average, a dissatisfied customer tells 11 other people.

5. Managers and Supervisors Must:

constantly look to make improvements.

put quality and service at the top of any agenda.

emphasise the longer-term needs of the Company, rather than short-term profitability.

ensure that employees know what is expected of them.

eliminate 'fear' of being criticised.

break down functional barriers.

listen to (and act upon, if possible) suggesstions from their staff.

ensure employees know who their customers are.

6. How to Begin a Quality and Service Programme

A controlled approach is necessary.

Do not introduce with a 'fanfare'.

It must overcome 'passive resistors'.

It must avoid destructive criticism.

Early successes are needed.

It must be kept going.

7. Quality and Service Programme so far

British Gas issued a Statement of Intent in which its principle aims can be defined as:

to provide an excellent service

to improve profitability

to be an excellent employer

to be active in the community

Crawley District has produced a Mission Statement, which states:

We are committed to being the best by:

getting it right first time

learning from mistakes

listening to each other

supporting each other

forming partnerships

sharing information

exceeding customer expectation

AND

having fun along the way!

District levels 2 & 3 have attended workshops to discuss quality and service.

From these workshops, the principle of 'groups' looking at 'things to do' has evolved, the groups being multi-functional and multi-layered.

Examples of 'successes' from the groups so far include:

letters with General Manager's name on instead of the Chairman's

switchboard operator reinstated who will answer all calls dialling the 'admin' number.

business cards are being reprinted with the 'admin' number instead of the 'public' number.

decision made to reintroduce business briefings early in the new year.

decision made to introduce depot administrative support.

Other examples of things looked at so far include:

Correspondence style of postcards.

telephone style (a charter to be produced).

production of a district handbook.

how information for service engineers is written on job cards.

how to brief engineers on giving bad news (e.g. PD's).

Also from the workshops, a Quality and Service Forum has been set up. This is a multifunctional group, of which each member is responsible for discussing quality matters with their colleagues and bringing them to the meetings for discussion and recommendation.

8. Next Steps

Our aim is to:

encourage staff to continually think about what they are doing and to look at ways of doing things better.

question systems

use judgement

consider themselves part of a team

consider internal as well as external customers.

We're looking at using 'case studies' in training to give examples of how we hope people would react to given situations of customer problems.

Appendix 3.2
Striving for Excellence with Customers

Crawley District has committed itself to being the best through, amongst other things:

- Getting it right first time
- Supporting each other
- Learning from our mistakes
- Exceeding customers expectations

Within Customer Management we have set ourselves a number of key principles and objectives which include:

- Placing the reasonable expectations of customers above the systems and procedures
- Treating the customers as we would wish to be treated in their situations

We also recognise that the people most important to the achievement of high customer satisfaction are the "boundary staff" who meet and speak with customers.

We have said that you are empowered to make decisions and that the only rule is to use your best judgement in all situations. We have also said that there will be no retribution for being wrong.

However, it has become clear that your best judgements are very different and that we need to have a more consistent approach to meeting and exceeding customer expectations.

To help us achieve this we are going to experiment with an open learning technique.

This booklet contains a number of fairly typical customer situations, each of which is described as a separate "Case". At the end of each Case you are asked to indicate what you would do to help the customer.

Please explain your intentions in note form in the space provided and be prepared to subsequently share your proposed "Action Plan" with colleagues as part of a "shared learning experience".

Remember that the objectives of the exercise are to support each other and to learn, and there will be no retribution for minority opinions.

Please also remember that the ultimate beneficiary of our work will be the customers who will hopefully receive a more consistent level of service and greater satisfaction.

Case 1

A customer has visited a showroom and purchased a new gas fire, making payment in full at the time. Two weeks later, the fire was fitted and, upon opening the box, the Service Engineer discovered that the decorative casing was so badly damaged that it couldn't be fitted. However the fire could be fitted and made to work without the decorative casing, and the customer was assured that a replacement case could be obtained.

Six weeks later a replacement case was delivered but this was also found to be badly damaged, and another replacement was ordered.

Four weeks later the customer telephones asking for news of the second replacement casing. You telephone the manufacturer and are told that delivery will be at least another two weeks.

What do you do?

Action Plan

Case 2

An elderly pensioner with limited income has visited her local showroom and asked to buy a replacement for the wire basket which fits over the balanced flue outlet of her boiler.

Her car mechanic son has written down the make, model and serial number of the boiler, and it was his intention to fit the part.

The customer has been persuaded that a Service Engineer should visit to check what is required and subsequently the pensioner is told that fitting a "flue protector" is a technical job which British Gas must do.

A Service Engineer calls and fits the wire basket and the elderly pensioner receives a bill for £65.00.

She telephones and complains that it was a simple job needing 4 screws fitting into the brickwork which her son could have easily done, that it took only 15 minutes for the Service Engineer to do the work, that the bill is exorbitant and that she can't and won't pay.

You check the VDU and discover that the bill for £65.00 is correct with the part costing £15.00, the Service Engineer's visit to identify the part correctly charged at £20.00, and the Service Engineer's visit to fit the part correctly charged at £30.00.

What do you do?

Action Plan

Case 3

A customer has bought a new cooker and after six months a problem arises which is preventing the oven from working, although the hob is still operating satisfactorily.

A Service Engineer visits and identifies a part which is required as an EFP. This becomes a manufacturers order because the cooker is so new that British Gas is not yet holding this part.

After two weeks the customer telephones asking for news of the part. You check with the manufacturer and learn that the manufacturer can give no firm information as to when the part will be available but hopes delivery will be possible within 2 weeks.

What do you do?

Action Plan

____

Case 4

An elderly gentleman who says he is 84 telephones during a cold December week when temperatures have been close to freezing. He explains that he has neither heating nor hot water because of a problem with his boiler.

You check the VDU and discover that he is not a Service Care customer.

The customer explains that he has had neither heating nor hot water for the last 3 days and that he has tried to get British Gas to visit each day and has been told on each occasion that we are "too busy" to help.

You check the radio system and discover that the "limiters" are in operation because we are already over allocated and that a previous request to remove the "limiters" has already been declined.

What do you do?

Action Plan

____

____

____

____

____

____

____

____

____

____

____

____

Case 5

A professional lady in her early thirties telephones and explains that some months ago she bought a "slide in" cooker to go with her new kitchen and that delivery was to be 9.00 this morning.

It is now 10.00, the cooker has yet to be delivered, the kitchen fitters are unable to work and the lady, who has taken time off work, wants to know when the cooker will be delivered.

You check the VDU and discover that the lady has bought and paid for the cooker so far in advance of delivery that it was not possible to schedule delivery at that time. The transaction was therefore booked as "wait customers advice for delivery".

You apologise and explain to the customer that a mistake has been made and that there is no cooker delivery organised for her today.

The customer is far from happy, given that her time off work is being wasted, and the kitchen fitters will be unable to carry on working.

The customer asks in no uncertain terms what you are going to do about it.

What are you going to do?

Action Plan

____

____

____

____

____

____

Case 6

At 9.00 a customer telephones and explains that their annual Service Care visit is planned for today. When arranging the visit the customer was offered an appointment but said that this was not necessary as they would be at home all day.

The customer apologises and explains that he now needs to go out after 2.00 p.m. and asks if we can make sure that the visit will take place in time for this not to be a problem. The job has been issued to a Service Engineer who is without a radio.

What do you do?

Action Plan

____

____

____

____

____

____

____

Appendix 3.3
Crawley District – Telephone Answering

THINGS TO REMEMBER ....

- Your telephone conversations will be the basis upon which many customers form their impression of British Gas [BG].
- You may spend as long as is necessary to deal satisfactorily with any one customer.
- The customer is not interested in how B.G. is organised, they simply want their problem solved.
- A dissatisfied customer relates their poor experience of B.G. to eleven other people, on average.
- A customer with a complaint is an opportunity to enhance the reputation of B.G.
- The best person to resolve a customer's problem is the first person they speak to.
- You should endeavour to meet the "reasonable expectations" of customers and you should put this before the "procedures".
- You should treat customers as you would wish to be treated in their situation.
- You are "empowered" to take the decisions necessary to resolve customers problems.
- We shall "stand by" you and your decisions, even when we disagree with them. There will be no "retribution" for being "wrong".
- You should not ask customers to "write in" with their problem.
- You have no need to "protect" your senior managers from customers. We are always willing to take calls from customers whenever you think it is necessary or the customer wishes this.
- You have a difficult and demanding task and we appreciate your important contribution to Crawley District being successful.

THINGS TO DO ....

- Keep to the agreed "opening" and "closing".

- "Smile" down the telephone.
- Be "ambassadors" and "sales people" for B.G.
- Be loyal to B.G., its products and your colleagues.
- Be "friendly and enthusiastic" not just "polite and efficient".
- Avoid transferring customers outside Customer Administration unless the customer is asking for this.
- If you can't deal with a customer's enquiry record details and agree a time to call back.
- If you do have to transfer a customer call give details of the customer and the problem to the new recipient.
- Please "support and encourage" each other and share together your good and bad experiences in order that we may continually improve.

THINGS NOT TO DO . . . .

- Never argue with a customer.
- Never suggest that a customer is wrong.
- Never transfer a customer "blind" to someone else.

QUALITATIVE STANDARDS FOR TELEPHONING ANSWERING

1. I should like us to agree a standard telephone answering phrase, which everyone will use. My preference is something like: "Good Morning/Afternoon, British Gas Customer Administration . . . How Can I help you?"
2. I should like us to agree that the penultimate "exchange" would be to ask the customer to note the name of the person they are dealing with and to ask for that person if they have any problems with the agreed arrangements.
3. I should like the final "exchange" to be "thank you for calling B.G.".
4. We need to explain to staff that, as the people who are in contact with the customer, what they say and do, and how they say and do it will be the basis of the customer's impression of B.G.

5. Because of this they all need to be both "ambassadors" and "sales people" for B.G. and they need to maintain Company, product and colleague loyalty at all times.
6. Because of this they also need to be "friendly and enthusiastic" not just "polite and efficient". We need to ask them to "smile down the phone".
7. Because of this we also need to ask them to accept the difficult proposition that they should never argue with a customer and they should never "accuse" a customer of being wrong.
8. We need to remind staff that there is no time limit to the duration of any call but that we hope they will use their skills to "control" a telephone conversation such that it will be no longer than necessary.
9. However the objective will be to spend as long as is necessary to deal with the issues to the customer's satisfaction.
10. Other objectives include:
    (a) meeting the reasonable expectations of customers and putting this before the procedures.
    (b) treating the customer as you would wish to be treated in their situation.
    (c) giving the customer a good experience of B.G.
    (d) ensuring that the person dealing with a customer's problem or complaint is "empowered" to resolve first time the issues to the customer's reasonable expectation.
11. Other guiding principles include:
    (a) the customer has no need to know how B.G. is organised and the person speaking to the customer must represent the whole organisation.
    (b) the person dealing with the customer must assume responsibility for the whole organisation, not just administration and respond accordingly.
    (c) the Bureau needs to provide an enquiry service for the whole organisation and must avoid transferring calls to other departments unless the customer wishes to speak to a "named individual".
    (d) Because of this the preferred option will be to take messages

or details of unanswered enquiries and arrange a return call with a timescale agreed with the customer.

12. In all but the most exceptional; very high expenditure claims, complaints should be dealt with on the telephone and appropriate action taken and no customer should be asked to "write in".

Customer Manager
Crawley District
British Gas – South Eastern Region

4. *The Metropolitan Police Service*

Introduction

The inclusion of a case study involving the police and total customer service may well bemuse some readers and bewilder others. This should not be the case. This chapter offers the reader an opportunity to digest, in one study, the plethora of problems and pressures an organisation has to contend with when facing the challenge of change. This is especially true of change which has been demanded, in greater part, by the customers' requirements; the needs of the people who live and work in and around London.

There are certain consistent challenges in service excellence organisations as illustrated throughout the book. Questions such as:

- What is our core business?
- How can we focus on that mission?
- Can we agree a mission statement?
- Can our culture manage that statement?
- If not, what do we have to do to get from where we are to where we've never been?
- How do we get everyone in the organisation to commit to our statement?
- What are the deficiencies in the system that prevent us from being as good as we could be at the business we are in?
- How do we get everyone involved in order to present a consistent public face, both internally and externally?

- How do we communicate what we are trying to achieve; both to our internal customers and to those we serve?
- What kind of communication and training emphasis will we need to support us on this journey?
- Can the system support the changes; do we have the leadership in our organisation to manage change?
- How shall we move from 'making it happen' to 'making it stick'?
- How can we measure how well we are doing with the change process; again, both internally and externally?

Believe it or not, The Metropolitan Police has had to address, and subsequently manage, each and every one of these issues. Given the traditions of The Metropolitan Police, the climate in which it operates, and its culture, one can only be impressed that its service excellence programme, known as PLUS, ever took off at all.

The contents of this case study are, therefore, relevant and rich for any organisation striving for service excellence. Case studies throughout this book illustrate the need for coming to terms with a changing market-place and customer community; the realisation that service is no longer merely optional. Customer service is not only desirable, it is the *sine qua non* of survival. That survival is by no means guaranteed, even in the police service. Knowing this, The Metropolitan Police took stock of their organisation and PLUS was born.

THE NEED FOR CHANGE

The public face of the police service is provided by its officers on the street; the policemen and women who take on a service directly to the general public. In the UK, the culture of traditional policing is characterised by these individuals, close to their community, only being able to patrol a beat with the consent of the general public. This consent can only be retained by the quality of service provided between the police and the public.

Towards the end of the 1980s, this concurrence had become contaminated, if not under commination. Media comment – along with various polls, surveys and studies – highlighted this, and demonstrated a growing concern about confidence in the police. They were in danger of losing contact with their customers, both physically and psychologically. Physically, as Area cars appeared to replace the 'bobby on the beat', and psychologically, as respect for, and confidence in, the police descended into outright opprobrium.

Market research, commissioned by the police themselves, did not improve matters. It did, however, help them appreciate what business they were in. The Joint Consultative Committee is a national forum for the Police Staff Associations – The Association of Chief Police Officers, The Police Superintendents' Association of England and Wales and The Police Federation of England and Wales. The Committee commissioned a wide-ranging study into contemporary policing issues known as the 'Operational Policing Review'. This included a national survey of public opinion, as well as a survey of police views and those of police consultative groups.

This report was produced at the end of a period that had sadly witnessed riots at Brixton and Tottenham, demonstrations at Wapping, and public complaints of abuse of authority at record levels; with jurors' increasing reluctance to convict on police evidence alone. The Metropolitan Police's customers – the taxpaying public – wanted change. These customers, paying over £1 billion each year for the policing of London, had every right to expect a cost-effective, non-discriminatory service that would work well at every level.

The change came through Sir Peter Imbert, who was appointed the Commissioner of The Metropolitan Police. He had an ambitious aim; to increase public confidence by improving the level of service provided to the people of London, whether resident or transient. However, Sir Peter did not just have a problem between his organisation and its external customers. Relationships between internal customers within the police service itself were also imbued with ignominy. This basically manifested itself in a gap between the workers and management.

Sir Peter was not as much concerned with the systems or the structures that had been brought about by, for example, huge legislative changes (e.g. the Police and Criminal Evidence Act). He was, however, deeply concerned with the 44,000 people that made up The Metropolitan Police Force.

Throughout this book, it is apparent how impossible it is to have positive external corporate excellence towards your customers, if this does not thrive within. Excellence organisations have a deeply ingrained philosophy and value system that says, effectively: 'respect the individual'; 'we're in this together'; 'make people winners – winners thrive, losers survive'; 'let us stand up and be counted'; 'hands-on, value-driven'.

Sir Peter sensed that some of these values were lost within the existing Metropolitan Police Force. His instincts, as a policeman, were confirmed with the publication of an externally commissioned report giving an independent diagnosis of the organisation. Known as the 'Wolff Olins Report on the corporate identity of The Metropolitan Police', it was entitled 'A Force For Change'. The study was primarily concerned with identity and with what the organisation stood for; how it operated and, as important, how it was perceived by its customers. These customers were not only the public that The Metropolitan Police served, but also those within the organisation who influenced its character.

This type of market research is often the launch pad for organisations who are changing direction, for whatever reason. Many companies undertake this through one of their internal research departments on the basis, albeit subconsciously, that if they don't like the message they can quietly shoot the messenger and ignore it. What was so convincing, or courageous even, about the 'Force For Change' initiative was their public announcement that the research was being undertaken; then, with a similar fanfare, announcing the results.

I mentioned 'courageous' for when you read the cultural background to how The Metropolitan Police had operated previously to the commissioning of this study – they are a structure shrouded in secrecy – you will appreciate how seriously The Metropolitan Police took the reappraisal of their identity and their image. Not only by allowing an outsider to carry out the assessment, but also to do so in public.

What the report primarily identified was that The Metropolitan Police lacked a strong sense of identity; this corporacy forms the foundation for many service excellent organisations. Six areas were identified for remedy within The Metropolitan Police:

- A sense of purpose.
- Improving a divided organisation.
- Improving poor management practice.
- Promotion of a service ethos.
- Improvement of internal and external communication.
- Improved visual appearance.

These were not superficial issues. They called into question many of the fundamental ways that The Metropolitan Police had been doing things and gave a very clear signal that there had to be change.

The 'Force For Change' report endorsed Sir Peter's original 'gut feeling'. It would have been very easy, on reading the report, for The Metropolitan Police to ignore its recommendations, return to obscurity, and become obdurate and oppressive. Sir Peter realised that The Metropolitan Police had no alternative but to redirect its organisation in order to improve the level of service provided to the public.

The PLUS programme was therefore established to turn the recommendations of the report into a framework for change. PLUS represents the most extensive strategy of change ever undertaken by The Metropolitan Police and, according to Sir Peter, 'will have the greatest impact on policing for many years to come'. PLUS embodies the firm intention of The Metropolitan Police to provide a quality service to the public and to put their needs and priorities first. For this to occur, all members of The Metropolitan Police Service must be more united in their purpose, with improved leadership and management, and the promotion of a more positive attitude towards the concept of service.

This case study reviews the major challenge that has faced The Metropolitan Police Service in its attempt to improve the level of service provided to all of its customers; internal and external. It highlights how this approach has made everyone more service aware, and the role played by those responsible for steering the service ethos through the organisation and making PLUS happen. As such, the study encompasses problems which are relevant to every corporation in the country attempting to strive for service excellence.

The Metropolitan Police Service's PLUS programme for total customer service has proved to be a major cultural challenge; a daunting, demanding path for it to follow in the 1990s. It is a journey which has taken it from being a Metropolitan Police 'Force' to a re-named Metropolitan Police 'Service'.

The Metropolitan Police Service – Total Customer Service

> *'Every one of us, whether police officers, or members of the civil staff, provides a service, whether directly to the public, or in support of one another. All our energy must be directed towards ensuring that those who actually deal directly with the public are given strong leadership and the fullest possible support. PLUS is all about being positive, overcoming our individual weaknesses and those of the Service. It is also about those individuals who aren't even going to attempt to meet these improved standards, realising that they do not belong in our Service. Those who cannot support our objectives should leave.'*
>
> Sir Peter Imbert QPM, *Commissioner of The Metropolitan Police Service.*

This opening quote demonstrates Sir Peter Imbert's seriousness towards The Metropolitan Police Service's PLUS programme; the springboard taking The Metropolitan Police from an organisation of 'sellotape customs', to a fully-fledged service culture.

Change is part of life, and in the service excellent companies illustrated in this book, change has become a way of life. As customers and the market-place change, those who serve – supplying products and services – must change alongside them, and come to terms with it. In some organisations this has been very difficult. British Gas, for instance (see chapter 3), proved to be an industry rife with ritual and trampled by tradition. It discovered that it could survive the changing market-place of the 1990s only by major organisational restructuring. British Gas, like the other service excellent organisations in this book, has needed to find leadership to see it through the change process.

What business are we in?

Sir Peter Imbert sees the problem twofold as far as The Metropolitan Police Service is concerned. First, he is more than empathetic of feelings shared by many of his own officers, of the dichotomy in the perception of policing. Should it be a Police *Service* or a Police *Force*? Second, society wants a service; it has indicated this through the media and opinion polls, by demanding more caring, community-orientated policing with improved standards of service. Nevertheless, when serious incidents arise (our house is burgled, or our car is stolen) we also want the firm law-enforcer of the 'blue and two' Area patrol car. One could therefore agree that members of the public, and some police officers, are not even certain what business the police ought to be in. This uncertainty, in itself, produces insecurity on behalf of both the police and the public as it perceives them. As Sir Peter says:

> *'The call upon The Metropolitan Police Service is immense. The workload is high, finances are limited, and the pressures are, at times, overwhelming. Looking after London means helping to prevent crime, targeting and arresting criminals, being professional and sympathetic to victims of crime and, when dealing with people, remembering that the people we speak to will be the people whose support we need tomorrow. At the end of the day, we must not forget that today's aggrieved customer could be tomorrow's juror.*
>
> *'We must not forget that we are accountable to the public, we depend upon them for co-operation and if we provide a service that they require, with honesty and courtesy, we, in turn, will receive the respect and*

co-operation that we deserve. The results will be more assistance and greater success. But if we fail in this, we all lose that respect and assistance, and the public may well look to other agencies for the support and reassurance that they require and which they are not getting from us. That alternative is unacceptable.'

On the one hand, therefore, we have a public which expects and, according to Sir Peter, deserves the highest standards of commitment and service promise. After all, we pay £1 billion a year for just that. On the other hand, the police have a duty to provide a service, to do a job within a very difficult society in the face of many pressures and broad responsibilities.

What do we, the customers, want from our police, and what do they think we want? That was very much the foundation for the operational policing review mentioned at the beginning of this chapter. There was no doubt that the community wanted to look to the police as a service. But what does providing this service entail? According to Sir Peter, service is about:

'Assisting victims, arresting criminals, responding to the everyday needs of the people of London. It is in our "Statement of Common Purpose and Values". Our Statement does not replace our traditional aims. Our purpose is still our 'Primary Objects', which are to prevent crimes, to protect people's property, to bring criminals to justice and to maintain the Queen's Peace. The Statement does, however, remind us all what the focus of our work must be, which is to care for the people of London. We must never forget that so many people depend on us, and look up to us. Perhaps, on occasions, their expectations of us are unrealistic; that is also part of the challenge. It is about responding to public needs. At the end of the day I am talking about you and I – the public and the police – working together for a better quality of life in London. Nonetheless, sometimes the public will find reason to complain or even to question our role. They must be answered, our customers must be reassured, and that is why we have brought about PLUS.'

However, can the police give a good service to the public if they do not consider they receive a good service themselves from within their own organisation, as appeared in the 'Force for Change' survey? The experience of service excellent companies says not. You simply cannot have one without the other. This is why much of the PLUS programme concerns itself with the six major areas highlighted in the 'Force For Change' report.

Also of concern to The Metropolitan Police, in striving towards improving service at all levels, is the enormity of the task. This is due, in part, to the convoluted nature and sheer size of the organisation. What has been revealed throughout this book is that excellence works best in simple organisations where basic values hold strong. Complexity in organisations causes inertia and indifference. Complex organisations tend to spend a great deal of their time on co-ordination; forming policy groups, who subsequently form committees, who then ask for more data and then more back-up from information systems. In fact, complexity breeds unwieldy systems, strict structures and closed management styles.

Life is not that complicated in service excellent companies; organisations which show a great deal of organisational flair and fluidity, much of which is achieved through 'visible' management, 'management by walkabout'. In the Digital case study (Chapter 2), for example, in order to change from being a product-based organisation to a customer-focused one, the usual organisational triangle became inverted. In other words, the organisation became very proactive, as opposed to reactive.

DETERMINING THE SERVICE BUSINESS MISSION

The 'Statement' was an attempt to rally the realm of the organisation, create focus and reinforce basic values (see Figure 4.1). It should be emphasised here that, in some of the other case studies in this book, the organisation's mission statement was usually a new document; a customer-focused approach to delivering a product or service, or improving the business they were in. This was not the case with The Metropolitan Police who already had their original goals set from 1829, their Primary Objects highlighted earlier by Sir Peter. The 'Statement' reinforced original objectives and built on the values required to improve policing for the future. As with other case studies, the reinforcement of the values 'Statement' throughout the organisation helped to create a corporacy. As Sir Peter says:

> *'I want us all to feel we are part of the same team – pulling in the same direction, remembering that what happens in one small part of the Service affects the whole. PLUS is not about going "soft", or simply about image. It is about getting things right within our organisation, between ourselves, and different parts of the Service, understanding why we are*

Figure 4.1 The Metropolitan Police 'Statement'

STATEMENT OF OUR COMMON PURPOSE AND VALUES

The purpose of the Metropolitan Police Service is to uphold the law fairly and firmly: to prevent crime; to pursue and bring to justice those who break the law; to keep The Queen's Peace, to protect, help and reassure people in London; and to be seen to do all this with integrity, common sense and sound judgement.

We must be compassionate, courteous and patient, acting without fear or favour or prejudice to the rights of others. We need to be professional, calm and restrained in the face of violence and apply only that force which is necessary to accomplish our lawful duty.

We must strive to reduce the fears of the public and, so far as we can, to reflect their priorities in the action we take. We must respond to well-founded criticism with a willingness to change.

in business. Of course it is about responding to public needs, giving the public the confidence to walk the streets, relying upon us in The Metropolitan Police Service, and being proud of the service that we provide. But it is also about ensuring that those officers and civil staff providing the service are being given the best possible support by the rest of us.'

How can this happen, however, in an organisation that for too long has lacked purpose and has a history of fragmentation. 'Sellotape customs' meant an organisation often running around patching things up, and not practised in proactive management. Nevertheless, in fairness, the police have always been very good (indeed, at their most able and comfortable) when operating in crisis situations; running around and being reactive. The type of management style, however, that is required of a service-centred organisation is very different, with much more emphasis placed on being proactive.

Launching the Mission for Customer Service

As with all the case studies in this book, the launch pad had to be the senior management. With The Metropolitan Police Service, this involved some 600 senior ranking police officers and civil staff.

They were given the opportunity both to discuss the adoption of The Metropolitan Police 'Statement' and to suggest ways in which its purpose and values could be translated down the line. As a result of these sessions a series of seminars was agreed, called 'Working Together for a Better Service', which everyone within The Metropolitan Police Service would attend. By November 1991, all 44,000 members of The Metropolitan Police Service had attended a one-day seminar; not only to appreciate why the PLUS programme was necessary for policing in the 1990s but also to give them the opportunity to discuss the values contained in the 'Statement'.

Much credit must be given to this management effort and the energy that went into the principle of ensuring that every individual within The Metropolitan Police Service attended a seminar. Eight sites across The Metropolitan Police District were selected and it took 60 weeks before everyone had participated. The seminars had a maximum of 20 participants with two facilitators; the participants being a mix of police officers and civil staff from across the organisation. This was vital, as it allowed cross-integration to occur, often between staff who had previously never come together. The Metropolitan Police Service has some 28,000 police officers and 16,000 civilians, known as civil staff, operating over 72 Divisions and elsewhere in The Metropolitan Police District.

Most of the 16,000 civil staff work behind the scenes and, although they are not in the public eye, their work is of great importance as they are the support staff to The Metropolitan Police. They could be working in one of the headquarters buildings, such as New Scotland Yard, or in one of the many police stations. There are also the Traffic Warden Service, Special Constabulary and many types of technical staff who are employed throughout London and its suburbs.

Peter Winship, the Assistant Commissioner, emphasises that seminars such as PLUS must have cross-integration across the organisation:

> *'You have to remember the culture of The Metropolitan Police. The internal dimensions were such that the police and the civilian staff were two nations, and what we were trying to achieve through our Statement was one culture, one organisation for the whole 44,000 staff. The communication throughout our size of organisation, with 72 Divisions, has always been very difficult. It takes a great deal of energy to get the ethos across, particularly to what were, in effect, two different cultures. I think that many people felt that The Metropolitan Police were too overtly macho on the uniform side of the organisation, therefore the one-day seminars, mixed with the civil staff, overcame much divisiveness. But this took a lot of energy.'*

The most discouraging fact about being this type of octopus organisation is the energy that needs expending to gain entrepreneurship. This can be, at once, exhausting and exasperating. Peter Winship mentioned the different styles of the civil and uniform sides of The Metropolitan Police Service and the need for emphasis on cohesion and corporacy. For example, the command-and-control culture of the police sometimes finds it very difficult to treat subordinates as entrepreneurs; as intelligent, creative and trustworthy people. I imagine it is a little bit like the *Dragnet* mentality that we used to see on our televisions: 'All we want are the facts ma'am, just the facts.' In other words: 'We do not want to know anything about *you* (the customer). We have just pulled up in our cars and we are macho guys who only want the facts, ma'am.'

That method of policing intentionally detached the police from the community. An organisation in that mentality can have a 'paramilitary' approach to management, and many of the officers I talked to in The Metropolitan Police Service felt this still existed at many intermediary levels. It is a management style designed to make sure that police officers do not get into trouble, certainly do not embarrass the department they work in and, even more important, do not get their supervisors into trouble. Anything that an officer does is prescribed for him or her; everything should be predictable with rules and regulations covering all. If a police officer violates any aspect of this regime then the disciplinary system will catch up with him or her.

This is a management style that does not allow individuals to be creative, to be entrepreneurial, to use creative thinking, or to take a risk in solving problems. These are, however, the very characteristics of customer-focused organisations. Conversely, don't lets knock this style of management, because it works very well when an organisation has to be disciplined and controlled, which the police have to be when in their enforcement role. However, what happens when they are in their service role? Often at the customer level, those people actually serving the public (e.g. officers on the beat) must portray a great deal of autonomy. This involves risk taking and rapid decision making. Police officers often have to think on their feet, and simply cannot keep ringing back to their station whenever there is a problem.

Making a customer service environment happen

The challenge for The Metropolitan Police Service – which, with all credit, it is now addressing – is that the organisation encompasses very different management and leadership styles. The command control type, which appears to dominate quite significantly in certain areas, is not at all synchronous with a service-centred approach.

Commander Des Flanders at 5 Area reminds us, however, that probably only 30 per cent of a policeman's job is enforcement compared with 70 per cent service. In my travels around The Metropolitan Police Service, I have, nevertheless, met a number of senior officers who seem to think it is the other way around! Perhaps their own management style is more autocratic and closed, directed towards discipline, control and checking rather than the more participative approach, geared towards communicating, developing, and motivating. I did meet a number of managers within The Metropolitan Police Service who truly believed they had a creative and participative style of management. But did they? When I asked their subordinates, they felt, as individuals, that they had no influence, no idea what was going on, and no feedback.

Of course, again, this commentary can vary depending on who you are talking to, and where, within The Metropolitan Police District. Some Divisions, more than others, have appreciated that work without feedback is a killing activity. For example, in 8 Area, Paddington Green Division, they place great store on not only passing information down the line through committed consultative briefings, but also on listening. Chief Superintendent Gerry McBride explains it thus:

> *'Five years ago it was all very authoritarian and it was a privilege here to be consulted. Now we have much more of a consultative approach. For example, we have a divisional policy meeting which will take on board any issue that has not been resolved from any of the line meetings.'*

These line meetings, which are held on a regular basis, are very similar to the team briefings mentioned in other case studies. Such briefings occur at the actual workplace and discuss issues affecting individuals, and their day-to-day work. At Paddington Green these meetings are minuted, in this way the minutes themselves actually become an action plan. If anything is not resolved to anyone's satisfaction at this level it can easily become an issue at a more senior level. 'What this means,' says Gerry McBride, 'is that individuals throughout the Division can see the chain of progress with regard to problem solving. Being minuted, these briefing groups become highly accountable forums, and on record.'

From my observations, morale always seems higher in service excellent companies. By comparison, morale never appears to be very high in an organisation where people are subject to the personal whims of their supervisors. That is why team meetings – of the type held consistently, and with Divisional management commitment at Paddington Green – are a credible communication cord. At the very worst, if something is not happening, at least they know why.

'Teamwork' is a word constantly used in service excellence environments. It is a way of pushing entrepreneurship right down the line in an organisation and, when managed properly, such teams can be major innovators for any company. Teamwork is the very essence of crime detection work. The team approach to criminal investigation has developed since the Crime Investigation Priority Project (CIPP) commenced in 1989. Chief Superintendent Brendan Gibb-Gray, in charge of detective training at Hendon Police College, explains the core recommendations of CIPP:

> *'We felt that, prior to 1989, there was not as much emphasis as there should be on making the needs of the victim more important within the crime investigation organisation. There was not sufficient emphasis placed on victims and witnesses, who are both our prime customers. Victims expect a good service, indeed they are entitled to one. Victims of crime want some straightforward services to be provided by the CID. For example, a sympathetic and reassuring attitude which indicates that they are being treated as individuals, a reasonable amount of time being spent with them at the scene. Victims also require reassurance, and they like to see or, at the very least, be kept informed of some positive in-*

vestigative activities. In fact, these victims' needs are very similar to the needs that would be expressed by customers of any other service.'

Brendan Gibb-Gray is correct, Why should a CID member of staff be any different from a member of staff in, say, the service department of the British Gas study? British Gas has set standards which insist that if a service engineer cannot make a call, or is running late, they must let the customer know, and the gas industry watchdog Ofgas insists these standards are public knowledge. Brendan Gibb-Gray saw no reason why such a service could not come from detectives to the victims of crime. (See Figure 4.2.)

However, to move to such a service-orientated CID, would mean moving away from the ad hoc type of reactive policing to more of a team-based approach. This is another example of proactive styles of management replacing reactive ones, which is the norm throughout an organisation trying to give improved service excellence. As a result of CIPP, the Divisional CID was formed into teams, usually comprising one detective sergeant, four detective constables and possibly one or two trainee investigators.

The management of the team became the role of each detective sergeant. This meant far greater responsibility for the detective sergeants, who found themselves moving from a checking and control style of supervision to a more hands-on, supportive leadership role. This was quite a change. Some readers may, however, remember the story of a supervisor who liked to keep track of every little detail. One day, the supervisor handed a job to a subordinate and immediately asked how long it would take. 'About two hours,' was the reply, 'but if you stand behind me, it will take two days.'

There are therefore differences with the management style for service-orientated teams at the workface. Detective Sergeant David Hills of Paddington Green Division CID explains:

'There is a tremendous responsibility managing a team rather than a given number of individuals. It requires a different type of management. For example, it is now a motivating role rather than a basic supervisory or control system one. Not only are we dealing with the supervision of

crime investigations, but as CIPP has made everyone more accountable I have a responsibility for their guidance, training, development, and well-being. In fact, if they are not happy with themselves it is unlikely that they are going to be happy towards people they are serving.'

Experience in service excellent organisations shows that the more devolved the decision-making process down the line, the more involved, and committed, staff are likely to be to *want* to give us their best. However, David Hills adds:

'It is the basic law of leadership – without credibility you are vulnerable. The team is every individual including their supervisor. I am not an "add-on". For teams to work effectively there has got to be a great deal of respect for one another as well as self respect. Additionally, there is a difference between managing individuals in the 80s and now in the 90s. Today we have to give "service" – there is no alternative. This means, quite simply, commitment to the public who pay our wages. We have to change from a "Force" mentality to a "Service" mind – but this cannot happen overnight.

'It is not easy, because we are still living in a bureaucratic ballast of paper pushing, form filling, checking, controlling and chastising. This is a major learning focus and to succeed there must be commitment and direction from the top right down the line to the team. Especially when you remember, teams are built upon challenge, contention and contest.'

Another word of warning that must be considered with strong team personalities and leadership is the question of competition. As David Hills sees it:

'Healthy competition is good, but it is a tight-rope – envy can breed contempt between teams and it could be divisive, but this is exactly where PLUS can help. PLUS is all about corporacy and therefore the management of the entire department, and the way it is led, is fundamental to breeding a healthy team spirit rather than a destructive one.'

Figure 4.2 Quality of Service

WHAT THE CUSTOMER EXPECTS

The crime victim

Telephone calls to be answered without delay and the expected arrival time to be given.

- **An immediate** *(though non emergency) response, both for cases of residential burglary or other emotive crime, and if the victim is at location other than home or work place.*
- *A telephone call back if delay occurs.*
- *A sympathetic and reassuring attitude including steps to allay the victim's fears.*
- *A thorough and conspicuous investigation, including comprehensive note-taking and search for witnesses.*
- *Officers to display listening skills.*
- *Information to be provided as to whether the crime is likely to be solved, including whether and when further contact is likely.*
- *To be told the likelihood of forensic evidence being found.*
- *Information to be provided on; what happens next, Crime Desk telephone numbers, crime reference numbers and general advice re insurance claims, changing locks, Victim Support etc.*
- *Promises of further appointments to be kept.*
- *Information on how to obtain crime prevention advice.*
- *Regular contact with the investigating officer or the Crime Desk. Regular updates on the progress of the case if arrests have been made.*

TALKING CUSTOMER SERVICE

A little learning may be a dangerous thing, but a lot of ignorance is just as bad. Excellence companies realise that leadership is about doing and about achieving. It is also about taking people with you and doing so with credibility. In the British Gas case study (chapter 3), for example, the cascading of the 'Striving for Excellence' mission would have withered if its seeds had not been sown at the grass roots of the organisation, through committed action plans right down the line.

Leadership is not only about taking people with you, it is actually about doing something which makes people realise that the organisation has, indeed, changed. Leadership is action, not position. This is a most important point because unless people further down the line actually see things happening – or are given a reason why they cannot happen – they will not take ownership of any new ethos, no matter how much they want to believe in it. In other words, if the blind lead the blind both shall fall into the ditch.

Organisations which have traditional civil service mentality-type management styles and structures – for example, the National Health Service study in this book and, indeed, The Metropolitan Police Service – also breed cynicism. In fact, complex cultures seem to cultivate cynics. The Commissioner has had to ensure that the philosophy of PLUS is built into the structure and working arrangements of The Metropolitan Police Service. To do this, he has had to ride out the cynicism, pre-empt the prejudices of those in the organisation who pay lip-service to what they believe is just another project, short-term, with a beginning and an end. There will be others, too, who believe that PLUS is all to do with cosmetic imagery. Both views represent some of the negative attitudes which have long lingered in this organisation and, indeed, reflect its culture.

As indicated earlier, PLUS is an entire cultural shift, changing attitudes and behaviour, with the whole organisation pulling together as one corporacy. It is worth remembering that any programme such as PLUS has to be a long-term initiative; a journey, not a destination. Positive change in organisations never just happens, it must be directed, encouraged and visible; people must see things happening. Above all it needs to be driven and in this regard the Commissioner has excelled. Positive change has, nevertheless, to be taken on board at all levels in The Metropolitan Police Service, and this requires an emphasis on leadership and communication.

Deputy Commissioner John Smith believes that there are some critical areas that PLUS must address in order to succeed:

> *'I have much concern over communication and bureaucracy within The Metropolitan Police. There is so much potential for frustration and resentment when situations are not fully explained. Taking the time to explain why the decision has been made, or cannot be made, can often relieve much of this frustration and resentment down the line. We must all take responsibility for ensuring that we pass on relevant information, clearly and concisely, this is particularly the mark of a good manager. However, there is also a responsibility on all of us to want to be receptive to information provided by others. Apart from that, I feel that we must all take a personal responsibility for the health and well-being of our Service. PLUS starts and ends with each individual's responsibility, in whatever job he or she does, to provide the best possible service to each other and to the public.'*

In excellence organisations the improvement of the communication structure is two-way. John Smith is right to suggest that in order to promote PLUS one has to communicate much more openly, and also to listen. Service excellent organisations, throughout this book, have all emphasised the importance of being a 'listening' organisation. Glenn Tilton, Chairman of Texaco UK, pushed the point very hard that organisational hierarchies have a tendency to throw up walls that preclude listening (see chapter 1). What results is an organisation perceiving any criticism as a negative. Staff, no matter at what level, become defensive and automatically argue the point. I've observed that you are then often left with an organisation that is both defensive and deaf, one that is a live laboratory for cynics; for cynics never listen to anyone but themselves.

Many of the organisation leaders in the book implicitly believe that, whenever you hear a manager say 'what is the point of talking to them, they just won't listen' that this is not the fault of the employees. Rather, it is more that the senior management have failed the organisation because they did not commit. Sadly, organisations can destroy themselves by cynicism and disillusion, just as effectively as by bombs.

That is why I believe The Metropolitan Police Service is absolutely right to concentrate a greal deal of its PLUS effort into the leadership programme now gathering momentum. Any service excellent organisation will insist that you must have the quality of leadership right before you can ever expect quality service at the customer interface level. Quality of service is always affected by the way people are led, and by the way they treat one another.

A WILLINGNESS TO CHANGE

The one thing that you notice when you spend a lot of time with members of The Metropolitan Police Service is that they do not always share a common sense of purpose. There is an inconsistency of views, as indicated earlier, on the overall objectives of The Metropolitan Police Service and, indeed, on policing itself. As also mentioned, the Service is fiercely fragmented which often makes it difficult for individuals to assess how they, themselves, as well as others, contribute to the whole. One wonders how such different standards of behaviour and action co-exist, sometimes with such a schizophrenia that it is noticed by the general public. Commander David Kendrick, of 2 Area, explains it quite simply:

> *'It happens because we, in The Metropolitan Police, are uncertain of our role. What is our business? What is our end product? What am I supposed to be? What am I supposed to be producing? Am I an Aunt, a Mother, a social worker in uniform? What is "proper" police work? Are we into "feeling collars" or "patting shoulders"? This was really what the debate was all about when attempting to agree our Statement. Policing has changed and so has society, and the public. Their expectations have become much higher, and as customers they are very*

sensitive indeed to our shortcomings. We know that society has changed, particularly in areas like respect for authority, and this is across the board, from schoolteachers to parents and indeed towards police officers. One work day it's stray dogs, then state ceremonial occasions, the next day on to road accidents and rape. It is a lot of pressure on the police. It is not surprising that as almost all of our work involves the public we are, the majority of our working life, involved in very stressful and emotional situations. However, whether we in The Metropolitan Police Service like it or not, the public change and we must change our ethos and our culture in order to have the partnership with the public that is so essential to us doing our jobs properly. There is no alternative.'

A lot of this service-role confusion can be eased if there is a keener dialogue between the organisation and its customer. The reader will recall this was very much the case in the Texaco study (chapter 1). The same is also true in the following Hyatt Hotel study (chapter 6) where the boardroom came to the kerb, so-to-speak, in order to find out exactly what the customer wanted, not what the organisation perceived them to want. This is happening more within parts of The Metropolitan Police, 'listen to your customer and act'. For example, the Notting Hill Police Station questionnaire, which gives members of the community (their customers) an opportunity to voice what they think about the service provided by their local police. This is where the listening part of the organisation is vitally important. (See Appendix 4.1, at the end of this chapter.)

However it is said, David Kendrick's point of view is reiterated throughout The Metropolitan Police Service. Given this dichotomy, coupled with the corporate complexity and cynical culture, it confounds me how PLUS happened at all.

Steering the Change Process

PLUS being launched is a great credit to The Metropolitan Police Service and its 'statesmen champions'; those, as indicated in other studies in the book, who lead an organisation towards service excellence. As with all other studies, a 'mission statement' is needed to drive new values and beliefs through the organisation. Mission statements such as The Metropolitan Police Service 'Statement' describe the business that an organisation is in and how the job is done, as well as the committed values of the organisation.

As has been seen in other studies in this book (particularly British Gas) agreeing a mission statement is often a painful process. I suspect this was particularly true for The Metropolitan Police Service. According to many of the senior officers I talked with, it was generally accepted that the launch of the 'Statement', as an exercise in communication, was not successful. Many confused the intention of the 'Statement', believing that it replaced the 'Primary Objects' and 'Blue Book' which were the original, much earlier, goals within the police service.

I suspect that many in the Service were simply confused about the need to restate the common purpose and values that they believed they were already upholding. This is a common mistake when introducing a change in direction, or emphasis, within any organisation. It is a point that should be remembered by other organisations about to launch a 1990s mission statement in their company. Do be certain when introducing new hopes and aspirations for the organisation that you are not suggesting that the way things were done previously was wrong. Rather, suggest that in order to survive and, indeed, excel we have to improve on what we were doing previously.

Organisations that develop major change initiatives need to be steered, monitored, directed and driven. For most organisations in this book, the 'driver' has been the top man in the organisation, and in the Sutcliffe Catering study which follows, its Managing Director explains how that job must be a domineering and tough one. The Metropolitan Police, under Sir Peter, put together a PLUS team, whose job was to look at the various key issues arising. Both those highlighted in the 'Force For Change' report and those which would obviously be raised subsequently as PLUS was cascaded through the organisation. (See Figures 4.3.)

Dr David Hickman was the manager for Component One, and was also selected as the representative of all the trade unions within

Figure 4.3 Directing and monitoring change initiatives

THE COMPONENTS

Joint teams of police and civil staff, drawing on external help where appropriate, have been set up to investigate the key issues. The areas being looked at by the component teams fall into three broad groups.

First, the adoption of the Statement of our Common Purpose and Values. Sir Peter Imbert introduced the Statement in April 1989 to provide the basic guidelines to the way in which the Metropolitan Police Service carries out its responsibilities in policing London. The task now is to ensure that everyone knows, understands and believes in the Statement – what it means to each and everyone in the Metropolitan Police.

Second, the group of components concerned with overall policy making and the operational management of the Service – Policy Making and Command Structures, Composition and Deployment of Teams, Rewards and Sanctions, Performance Indicators.

Third, there are three components concerned with the way the Service behaves and presents itself – Paperwork and Bureaucracy; Communication; The Appearance of the Force.

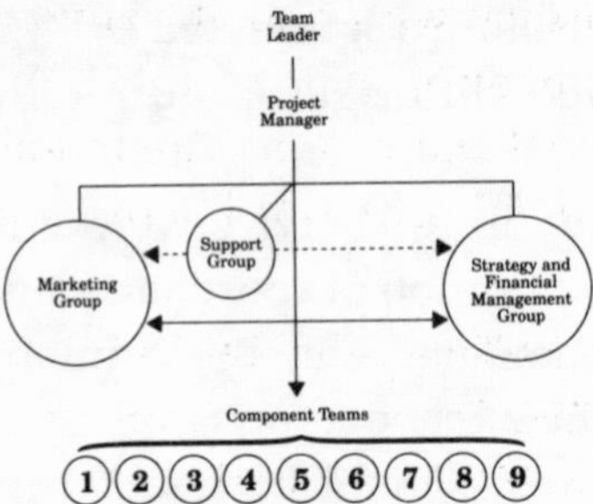

Component 1 **Adopting the statement of common purpose and values**
Ensuring every member of the Metropolitan Police Service understands and practices the organisational values.

Component 2 **Policy making and command structures**
A top-to-bottom examination of the decision making levels of the organisation, beginning with the Policy Committee. A radical review of the whole system of policy making so as to ensure that it works. Determining a structure or level of decision making. Examination of the allocation of resources.

Components 3 & 4 **Composition and deployment of teams**
Ensuring a balance of talent throughout the organisation. Effective deployment of manpower. Establishing a consistency of standards, a quality of service both externally and internally. The organisations exists to support front-line personnel. Appraisal of skills to ensure that they are being put to best use. Postings policy.

Component 5 **Rewards and sanctions**
Complaints, commendations and management's responsibility for discipline. Good behaviour rewarded, poor behaviour identified and tackled. Effective staff appraisal, merit awards, promotion and selection procedures.

Component 6 **Communication**
Both internal and external. Encouraging trust. Examining internal communication policy. Encouraging briefing, consultation and feedback. Improving standards of written communication. Developing training. Examining communication with the public, direct and via the media.

Component 7 **Paperwork and bureaucracy**
Cutting down and streamlining paperwork – challenging the "put it on paper" syndrome. Encouraging trust. Examining retention and storage times and retrieval process. Examining unnecessary bureaucratic systems. Encouraging personal communication.

Component 8 **Appearance of the force**
Buildings, vehicles, uniforms, print material. Working towards a coherent, consistent and instantly recognisable visual identity. Creating a Metropolitan Police Service style.

Component 9 **Performance indicators**
Promoting an effective customer survey. Striking a balance between value for money and quality of service. Establishing simple, effective indicators, linked to personal performance, rewards and sanctions.

the organisation for the PLUS team. The central PLUS team were responsible for ensuring that initiatives were co-ordinated and focused. This central PLUS team worked under the direction of a team leader, and was organised into three groups:

- **The strategy group:**
  – is concerned with the overview, the strategic plan
  – provides support for the component teams
  – co-ordinates recommendations to ensure corporacy and consistency;
  – balances expediency with radical solutions.
- **The marketing group:**
- – stimulates internal and external communication about PLUS;
  – carries out (in the short term) internal and external opinion surveys;
  – seeks to provide feedback about PLUS initiatives.
- **The support group:**
  – provides administrative support;
  – develops and maintains the data base.

Therefore the task of the central PLUS team was to co-ordinate the issues being explored separately by the nine component teams (see Figure 4.3), and also to focus on solutions and recommendations that would be emerging from all of the PLUS seminars. 'There were a lot of teething problems getting the PLUS initiative off the ground,' said David Hickman, 'choosing the right people for the PLUS team was a bit hit-and-miss. We all had a lot of learning to do.'

This problem, of choosing people to help steer and monitor initiatives of the PLUS type, is consistent throughout many organisations who have evolved similar vehicles for change. It probably is 'hit-and-miss' in that often such initiatives are reliant on volunteers. Sometimes, those who think they might enjoy training, communicating, facilitating and so on prove to be mediocre, or simply no good whatsoever. In some companies, for example Texaco, a number of facilitators volunteered to join the steering process for total customer service and discovered that it was a very difficult job indeed. This feeling is reiterated by those who acted as change-agents in the NHS study, later in the book (chapter 8).

The success of initiatives, such as the PLUS seminars, very much depends on the facilitators. As can be seen in other case studies, organisations trying to achieve change must have people within them who will take ownership of the value system and help steer and motivate it through the organisation. There was no doubt that getting all members of the organisation united was an important contribution of the PLUS programme, particularly as it brought the police officers and civil staff together and helped create corporacy.

I have attended a number of seminars similar to the PLUS type. There are certain problems that can occur at these sessions especially with the following:

- The presence of senior management.
- The presence of management who are not committed.
- The presence of management who say they are committed but who are actually deliberately sabotaging the process.
- The facilitator.
- The basket of recalcitrants, and 'bad mouthers'.

Most of the organisations in this book have undergone the type of awareness sessions that the PLUS programme initiated. They have been cross-functional, some being led by internal managers and some by external trainers not associated with the company. Depending on the culture of the organisation 'you takes your choice'. Often the problem with using an internal facilitator on seminars like PLUS is the difficulty an insider can have in managing the gripes, groans and grievances which emanate from the discussion groups. According to David Hickman:

> *'Top management must be committed and enthusiastic about PLUS and must demonstrate these qualities visibly. There are not usually any problems with this top layer, but there can be within intermediate levels who are not "signed up" or who deliberately sabotage the process. One area*

where we could, and should, have done more work was in identifying the blockages in the system and ways of overcoming them.'

Another vital influence on the success of these PLUS type seminars is not only how they are managed by the facilitators, and their capability, but who opens and closes them. According to Chief Inspector Tony Brooking, of the PLUS team:

'The successful seminars were certainly those where the senior officer, police or civil staff attending displayed a positive attitude towards PLUS, and was highly respected with a lot of street credibility. We were overcoming a lot of cynicism and, therefore, wanted senior management who carried presence and who did not inhibit the day. The point about these one-day seminars was everyone looking at what they did within the organisation, and discussing how they did it and where they could improve.

'The success of a seminar relies on participation by those attending. The facilitator has a crucial role in encouraging this participation, but also the senior officer can have a great influence. For example, they initially opened and closed the seminar days, then experience showed that there was much value in their being present throughout the day. This was particularly helpful when they could respond immediately to moans and groans which really only required feedback, as many of the grievances were based on lack of knowledge. The senior officer needs to be highly respected, have street credibility, and be able to put across the ethos of PLUS in order that it may be easily related to an individual's day-to-day work. It is vitally important that the presence of a senior person does not inhibit open and honest comment from participants.'

Companies that have gone through a similar PLUS process have discovered that the best way for organising the seminars, and ensuring that everyone attends, is to get more people on board ('champions') and have as many people involved as possible. Many of these champions can themselves be the facilitators, trained to lead the seminars. Further down the line there will be other champions, responsible for ensuring that the staff in their departments attend the seminars. After the seminars staff attitudes and behaviour can be monitored by executive champions, as discussed in the British Gas study (see chapter 3), who develop the ethos of PLUS through workplace action.

If an organisation does choose to use its own facilitators, and asks for volunteers, it runs another risk. For example, The Metropolitan Police Service did not want to see PLUS being a centrally-controlled initiative. As David Hickman says:

> *'We wanted to spread the ownership of PLUS across our Metropolitan Police District. Initially some inappropriate people were nominated locally; too junior staff, or personnel who did not possess the qualities necessary to be an effective facilitator. This had an adverse effect in the beginning, and we had to apply some pressure to get better quality staff.'*

As mentioned earlier, and in keeping with other studies, facilitators are a definite factor in the success of any seminars of this nature. Amongst the skills they must have are the following:

- Being confident.
- Enjoying communicating.
- Being erudite.
- Having a sense of humour.
- Ability to organise and participate.
- Ability to manage time, and recalcitrants.

It is vital, as Tony Brooking mentioned, that they have credibility. This is particularly necessary in an organisation such as The Metropolitan Police Service with its cautious and circumspect culture. It is these street-wise product champions who will act as the apostles, the advocates down the line, without whom the majority may become highly cynical towards the PLUS initiative or, rather, more cynical than they already were!

The training course that teaches the facilitators is absolutely crucial in ensuring the quality and dedication of those who are finally nominated; an area where many organisations do not devote enough effort. This is a pity because, as indicated, facilitators could be your product and service champions, particularly when they return to the work environment after the seminar stage is completed.

Diane McNulty is a traffic warden at Stoke Newington and she was selected as the best facilitator on 2 Area. She says:

> *'My main fear was my lack of confidence in acting as a facilitator but this soon disappeared as I became more experienced. My perceived concern, about being a traffic warden having to facilitate a group of people largely made up of police officers, did not in reality prove to be a problem. The most satisfying aspect of the role was to see the change in the group's attitude as the day progressed. Often there was a significant amount of cynicism and resentment towards the PLUS programme and the one-day seminar. However, once the group appreciated the purpose of the day, and the value of PLUS to themselves and the public in general, their attitude changed and most seminars finished on a positive note.'*

Superintendent Tony O'Brien (known as 'Mr PLUS' at 2 Area) spent a great deal of time involved with ensuring that the 3,500 staff in his Area attended the one-day seminars. He endorses the vital role of the facilitators:

> *'It was essential, in retrospect, that we had mixed group seminars from right across the organisation. It helped to increase the corporacy of the police family, and increase value. Of course there were resentments, and I certainly think that a great many of the civilian staff were shocked by the way the police side of the Service "bad mouthed". The refuse dump of moans and groans usually lasted for the first hour. This was where the strength of the facilitator was vital. Some facilitators could not manage this situation, whilst others turned problems into opportunities. Others were quite refreshing, in the way they opened people's eyes to how they could do things better.'*

Tony O'Brien believes that, after these seminars, 70 per cent of the delegates had a 'sense of ownership' of the PLUS programme. However, one thing is certain; if you do not do something with those 70 per cent when they return to their jobs, then there may well be a significant loss of that commitment.

With such a highly defensive, and sometimes derisive, organisation as The Metropolitan Police Service, I suspect that the PLUS seminars were very difficult to manage indeed. As mentioned earlier, organisations which are hierarchical preclude listening and take criticism as a personal attack. This is not peculiar to The Metropolitan Police Service. I attended a similar type of Customer Service training programme with British Airways. At the beginning of that seminar day there was a consistent concurrence that at least 10 per cent of the individuals in the room at that time were letting down the organisation 90 per cent of the time, and the other 90 per cent were not. By the end of the day, the fearless facilitator had us all believing that 90 per cent of everyone there were letting down the organisation 10 per cent of the time, including myself!

From the many staff I have talked with who attended the PLUS seminars, the majority felt that effective communication of the philosophy of PLUS, and of what was happening throughout The Metropolitan Police Service with regard to the 'Statement', was essential. It was felt this was important in order for everyone to regain some of the value and respect for the Service, and those they were serving, that had been lost. In this regard, the PLUS seminars could be considered successful. As one policewomen said to me:

> *'Yes, I certainly came away feeling that I had understood more about what PLUS was trying to achieve and why we had to go down this road for the 1990s. But, on my seminar there were some who deliberately sabotaged the day and this was not handled very well. This was a pity, especially as one had recently reached rank.'*

As has been discussed in other studies in this book, the important issue after attending a PLUS type seminar is to ensure that the momentum is reinforced by action back at the workplace.

MAKING IT STICK

One must act very quickly after such seminars to ensure that the momentum is reinforced into action plans at workgroup level. With the PLUS programme this was, again, very much a hit-and-miss affair. It also very much depended on what Area and Division you were working within. At 5 Area, Commander Flanders was quite insistent in the way he would recognise and manage any malicious obedience. Coping with those who pay lip-service to any change proposal, and who then go out of their way to sabotage new ways of working or behaving.

One of the problems with this stage of any change initiative is the fanatic. Oscar Wilde said that the worst vice of the fanatic was his sincerity; and there is nothing worse for an organisation than someone going around pretending to be 'PLUSed'. These are the pretenders, those who merely pay lip-service. They go through life with their mouth open and their mind closed, primarily to appeal to superiors. They are the 'yes' men and they are a problem. Chief Superintendent Peter Twist of 2 Area agrees there are a great many 'yes' men around:

> *'A lot of senior officers are foot dragging, because they lack commitment to PLUS. They do not believe that PLUS is the Service they joined. Further down the organisation some police officers feel their status is demeaned by being seen to be helpful, that it is not macho to be courteous. Fortunately, PLUS is now getting through the system and individuals are beginning to realise that a daily transgression, of rudeness for example, contaminates a whole public service and, indeed, the whole police service. Also, you must remember that PLUS has its supporters, those who say "this is the type of police I always wanted to follow," and after a while it pays off. You will find that the officers you meet around here truly believe that it is right to be helpful to the general public.'*

In many organisations, one has to be able to identify the disbelievers and the fanatics. They can be a thorn in the side of any organisation which is trying to be rosier; they can even prevent some of the initiatives getting off the ground. Making PLUS stick can, therefore, depend on what Area and Division of The Metropolitan Police you happened to be working in. Commander David Kendrick at 2 Area agrees, and asks: 'Why should you get a different kind of policing if you live in one part of London rather than another?' This is a problem within a fragmented structure, and that of devolving customer service responsibilities. Some Divisions have their champions more than others; in these cases there is a raising of morale in both that police station and their community.

In a later case study in this book, Simon Access (chapter 10) are quite insistent that their 'Best of Both Worlds' initiative should be managed centrally at a global level; despite being an entrepreneurial organisation with autonomy pushed as far down the line as possible to the individual companies. (This also happens to be the case in the Sutcliffe Catering Group study in chapter 5.) The reason there is a tight control on the change process at a central level is to ensure consistency throughout the whole corporation.

This is not a philosophy enjoyed by The Metropolitan Police Service, and it is a question of getting the right balance. A Commander told me that there were, in fact, eight separate police forces within London. I only thought, and hoped, there was one. However, his views illustrate why some Divisions have taken on the PLUS ethos more than others, and are so much more tuned into what PLUS is all about than their counterparts in different parts of London. This is where it is vitally important to have champions, particularly at the team or section level, putting the message across and enforcing standards. The central PLUS team, even with all its component parts, simply cannot do it alone; it must have devolved devotees.

Leading customer service at the frontier

In service excellent organisations the team is the critical factor. Inspector Paul Ramsay, at Paddington Green Division in 8 Area, feels: 'The ultimate aim of The Metropolitan Police is to enhance the quality of life of the community.' To achieve this, he believes that PLUS has tried to promote corporacy amongst all employees in order that they are all pushing in the same direction; trying to improve relationships with each other, and the community.

> *'We have realised over the last few years that what we, as police officers, think is important is not necessarily what the public think is important. Also, we know that police alone cannot tackle the problem of crime. Because the fight against crime is a major part of our work we need to involve the public, and through this partnership hopefully satisfy both their needs and ours. However, this search for service and quality is continuous, and part of the programme of change is the implementation of "sector policing", which I believe is a major step forward if done properly.' (See Figure 4.4.)*

Figure 4.4 Sector policing in the MPS from 1992

WHAT IS SECTOR POLICING?

The division is divided into smaller areas or sectors with each division deciding upon the most appropriate size and number.

Each sector is then policed by officers grouped into teams led by sergeants, with an inspector in overall charge.

These teams deal with all calls on their sector over a 24-hour period.

Apart from identified central divisional posts (CAD, front and custody offices, R/T car, van) operational officers are deployed on sectors. Divisions may choose to create a dedicated team to fill central positions or post officers from the sectors.

However, as Paul Ramsay insists:

> *'In these changes we need to take the officers, who will be delivering the service to the public, with us. "Us", being the management teams on Divisions. It will be no good if the officers delivering the service do not believe in what they are doing or why they are doing it. This, of course, has implications for the management of change and leadership.'*

It is very much this issue of leadership which The Metropolitan Police Service began addressing seriously in 1992. I was very impressed with the meeting that I attended in 5 Area where, at workplace level, they are developing 'quality of service' programmes. Commander Des Flanders, at 5 Area, believes that:

> *'The quality of service that we give to our customers is very much affected by the way that the people, those directly in touch with the general public, are led and also by the way we treat one another. We must improve the standard of leadership within our organisation. I firmly believe that improving leadership standards down the line to those who are managing front-line teams – for example, our sergeants – will ultimately give impetus to local things happening. What is the point of going through all of the PLUS seminars if, at the end of the day, no one at the front end notices that anything is different. All that will happen is our police and civil staff will have seen it as yet another torch and simply will not believe that anything different is going to take place. Unless we commit how can they possibly connect?'*

At 5 Area a working group come together from the different Divisions and the 23 operating police stations within the Area. Primarily, they discuss ways they can improve customer service throughout the Area. The representatives are broadly based across the various Divisions. They include civil staff representatives, as well as operational and area-based units, and comprise various ranks with at least two sergeants. These groups generate issues that directly affect people giving customer service, whether from Support, Crime or Operations. These are not 'talk' shops. Some of the matters will improve the lot of their own staff, and some are geared to the general public, while other matters help the police themselves to feel more professional.

One point that has been consistent throughout the customer service excellence studies is that those companies that are really striving for excellence are those which are very close to the customer, whilst also discussing issues specifically related to improving quality and service at the workface. The Japanese would call this concept 'quality circles'. Whatever name you give it, it is a way of getting change off the ground with frightening alacrity.

At 5 Area they are looking at various contact points where they feel they can concentrate upon providing a top level quality of service. These involve 'putting people first':

- In the street.
- At the police station.
- On the telephone.
- By letter.
- Through the media.

It is one thing to identify the contact points but, as one of the police sergeants said at the Area meeting I attended: 'It is another thing to make sure something really does happen, and that is why we have "do it now" activities.' In other words, representatives leave the meeting and must go away and do something. Some 18 'do it now' initiatives have resulted from these meetings emphasising the point that if people actually see things happen then they will take ownership much more of the PLUS initiative. As an executive officer said:

> *'It is all to do with meeting the needs of our customers. For example, some of the things we are now doing – especially at the front line, as in some of our police stations – is nothing short of what our customers expect. Regrettably we were just not always doing them before and that is why it is so important to find out what the customer wants.'*

In other words, they are closing the gap between customer expectations and service delivery. (See Figure 4.5 and Appendix 4.2.)

Figure 4.5 Quality of Service delivery: defining quality

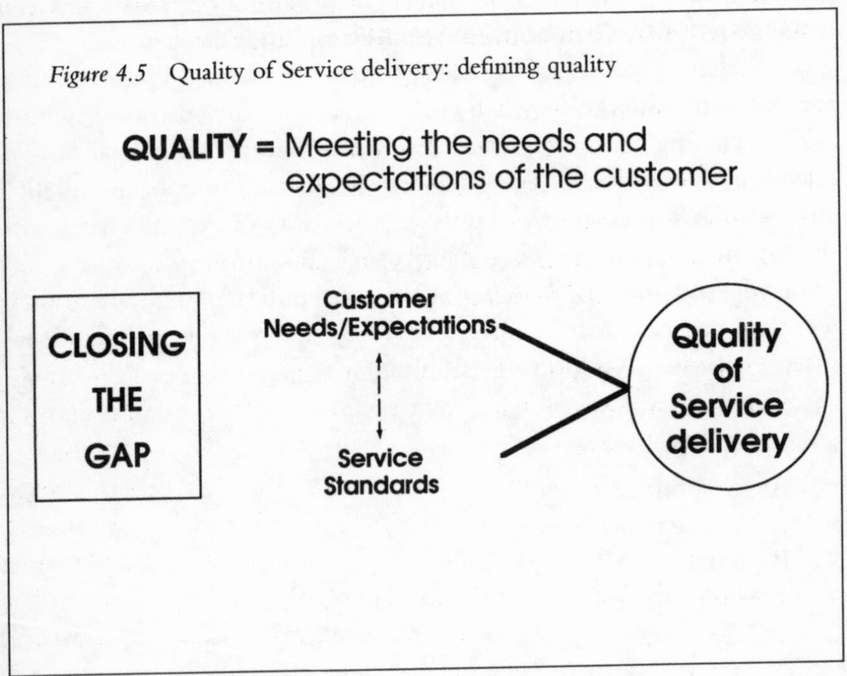

Another 'shop window' for The Metropolitan Police Service is provided by their Area cars, which are the fast response vehicles. The reader will recall Peter Winship speaking earlier of the 'overtly macho' image that the uniformed police officers portrayed. Certainly, as far as the public are concerned, this conception concerns police officers in cars not those 'on the beat', and is one of the areas that The Peel Centre at Hendon Police College also addresses itself to in its Driver Training School. The Superintendent in charge of the school is Brian Lunn, and one of his challenges, when students arrive to be trained as drivers of Area cars, is to make them realise that they must be service-orientated and not status-centred:

'It costs £12,000 to send a police officer on our six-week advanced course and, again, the PLUS ethos is very much built into their training pro

gramme. They have to be very conscious of their image. After all, they are in a marked car which people immediately identify as belonging to The Metropolitan Police Service. It is probably this vehicle which is our largest shop window to the public, and as such the way that the car presents itself, is driven, and the appearance of the driver are all extremely important. We work to the Four S's; Safety, System, Smooth, Speed. Many people are surprised at the length of the training course, but whenyou consider these officers have to drive safely, to a police system of driving which is smooth and not erratic, often at high speed, and always at a high degree of concentration, you can appreciate the technical skills required.'

Brian Lunn endorses points made by other members of the Peel Centre, in that it is not just being proficient in your end product – in this instance the ability to handle a vehicle – it is also training in how that end product is served:

'There is a great deal of leadership training needed when these students come to the driving school because they also have to learn the ability to make decisions and become the leader at a scene or major incident; mainly, because they are often the first person on the scene and must manage that situation. Therefore they must have correct attitudes, and be able to make judgements. In effect, planning for the worst thing that can happen.'

If only other organisations with large car fleets would appreciate the importance of such a training and image commitment to their drivers.

An interesting point emanating from these 'shop window' examples of change is that, as we have seen before, you just cannot become 'PLUSed' overnight. In order to give quality of service, the giver must be trained, must have the right attitude and accompanying behaviour, to *want* to give that service to the customer in the first place. Again, this type of training attitude is consistent throughout service excellent organisations and is highlighted in many of the studies in this book.

ENTHUSING CUSTOMER SERVICE

In 2 Area, Commander David Kendrick is totally committed to PLUS because he firmly believes that it must come from the top:

> *'My challenge is to make the weakest link in this Area more effective. You do this through the 3E approach:*
>
> - *Energy to all aspects of PLUS.*
> - *Enthusiasm for all aspects of PLUS.*
> - *Example of PLUS.*
>
> *Of course there is a major reluctance by some people to change, especially by those in the Service who are asking: "What am I supposed to be doing as a police officer? I mean, what is the end product? Does it need more salt and pepper?" However, if you constantly have the 3E approach, after a while, the message gets through but it must go right down the system, I simply will not tolerate a non "PLUSed" middle manager here.'*

A way of getting the message across in 2 Area is through 'work-shadowing' (interestingly, the opposite approach to Hyatt Hotels' 'In Touch Day', explained in chapter 6). When Commander Kendrick was fed up with certain officers constantly 'having a go at the guv-'nor', he decided that some of them should be one for a day.

Barry Cowsey is a police constable attached to Forest Gate Police Station in East London who has completed some two years' service in The Metropolitan Police. He 'work-shadowed' Commander Kendrick for a day:

> *'One day, at the Area Training Unit at East Ham, we were asked for our views about senior police officers, which we wrote on a large sheet of paper. They came in for a bit of flack. I said I thought they were distant and aloof and that we never saw them. Commander Kendrick, who unbeknown to us all was waiting outside, then came into the room.*

When he heard my views, he invited me to spend a day with him, which we arranged to do two weeks later.

'We went all over, with me acting as his "shadow". It gave me a tremendous insight into senior officers, with whom I (usually) had hardly any contact. We went from touring a police station to a football match briefing, followed by a medal presentation ceremony in the evening at New Scotland Yard, where I was introduced to a number of other senior officers who were amazed at what Commander Kendrick was doing. The wife of one of them thought that I was Commander Kendrick's bodyguard! It was a very, very enjoyable day. I realised how senior officers have no time to themselves. Their working day is just like 24 hours really. Since then I have been impressed to hear him on the radio early in the morning. He's one of the few Commanders I've seen visiting the stations.'

As with all service excellent organisations, a consistent theme is 'visible' management. Management by walkabout becomes the norm. This apparently simple concept does, however, occupy a major portion of management time in excellence organisations.

Without this visible management, even those parts of organisations where the champions are working can diminish in excellence. All service excellent companies remember that their champions are the mission messengers. As mentioned earlier in this study messengers can get shot. Service excellent organisations that develop their champions have strong support systems, and networks, in order that the messengers themselves continue to be motivated to pass on their mission. This is why leadership in quality service is so vital; in fact, it cannot be stressed enough. Quite simply, if you do not have committed, enduring and visible leadership, there will be no support system, no champions and therefore limited 'happenings' at the point of delivery to the customer.

However, visible management, such as Barry Cowsey's Commander visiting the station, has to be genuine. The balancing act between being value-driven or giving supportive leadership, and being perceived to be on a 'witch hunt', is very fine. There is simply no point in putting your head round the door and seeing how everyone is getting on because you have been on a management training course and been told that it is good to be 'visible'. Leadership is all about winning hearts and minds and that is why organisations who are striving for excellence put so much effort into leadership development.

CONTINUAL IMPROVEMENT THROUGH CONSTANT REVIEW OF SERVICE

In many organisations quality of service fails at the front line, particularly at the supervisory level, and the reason for this is twofold. Far too often those directly managing staff dealing with customers have very little training in leadership skills. Some are promoted to supervisory levels for what are often the wrong reasons. Perhaps they have obeyed all the rules and regulations well and therefore will not upset the system; they are very good 'yes' men. They may alternatively have served the required years and on that basis of tenure are due promotion, or they may have been promoted because they are very good at passing exams. Whatever the reason, and all of the above are unsound and unjust, no one in a supervisory position should be there without leadership skills; especially when you consider the more demanding management style required in a team-centred environment (as mentioned earlier by David Hills of Paddington Green CID).

At The Metropolitan Police Service PLUS seminars there was much criticism levelled at the quality of leadership within the Service. The criticisms were varied; e.g. too many managers were quick to complain but slow to praise, they did not motivate their teams but were very good at checking, controlling and disciplining. Many staff at the seminar complained that they never saw their respective manager. I can believe this, I met some people in New Scotland Yard who had not seen their 'guv'nor' for seven months!

Many members of the Service I talked to believe The Metropolitan Police should put much more into training – particularly for those who have occupied the same position for some time. Nowhere is this more appreciated than at The Metropolitan Police Service's

Hendon Police College, Peel Centre. Superintendent Brian Boon, who is head of their Management Training and Development Branch, is conscious that many sergeants and inspectors who trained a few years ago require further development in those areas that are more relevant to their job role in the 1990s. Hendon is looking at the possibility of more modular training, getting line officers and civil staff back to Hendon on specific training inputs, linked to the PLUS ethos and to present day jobs. For sergeants and inspectors new to their ranks Brian Boon's department particularly wants:

> *'To enhance the leadership training, as a means to drive PLUS and produce a quality service to the public at the "cutting edge". Inspectors and sergeants will undertake imaginative and effective training as far as leadership is concerned, and much more time is being spent on role playing as a powerful means of establishing self awareness. The whole programme is inextricably linked to the PLUS ethic.'*

However, many police officers believe that the management development they receive is far too insular. Apart from benefiting from cross-integration within the Service, many feel that they could learn from mixing much more with management in other sectors of commerce and industry. At Hendon, Brian Boon has taken these comments fully on board during 1992. For example:

> *'We have entered into a most interesting partnership with the National Trust, where our police officers and civil staff will carry out joint projects at work on Trust properties. Currently we are looking at other initiatives where police management can work alongside other organisations in the community. For example, Hampstead Division and the Royal Free Hospital are presently discussing sergeants testing their leadership qualities and abilities, through the preparation and enactment of an evacuation plan for that hospital's dialysis unit. This training actually yields benefits for people other than the police, such as the hospital itself, and the general public and their safety.'*

In service excellent companies, training is seen as a major commitment underpinning the entire ethos and change process. This is very much the case in The Metropolitan Police Service. Whoever you talk with at Hendon, whether it is their Commandant, Chief Superintendent Colin Shew, or their Chief Instructor, Chief Inspector Bernie Hall or Chief Superintendent Brendan Gibb-Gray, Head of Detective Training, they are all agreed that training input must be married to the ethos of PLUS. Hendon is a highly competent training establishment. They are aware of the negative attitudes within The Metropolitan Police Service indicating there is simply not enough training to help police officers move from their reactive style, which many are comfortable with, to more proactive behaviour. As John Grieve, Commander of Training at Hendon, states:

> *'Basically we are asking people to change their attitudes, many of which have been based on military principles, to those now based on corporacy. For years the emphasis was always on procedures, but now it has to be on how the customer thinks, and much of our training here now is geared towards changing their behaviour.'*

The tendency to take a lot of police training to community-based projects, as mentioned earlier by Brian Boon, has another benefit as well. Sergeant John O'Driscoll is responsible for the training of sergeants and inspectors, and he sees a major pay-off in these community-integrated projects being the fact that more police officers will: 'Work with the community, which will help in changing their attitudes. Basically we are trying to change the emphasis – which has always been on the end product – more to how it is now being served.'

Commander John Grieve appreciates that more training needs to be pushed down the line. He views Area and Divisional training as being 'much more responsive to the needs of everyone working at the sharp end'. In service excellent organisations, training has always been devolved right down to those individuals in direct interface with the customer. Hendon agrees. More guidance will be given to the training units at Divisional level for them to deliver to their teams themselves. This is already happening with initiatives such as the 'Leadership and Quality of Service' workplace discussions (see Figure 4.8). Service excellent organisations such as those mentioned in this book are constantly involving their staff in such training. The readers will recall from the Texaco study (chapter 1) just how much Barry Limb's training budget increased in one year (£150,000 to almost £2 million) due to the importance being given by the boardroom to the training of supervisory staff. In many instances these supervisors are managing the staff operating at the sharp end of the business.

Many of these case studies find middle and line managers, plus their entire team, in training environments where they are specifically talking through problems that occur on the job. This, at present, does not seem to happen as often as it should within The Metropolitan Police Service. However, Assistant Commissioner Peter Winship is hoping that: 'The new "Service Standards of Leadership" initiative will develop, which will ultimately mean managers being assessed against criteria and benchmarks, some of which will be linked to the philosophy of PLUS.' Some Divisions are practising a type of job-related service training, via a team approach, similar to that in the Texaco study. This is where a team would take an issue (for example, see Figure 4.8) and they would deliberate on how best to manage such a given situation.

In 1992, this 'team leadership' approach is finding a more natural habitat within The Metropolitan Police, as the Service moves towards what Paul Ramsay earlier referred to as 'sector policing'. This will provide excellent opportunities for inspectors, sergeants and their teams to live through training models that ultimately reflect on developing not only their own job skills, but also the type of interpersonal skills that are required to achieve improved service.

Sir Peter Imbert indicated at the beginning of the study how he believes that the assessment and appraisal, now being considered through the 'Service Standards of Leadership', will soon become the norm, at all levels, throughout the Service. He said: 'PLUS is also about those individuals who aren't even going to attempt to meet these improved standards, realising that they do not belong in our

Service. Those who cannot support our objective should leave.' Discussions are now occurring with the Home Office to agree areas of renewable contracts for senior police officers. This appraisal will enable The Metropolitan Police Service to deal with its basket of recalcitrants; those who do not perform under the new PLUS ethos.

This would be good news for those 'executive' champions who do carry the torch for the ethos of PLUS. At the present time, if managers do not want to come on board, and they do not voluntarily leave the Service, they are shunted into sidings where they can do the least possible damage. For many of the officers I talked with in The Metropolitan Police Service, the Service has some crowded sidings. Certainly, more than 90 per cent of those I spoke with would like to see a policy of 'renewable service contracts'. This dominant approach to only having executives in the organisation who are committed to customer quality service improvements is a norm in all excellence environments. Most of the companies in this book actively recruit, appraise and reward both managers and staff, in line with standards which are very much linked to their mission statement. The Dell case study (chapter 9) is an excellent example of this; the Metropolitan Police Service leadership is considering no more, no less. To those who whinge 'Why should there be renewable service contracts throughout The Metropolitan Police Service?' many observers reply: 'Why not?'

The Value of Satisfied Customers

Sergeant Andy Norfolk, of Paddington Green Division, was a facilitator on the PLUS seminars. He believes that:

> *'As a result of PLUS, 95 per cent of the force recognise policing in The Metropolitan Police Service, is a service. We accept that we have customers but it is only through constant reinforcement back at the workplace that, ultimately, the pay-off to those customers will begin to be realised. We have to look at both our strengths and our weaknesses and see where we can improve.'*

Figure 4.6 Quality of service delivery: meeting the needs of customers

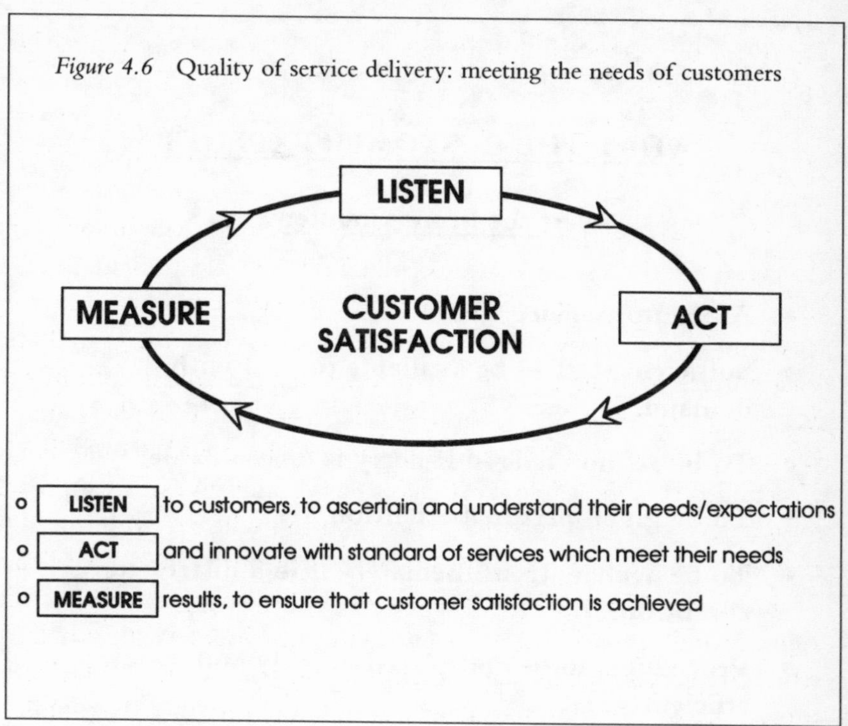
LISTEN
MEASURE
CUSTOMER SATISFACTION
ACT
LISTEN to customers, to ascertain and understand their needs/expectations
ACT and innovate with standard of services which meet their needs
MEASURE results, to ensure that customer satisfaction is achieved

His comments are very much endorsed by those in The Metropolitan Police Service who monitor customer satisfaction, and Metropolitan Police performance.

Component nine (see Figure 4.3) have established a range of performance indicators, for various levels of The Metropolitan Police Service. These enable it to measure achievement in whatever it does and how it does it, whilst also assessing the public's perception of how it does it. All place emphasis on quality of service. This is a case where a Centre can support all eight Areas of The Metropolitan Police Service, by using Service-wide performance indicators as a significant management information tool which assists in gauging levels of service impact achieved.

With the emphasis on the service impact at the point of delivery (the customer) surveys have been undertaken to assess performance. For example, a survey was conducted on four Divisions. This used customer service cards available at police station front counters, and

Figure 4.7 Quality of service: what the customer expects

WHAT THE CUSTOMER EXPECTS

At the Front Counter

- **A prompt service.**
- **Sufficient staff to be available to deal with demand.**
- **To be acknowledged if delay is unavoidable.**
- **To be given personal attention.**
- **To be dealt with immediately if in a distressed condition.**
- **Procedures to be completed quickly and efficiently.**
- **A degree of privacy to be afforded, especially when taking reports or statements in crime cases.**
- **Reports to be taken, even if the incident did not occur within the Division.**
- **A sympathetic and reassuring attitude.**
- **Not to see officers apparently idle, whilst crime reports are being taken.**
- **An explanation to be given as to what will happen next.**

customer service questionnaires (an example of which is at Appendix 4.3) completed by visitors. Continued customer measurement is a very strong side of the PLUS initiative and completes the loop of meeting the needs of customers (see Figure 4.6):

- Listen.
- Act.
- Measure.

Information retrieved from such customer surveys can be acted on at the point of service and subsequently incorporated into PLUS standards. This is also the case with service to victims of crime, which has been taken on board at Paddington Green Division, who now appreciate that victims of crime are indeed their customers. (See Figures 4.2 and 4.7.)

WINNING YOUR CUSTOMER

The ultimate criterion, of course, is whether you carry the 'partnership' of police and public with you. Detective Chief Inspector Heather Penna, at Paddington Green Division, believes that improving the quality of service and responding to the community's needs and wishes is vital:

> *'This is the only way a stronger partnership can be created between the police and the public we serve. The overall quality of service that we can provide is dependent on the strengths of that partnership. Really it is all about harnessing goodwill.'*

I was present at a Divisional consultative group meeting attended by members of the community representing Heather Penna's 'Parish', as she calls it. She saw attendance at this type of meeting as a vital part of her job role and an example of 'partnership' at work: 'I feel that the public have a right to know about what we at Paddington Green CID can do for them but, equally, we do need them to help us.'

Figure 4.8 'Leadership and Quality of Service' discussion example

WHAT IS THE ISSUE?

A member of staff is not making a full contribution. Lack of punctuality, deterioration of work, attitude and appearance are causes for concern.

WHAT DO WE NEED TO DO?

By personal observation, examination of workload and discussion with first line supervisors, or others who can contribute, confirm the individual's level of performance.

If confirmed, discuss each matter of concern with individual, seeking underlying problem.

If identified, work with the member of staff to alleviate or remove cause of under performance and monitor.

Consider:

- re-allocation of workload;
- additional training;
- flexibility of hours;
- alternative post;
- granting of compassionate leave;
- referral to CMO;
- referral to welfare officer.

Revisit these issues as deemed necessary.

If individual refuses to co-operate and remains unresponsive:

- comply with any current cautioning procedure and record;
- make it clear that close supervision will be maintained;
- emphasise that progressive steps will be taken to monitor conduct and performance looking for improvement.

If performance remains unacceptable and attempts to provide assistance continue to be ignored – refer for a formal enquiry to be considered. Keep the member of staff informed at every stage of this process. Do not avoid this difficult obligation.

WHAT HAVE WE ACHIEVED?

We have responded to the individual and preserved team integrity.

Part of this 'partnership', as indicated by Heather Penna, is to have the public become more involved. The equivalent of the user groups and customer clinics referred to in other studies in this book are the joint partnerships between police and public: Neighbourhood Watch Schemes; Divisional Consultative Groups; Crime Prevention Panels; and so on.

There has to be that strength of 'partnership' on both sides, however, for people to *want* to be involved. There are still far too many members of the public who feel too alienated from their local police station to want to help. Conversely, there are still too many police officers who unfortunately pay no more than lip-service to the community who pay their wages. Nowhere is the need and bond better seen between police and community than with 'CRIMESTOPPERS' (0800 555 111). According to Detective Inspector Adrian Holder: 'CRIMESTOPPERS is an excellent example of the partnership approach at work, with the police, assisted by Community Action Trust, actively involving the media, industry, commerce and the community in the constant fight against crime'. If a member of the public has any information which can help the police they can make a free call from anywhere, at any time. They will also not be asked their name or address. In its first three years, this 'partnership' has resulted in over 3,000 individuals being arrested, more than 10,000 crimes being cleared up, and £6 million worth of property being recovered (the numbers are still growing).

Of course, there is a long way to go to achieve total customer service through the PLUS initiatives. Nevertheless, it is those at the frontier of The Metropolitan Police Service who know the business best. They will have the ultimate say on whether the quality of service to the people of London has improved as a result of PLUS.

Earlier in this case study, Sir Peter Imbert referred to those people at the front line who actually deal with the public being given 'strong leadership, and the best possible support', from their senior officers. In keeping with the other service excellent organisations in this book, one hopes – or does one do more than that – that those at the front line will not be disappointed. Sir Peter remains as emphatic as in his opening quote: 'Those individuals who do not attempt to meet the required standards of leadership do not belong in our Service. Therefore, those at the front line will not be disappointed.'

Appendix 4.1

Notting Hill Police Station

Questionnaire

Please help us to help you by letting us know what you think about the service we provide.

1. There are a lot of different sorts of offences and the time police have is limited. Here are a selection of offences. Which four of these do you think the police should spend most time and energy trying to combat. And, of the remainder, which three do you think the police should spend least time and energy trying to combat? Please indicate by placing ticks in the columns alongside.

	4 Most Time	3 Least Time
Burglary from offices, shops, factories, etc.		
House Burglary		
Thefts of Cars and Thefts from Cars		
Racist Attacks		
Attacks on Women		
Street Robbery		
Parking and Traffic Problems		
Anti Social Behaviour (fighting, vandalism, etc.)		
Drink Driving		
Use and Sale of Soft Drugs (e.g. Cannabis)		
Use and Sale of Hard Drugs (e.g. Heroin, Cocaine)		

2. The Police are asked to do a lot of different jobs. These are some of them. We have limited resources and cannot always cover everything. Please indicate which three jobs you regard as most important and which three jobs you regard as least important by placing a tick in the columns alongside.

	3 Very Impt.	3 Least Impt.
Respond Immediately to Emergencies		
Investigate Crimes and Detect Offenders		
Give Crime Prevention Advice		
Patrol the Area on Foot		
Patrol the Area in Vehicles		
Provide Help and Support to Victims of Crime		
Control and Supervise Road Traffic		
Work Closely with Local People and Schools etc.		

3. This is how we the police in Notting Hill divide our resources. Please show how you would divide these resources, and do this by using the boxes below. Remember if you move units from one box to another it will adversely effect police resources in one area (if you move one from Emergency Response to Community Work it will take police more time to answer an emergency call).

	Uniform Patrol	Plain Clothes Patrol	Investigating Offences	Emergency Response	Community Liaison
How Notting Hill Police divide their resources	9	2	2	3	1
How you would arrange Police resources					

(Figures represent number of Police officers)

4. What do you think of the services we deliver in relation to the subjects in Question 2.

	V. Good	Good	Poor	No Opinion
Respond Immediately to Emergencies				
Investigate Crimes and Detect Offenders				
Give Crime Prevention Advice				
Patrol the Area on Foot				
Patrol the Area on Vehicles				
Provide Help and Support to Victims of Crime				
Control and Supervise Road Traffic				
Work Closely with Local People and School etc.				

5. Is there anything particularly good in your opinion about the service we deliver?

____

____

6. Is there anything that needs a lot of improvement in the way we deliver these services?

____

____

7. Have you any other comments you would like to make?

____

____

It would help us if you could complete this section.
Name
Address
Tel. No.
Please return the Questionnaire in the envelope provided. Thank You.

Appendix 4.2

Quality of Service

At the Station We Will:

Provide a prompt and reassuring service to *all*, in a way that inspires confidence in our ability to help and advise, and in our readiness to do so.

Ensure sufficient staff are available to deal with members of the public. All callers will be dealt with immediately. When one member of the public is being dealt with and others arrive they will be immediately acknowledged and reassured. Anyone obviously distressed will be given priority and the reason explained to other callers. Callers will be given as much comfort as possible; e.g. use of of telephone to contact relatives or friends. Staff working reception will introduce themselves by name; e.g. 'Good morning, I'm Alison Day. How can I help you?' People who attend the station to give assistance will be thanked prior to leaving and where necessary contacted later to be told the final outcome. An explanation will be given to callers as to what will happen as a result of their call; e.g. process procedures, property found etc.

Employ trained staff on front counter enquiry duties. Those staff will be easily identifiable and will portray an efficient and approachable image. The service provided at front counters will match the demands of the public and will be supervised appropriately.

Reception duties will be undertaken by members of the civil staff. Reception staff will be selected on the basis of their interpersonal skills. Comprehensive local training will be provided prior to taking up their duties. Supplementary training will be provided to keep staff abreast of new procedures. Rosters for reception staff will be devised, based on an analysis of peak demands. Reception staff will wear name badges. Overall responsibility for reception staff rests with the HEO whilst duty officers will be responsible for day to day performance of duty. Reception staff will be consulted when rotas and working practices are being devised.

Facilities at the station will be kept clean, tidy and comfortable and will be treated with respect by all personnel.

Refreshments of any sort will not be taken into the reception area or consumed in view of members of the public. Books and forms will be neatly stored, clearly marked and readily available. The reception area will be the priority for station cleaning staff. The station notice board will be clearly visible and regularly updated with useful information. A supply of pamphlets and leaflets giving advice and guidance will be available. Particular needs of individual callers must be met; e.g. seats for the elderly.

In Written Communication We Will:

Every piece of written correspondence will be acknowledged promptly, the aim being to reply fully within ten working days.

All letters received through the post which cannot be answered immediately will be acknowledged. Acknowledgment letters will be sent as interim replies where the relative importance of the person or the topic justifies it. Save in exceptional cases a full written reply will be sent within two working weeks.

The content of written communication will be simple, clear and precise giving as much information as possible.

Replies will be professionally set out using clear and precise language and will be typed unless of a personal nature. Replies will be as informative as possible. All replies will be on official headed paper and sent in white envelopes.

An organised registration system will be established and maintained to ensure that correspondence is dealt with appropriately and within the set time scale.

The receipt and despatch of letters through the post will be recorded in the

Correspondence Register. A member of the civil staff will be designated for the responsibility of recording the receipt and despatch of all letters. The Correspondence Register will be regularly supervised by a designated member of the senior management team to ensure that the above specifications are strictly adhered to.

External communication will be prepared by specialist typing staff and will be monitored within a quality control system.

The typing manager will be responsible for the quality of all typewritten letters. Where appropriate, staff involved in the preparation of replies and in the use of the Correspondence Register will be trained.

Appendix 4.3
Customer Service Questionnaire

Thank you for taking the time to fill in this questionnaire. Please fold and seal this form and return it by normal postal service. NO STAMP is required.

Please tick appropriate boxes

1. I attended the station:
- To produce driving documents ☐
- To report an accident ☐
- To report a crime ☐
- To ask for advice or directions ☐
- To enquire about a person in custody ☐
- Matter not mentioned above (please specify) ☐

....

2. I was attended to:
- Immediately ☐

FOLD HERE

- Promptly ☐
- With delay ☐
- With unacceptable delay ☐

3. I found the staff:
- Very helpful ☐
- Helpful ☐
- Not very helpful ☐
- Very unhelpful ☐

4. I would describe the service I received as:
- Highly professional ☐
- Professional ☐
- Not very professional ☐
- Very unprofessional ☐

5. If we could improve the service provided in this Police Station which of these would you like?
- Additional staff ☐

FOLD HERE

- Better decoration ☐
- More privacy ☐
- More information ☐
- Other reason (please specify)

.... ☐

6a. My age group is:
- Under 17 ☐
- 17-24 ☐
- 25-34 ☐
- 35-44 ☐
- 45-54 ☐
- 55 plus ☐

6b. I am:
- Male ☐
- Female ☐

7. Please show the day and time you attended the station

Day
- Monday ☐
- Tuesday ☐
- Wednesday ☐
- Thursday ☐
- Friday ☐
- Saturday ☐
- Sunday ☐

Time
- 7am-11am ☐
- 11am-3pm ☐
- 3pm-7pm ☐
- 7pm-11pm ☐
- 11pm-3am ☐
- 3am-7am ☐

8. What do you think should be the main concerns of the Police in this area? Please tick 3 from the following list:
- Burglary ☐ Vehicle Crime ☐
- Robbery/theft from person ☐
- Rowdyism ☐ Traffic ☐
- Vandalism ☐ Drugs ☐
- Sexual offences ☐
- Racial harassment ☐
- Other (please specify)

.... ☐

9. My impression of the Police generally is:
- Very good ☐
- Good ☐
- Poor ☐
- Very poor ☐

10. I would describe my ethnic origin as:
- White ☐
- Afro-Caribbean ☐
- African ☐
- Asian ☐
- Other (please specify)

.... ☐

I do not wish to say

.... ☐

Please use this space if you have any further comments:

5. *Sutcliffe Catering Group*

INTRODUCTION

Sutcliffe Catering operates within the UK contract catering industry which has a turnover of around £1 billion, employs some 75,000 staff, and provides almost 600 million meals a year in a wide variety of locations – industry and commerce, healthcare, local authorities, education, Ministry of Defence, and other sectors of industry, such as leisure centres.

Catering contractors provide over 66 million meals a year in independent schools in the UK, 47 million meals in the Ministry of Defence, and 42 million meals in hospitals and healthcare. Contractors provide almost 55 per cent of meals served in UK industry and commerce.

During 1992, there has been evidence of greater penetration of the local authority, healthcare, education and Ministry of Defence markets. In total, contractors provide a catering service at nearly 10,000 outlets and Sutcliffe Catering Group has itself seen an average growth rate of 25 per cent each year over the last three years. It is expanding at twice the rate of its nearest competitors. Sutcliffe Catering has increased its profits by 21 per cent over the last year and achieved a turnover of some £340 million. Sutcliffe services clients across the UK: from the shipyards of the Clyde to the BBC; from major banks to Glamis Castle; from the Charing Cross Hospital to Roedean School; from the *Daily Mail* to the oil industry; from Ford Motor Company to P & O European Ferries' on-board catering;

from Bradford City Technology College to British Airways' staff restaurants and their branded lounges such as 'Concorde' and 'Club World'. Sutcliffe employs 22,000 people, with only 22 at its group headquarters at Aldermaston in Berkshire, England. It is one of the top three contract caterers in the UK, servicing over one million meals a day.

Sutcliffe has a highly devolved management structure, operating through eight autonomous regional companies. Integral to its success is that clients see the company as a local organisation, with senior management located in their area who are accessible and who have strong local identities with perceived autonomy.

This case study illustrates how Sutcliffe's major competitive edge in total customer service is achieved through its structure and ethos of devolved responsiblity. Within a learning environment, Sutcliffe forces all staff to look to themselves to get a result, as opposed to looking at a central organisation to help them.

SUTCLIFFE CATERING GROUP – TOTAL CUSTOMER SERVICE

> *'To change a culture you need to be tough and dictatorial and approach it with resolve.'*
>
> Don Davenport, *Managing Director, Sutcliffe Catering Group*

Readers may find it alien that such an authoritarian comment should emerge from the managing director of an organisation which prides itself on a highly devolved structure. After all, Sutcliffe operates through eight totally autonomous regional companies: Scotland; Midlands; Southern; South East, West, North; City (their executive hospitality and special events division); and Fairfield Catering (their specialist schools and local authority business division).

This word 'dictatorial' is, nevertheless, used a great deal by leaders in service excellent companies (such as those in this book). They use the word relating more to absolute than autocratic or domineering; about being value-driven, rather than despotic. Don

Davenport is domineering, particularly in driving through, with sustained personal commitment, the values he seeks to implant throughout the organisation:

> *'You have to be tough. In a way, being dictatorial is effective leadership, as you push the values of your mission statement through the organisation down to the customer-face, and constantly persist in reinforcing these values. Persistence is vital.'*

Service excellent organisations have two powerful characteristics. They are 'value-driven' and have highly 'visible' leaders. There is no point having a vision – such as that expounded in Sutcliffe Catering's 'Mission Statement and Philosophy' (see Figure 5.1) – unless all the staff have tangible evidence of its ethos being put into action.

In the Texaco case study this was illustrated through the belief, from the top of the organisation, that the boardroom must come closer to the customer. This meant, quite simply, the mahogany corridor of head office touching base with the forecourt at the service station where the litre of petrol is sold. In Sutcliffe, this 'hands-on' approach is realised through the devolved structure which encourages entrepreneurial flair, the capacity to innovate and have strong local identities in the field.

When I met Ian Mitchell, the General Manager in charge of Sutcliffe's client British Airways, I was impressed by how he embraced this approach. Not only was he driven by the same coherent value system as Don Davenport, but he was also always out in the field, wandering around, staying in touch with his territory most of the time. This is an interesting point in service excellent companies such as Sutcliffe. On the one hand, there is a value-shaping leader generating excitement, enthusiasm and energy throughout the staff; on the other hand, doing so by being visible, and instilling that excitement, enthusiasm, and energy through a multitude of simple, everyday actions as opposed to words. Leadership in excellence companies is, therefore, at once attention to doctrine and attention to deeds.

Ian Mitchell's 'management by walkabout' stems from the feeling of being part of one big family; and this in a corporation that

Figure 5.1 Sutcliffe Catering mission statement and philosophy

MISSION STATEMENT

We aim to further enhance our position as the United Kingdom's leading contract caterer for the quality of its products and services.

We will do this by forming a unique 'quality partnership' with our clients, our customers, our staff and our suppliers.

We shall continue to encourage our regional companies to grow their business through the use of their entrepreneurial flair, their strong local identities and their ability to innovate.

PHILOSOPHY

Our actions will at all times reflect our key values. We believe in freedom with responsibility, in strong leadership and in flexibility. Above all, we believe it is our duty as a company to allow every person within it the opportunity to fulfil his or her potential and to make the maximum possible contribution to the achievement of quality.

employs some 22,000 staff. Frank Whittaker, Director of Sales and Marketing of Sutcliffe Catering, explains:

> *'The notion that every one of our people owns a business is fundamental to our competitive edge, and this is particularly important when the perception of the product or service cannot be differentiated against others in*

the market-place. For example: each area manager in the Sutcliffe Catering Group feels they own a business of 14 contracts; each Operations Director feels they own a business of 70 contracts; and each company Managing Director feels they own a business of 250 contracts. This philosophy breeds certain types of people, i.e. entrepreneurs, natural leaders and personal achievers.'

Other case studies illustrate that service excellent companies must have consistency when it comes to the sharing of the value statement or corporate philosophy. This 'speaking with one voice' throughout the organisation is, of course, important. It instills critical business values and objectives in a constant, dependable, undeviating way towards the customer. This can be witnessed, for example, in the retail sector throughout Marks and Spencer. Here, the boardroom mission for quality and service excellence is consistently seen by the customers, whether shopping in Edinburgh or Eastbourne. It is important that customers know they can rely on service at whichever store they choose to visit, and that the quality is compatible throughout the Marks and Spencer operation. This is also true at Sutcliffe. But they are also conscious that too much homogeneity can lead to the 'yes-man' syndrome, which merely engenders lip-service to the ethos of service excellence, rather than any firm personal belief, commitment and ultimately ownership.

The above is a vital point in excellence companies. It is achieving the balance. After all, where all people think alike no one thinks very much. Of course you want a lot of 'yes, yes, yes' people around; these can be your 'champions' who help with the reinforcement process of the customer service mission. However, saying 'yes' from the vocal cords does not mean it is from the heart. This is where the 'visible' management by walkabout is so vital, and where Don Davenport's 'resolve' mentioned in his opening quote becomes voracious:

'The basic value for everyone in this organisation is quite simply to believe in being "the best". It is a belief that, in this highly competitive market of contract catering, we can only succeed by giving superior service. A belief in the way the job is done; the nuts and bolts of doing that

> *job well. A firm belief that most of our organisation should be, and can be, innovators; with explicit belief in, and recognition of, the significance of continued growth and profitability.'*

At Sutcliffe that is what entrepreneurial leadership is all about; getting out of the office and doing it better than anyone else.

Don Davenport is 'dictatorial' about this belief system. If he wants everyone throughout Sutcliffe Catering to believe that they are working for the best contract catering company in the world, he and his senior management team must set, and demand, standards of excellence throughout the entire organisation. Whether it is Don Davenport at national level, or Ian Mitchell at local level, when discussing their service goals for Sutcliffe they are quite clear; that is to give the best customer service of any UK contract catering company. Neither will compromise on this ambitioin, in the belief that when the manager and leader compromise, the whole of Sutcliffe Catering will compromise.

The managers in the Sutcliffe Catering Group all admit that none of this is easy. Basically you have an organisation which is constantly striving for excellence in a highly competitive environment, with a mania for perfection. However, all will admit that aiming for perfection is the engine of progress, and one of the ways of moving towards excellence and perfection is for everyone to do their job better. This can mean every individual looking at the way they currently do a task and discovering ways that it could be done better, more effectively or more productively. According to Frank Whittaker: 'This calls for an innovative organisation, and at all levels. That is the sad thing about large organisations, it is the fact that they have lost sight of what got them large in the first place; innovation.'

In Sutcliffe Catering there is the belief that growth through innovation ultimately has a pay-off in profitability. Given Sutcliffe's financial records, this has certainly proved to be the case. Sutcliffe Catering has the facility to be a large organisation that is also able to retain the 'family' spirit mentioned earlier. This is encouraged through the entrepreneurial flair that results when you push autonomy as far down the management line as possible.

We have emerging, therefore, in Sutcliffe Catering, a number of consistent factors which are true of all the service excellent companies in this book:

- A strong, yet simple, vision and values system incorporated into a 'Mission Statement and Philosophy' which everyone in the organisation understands.
- The belief, again simple, that their company is the best.
- The innovative and entrepreneurial style that permeates the organisation, committing all staff to self assess how any job can be done better to ultimately improve service.
- The constant reinforcement by management of the values system, by getting out into the field regularly and keeping in close touch with staff and customers.
- The value-driven organisation being led by a hands-on management style, and by people who know the business inside out. Most of the managers at Sutcliffe, for example, come from operational backgrounds in the industry and they are therefore extremely at ease with the nuts and bolts of the business. They, themselves, have often come up through the kitchens of the industry. As a result, they may find it easier than many to get out and about within the company, and with their clients and customers, and to listen to criticism.
- Through a highly autonomous structure, managers become very much more accessible and approachable. It is much easier for them to manage by walkabout.
- By being much more visible, managers are at greater liberty to talk much more to staff about what is going on in the company, and why. In other words, service excellent companies are well-informed companies.
- The company treats the individual well and with great respect; people being more important than systems.

This last point is substantial. Many companies put too much emphasis on technology and systems, minimising the role of individuals. In many industries, including catering, front-line customer contact jobs have been designed to be as simple and narrow as possible in order that they can be filled by almost anyone. Many companies are now building 'idiot-proof jobs', although this model often flies in the face of what service sector customers want most; the things that technology cannot do as well as thinking human beings, or cannot do at all. The more technology becomes a standard part of delivering service, the more important the personal interactions are in satisfying customers and in differentiating competitors.

Of course, some would argue that technology is proving to be cheaper than people. However, the Digital study in this book (chapter 2) indicates how technology can become a friendly face behind customer care. What is happening in many organisations – and this is particularly apposite in the catering industry – is that companies offer unrewarding jobs, low wages and poor training. They then, as a result, attract mediocre staff, with limited loyalty. The organisation then suffers high rates of labour turnover which further undermines customer service and total quality. That is why excellence companies, such as Sutcliffe, are so successful. They are not locked into this standardising, production-line mentality; there is major emphasis on training, developing and enhancing the skills of staff, managers and team leaders. I find it amazing how seldom the word 'systems' gets a mention in those service excellent companies.

Training for excellence

There is another recurring theme in excellence companies, and that concerns the input to training. In Sutcliffe Catering training is also devolved as far down the line as possible. When I was in Sutcliffe, it seemed everyone was training; not just for the sake of it, however, as it was all geared to their mission statement. In fact, in its commitment to training, Sutcliffe is quite extraordinary within its industry. Its management system would not operate without the major ingredient of education. Sutcliffe spends three per cent of its salary bill (15 per cent of its profits) on designing, implementing, and monitoring its training programmes. This is the highest percentage within the UK contract catering industry. Sutcliffe was the first, and only, contract caterer to be awarded the National Training Award for Total Training Provision; for the complete range of training activities it offers long term. The company employs the largest team of full-time trainers within the industry, meaning the best ratio of trainers to units. For example, Sutcliffe employs 52 trainers to oversee 1,850 units; its nearest rival employs 28 to oversee 2,800.

Sutcliffe awards three times more qualifications in trained skills than any of its competitors. It is the only company in the industry to insist that all 22,000 staff undertake a food hygiene training scheme, and pass an exam marked independently by the Royal Society of Health. They are also the only major contract caterer to make the holding of this qualification a condition of employment. This scheme is the biggest distance learning exercise of its type ever undertaken in British industry. In addition, those recruited to the company direct from school start on a staff apprenticeship scheme and have the opportunity to attend college for the first three years of employment, with Sutcliffe paying the bills.

Bottom-up, all employees who join Sutcliffe go through what is known as an 'Essentials Scheme' which is a comprehensive induction course. This not only covers job skills and detailed information about the company, but also encompasses 'The Ambassador Scheme' in customer care, which trains employees in customer relations. This is a crucial requirement for anyone working within the hospitality industry. I am reminded of an incident involving two colleagues of mine at their staff restaurant which, not surprisingly, given this story, is called a canteen!

> *'Sally and I went down to the canteen place and ordered one of those pizzas where you put the topping on yourself. I chose one with anchovies. When I ordered it, and the young man had rung it through the till, I realised that the friend I was going to share it with doesn't like anchovies, so I asked if he could take the anchovies off. He said "I'm sorry I can't do that because I have already put it through the till". It wasn't as if the pizza had yet been made or anything, he had just put it through the till. I took that as the reason for him not getting the anchovies off the pizza, which was really weird. On reflection, as I ate*

my pizza, I realised that it had come to a point where I might as well have had a relationship with the computerised till rather than with the person behind it, because the person behind it had no power over the situation, and neither did I.'

I am also reminded of shopping at my local supermarket and spending a great deal of money. At no time in the five minutes it was taking to ring my produce through the till and pack it, did the assistant once speak to me. Before leaving, I suggested that it would have been nice if we had spoken during our transaction. 'No need to' said the assistant 'it says goodbye and thank you on the receipt.'

Sutcliffe view training as absolutely imperative to good customer service. Certainly going through a programme like 'The Ambassador Scheme' you would be unlikely to have a Sutcliffe member of staff talking along the lines of these comments, made to me by a catering assistant in a rival firm:

'Before, we were able to be more relaxed with the customers, we were serving them and that was what we had seen as our job, to serve the customers. We could take time to talk to them and we were getting regulars coming in to the cafeteria . . . we would be able to chat with them and have a laugh. Any new customer coming in and standing beside that customer would be involved in the conversation. Now the pressure is on to keep the customers moving. We are not really to be seen to be chatting to customers. That is not our role. We are selling to the customers. We are asking a question, waiting for the answer, so that we can ask the next question. If I'm asking you "do you want peas, beans or carrots," I am waiting on a response to that question, so I can put carrots on your plate, so that I can go on to the next question, "do you want chips or potatoes?" Sometimes customers can start talking and I haven't actually been listening to what they are saying, because I'm too busy going through this routine I have to do. You are not even looking at them as customers, you are just getting on with your job. They are not customers any more, they are just the people that you are taking money from.'

There is, therefore, a major emphasis placed throughout Sutcliffe on interpersonal skills. This is another consistent theme in excellence companies; technical skills training at operational level synchronous with behavioural and relationship skills. Managers take modular courses in communications, finance, group training, administration systems, business retention and supervisory skills. Sutcliffe believes that training should continue right to the top of the management structure and consequently is the first company in the industry to run its own MBA. Seven members of the company's senior executive have graduated from an MBA programme specially designed, in conjunction with the Middlesex Polytechnic Business School, to be practical and relevant to Sutcliffe's business.

Sutcliffe has also been able to incorporate measurable payback into the MBA, despite the programme costing £15,000 per head. Through undertaking a project relevant to an area of Sutcliffe's business – for example, researching and implementing new time efficient and money saving systems – the company has already more than recouped the money spent. Not only that, but the MBA has broadened the abilities of the managers. It has made them financially minded, able to deal with marketing concepts and analyse and compile statistics; the competence skills for operational autonomy to succeed.

The observation I made of all their training programmes was that they were not tunnel-orientated, in that they were not specifically job-related. Rather, at all levels, they encompassed areas outside of an individual's narrow job base to embrace much more information about Sutcliffe, its business, and the industry within which it was operating. This seems to underpin the entire learning environment. According to Frank Whittaker, it is this that encourages people to look to themselves to get results, rather than always looking to somewhere else in central organisation for help:

> *'The whole process gives our people a different type of education. An outlook on cause and effect which enables them to have a better and more productive view of the environment within which they have to operate. It is an education process which assists everyone to ask the right questions of customers, clients, and the people they work alongside within the*

organisation. We believe, for example, if you deal with clients that you have to be able to hold a mature business discussion with those people, not necessarily about the business we are in – catering – but about real issues that affect their business. Our managers are dealing with clients and customers whose business, for example, could be affected by international finance; Europe or the Japanese influence. Therefore their training and education within Sutcliffe must give them a business exposure which enables them to have better, and more productive, views on the environment within which clients and customers are working. The whole process leads us to becoming a learning organisation by doing it better; and if we do it better it will cost us less.'

STICK TO WHAT YOU KNOW

A devolved structure, even with all of this massive learning input, can have its problems, of course. With devolved management, people can interpret senior management's wishes in different ways. For example, Sutcliffe's ethos and structure encourages entrepreneurs and people with flair and initiative. Recently, one of their managing directors saw an opportunity to broaden his local business base and get into staff agencies. On the surface, this seemed a reasonable business venture. There is synergy, in that relatively high staff turnover is expected in the catering business and so they regularly use agencies. It therefore seemed logical to Sutcliffe to run an agency themselves. Having acquired one, however, Sutcliffe soon found that – although on the surface this business was closely allied to their business – they lacked the core competence to manage it effectively. Also, Sutcliffe lacked the pool of people necessary to provide an instant service. Sutcliffe admit, from this experience, that they learned to concentrate on the one business. As Don Davenport says: 'At Sutcliffe we have learned to concentrate on the core business, where our core competence lies.'

Basically, Sutcliffe was trying to take on a business that it did not know how to manage, or operate, and this is a lesson well learned from excellence companies. All the organisations in this book have stayed very close to businesses they know, and seldom transgress from their competence base. Ironically this 'niche' strategy, or singular devotion to the core product, is the very reason why clients come to Sutcliffe Catering in the first place. There is a general trend in the market-place for companies to contract out their non-core activity and concentrate their management resource on their mainstream business.

Although Sutcliffe may be in the catering industry, the business it is actually in is, according to Frank Whittaker, 'the management service business'. Clients vary, but on average, when Sutcliffe takes over an existing client-run operation it can increase the number of staff using a restaurant by between 10 per cent and 40 per cent; simultaneously achieving cost savings of some 10 to 20 per cent on the running of the restaurant. The bulk of this saving is achieved through the vast central purchasing power of a company such as Sutcliffe which manages over 1,700 restaurants, and serves more than a million meals per day. The quality of food that Sutcliffe serves does not just depend on catering practices in the kitchen, but goes far beyond that to the beginning of the food-chain. Sutcliffe spends a massive £150 million a year on food, which translates into cost savings for clients of 10 to 20 per cent over contracts run in-house.

During 1992 Sutcliffe has undergone a rationalisation of its suppliers, to ensure that all its restaurants purchase from far fewer national suppliers. The effect has been to significantly increase bulk purchasing power and thus enable Sutcliffe to improve quality for the same price. In addition, general cost efficiencies are made possible by the specialist management expertise of contract caterers, in such areas as systems control and productivity. In the 1990s, as companies concentrate more on their core industry and streamlining, businesses are increasingly unwilling to devote large amounts of management time to peripheral activities. Contract caterers can achieve considerable savings in terms of the hidden costs of management time. Many companies have made it part of their declared business philosophy to contract out all peripheral services in order that their management resource can be concentrated on the base business. Effectively, what Sutcliffe's clients are buying is a catering insurance policy which reduces costs and allows them to concentrate on their core business. By using Sutcliffe, clients also ensure a high quality, visible company perk to staff. Therefore, there is a tremendous need on the part of Sutcliffe to ensure quality of food and service.

The importance of staff restaurants to employees is demonstrated in annual surveys by the UK Institute of Personnel Management. They consistently identify company catering as being in the top three of employee perks; rating it as important as a pension and a company car. On average, Sutcliffe's clients pay a subsidy of around £140 per annum for each member of staff. This is a relatively small price to pay for a visible perk and, unlike other benefits, employees are constantly reminded of their company's attitude every time they sit down to eat a meal. Perhaps the Metropolitan Police Service should remember this!

Sutcliffe, therefore, is an industry which has benefited from the increased demand for its services since more companies have contracted out their staff restaurants in order to reduce costs in the recession. According to Don Davenport:

> *'The overall effect of the recession has been to increase the rate at which contracts change hands, as clients seek to reduce costs. Therefore, to grow in this environment, we have not only had to carry on winning new clients at a very high rate, but we have also had to make doubly sure we keep all our existing clients through relentless attention to quality and service.'*

Sutcliffe holds each catering contract for a lifespan of, on average, 12 years. Good news. However, the contract with the client is initially 12 months, then rolling-over every four months. This means that there is a major concentration on constantly introducing proactive initiatives that reflect different client's priorities and, in an innovative way, that ensure the client still wants to do business with Sutcliffe. In such a competitive environment Sutcliffe is conscious that there are competitors constantly knocking at its existing client base. Customer service, therefore, is dividing the winners from the losers. At Sutcliffe, they believe it is the ultimate competitive advantage.

THE CUSTOMER IS KING

The success of Sutcliffe's customer relations depends upon its ability to handle a unique triangular relationship; its client is the company who employs it, but its customers are the client's workforce who eat in the restaurant daily. This is why the automony and entrepreneurship of the Sutcliffe organisational structure is so important. Ian Mitchell is totally responsible for Sutcliffe's client, British Airways. Some 23,000 staff eat daily at London Heathrow Airport and Ian Mitchell has to be flexible enough to not only satisfy his client's demands, but also those of his eventual customer.

Graeme Thomas, Senior Manager, Restaurants and Clubs, British Airways, has no doubts why he hired Sutcliffe Catering:

> *'They have massive autonomy, and Sutcliffe's greatest strength to us, as a company, is they seem to be infinitely flexible. They always have a response or a proposal to us within 24 hours, and it is always, but always, directed to not what is in it for them but, rather what is in it for the customer, for British Airways and our staff, and the customers who use Sutcliffe's products. They have tremendous innovation which links into our own airline philosophy.'*

Graeme Thomas cites a typical example of this marriage between company and client. British Airways have a 'Fit for Business' programme (see Appendix 5.1). An innovative initiative was introduced within 24 hours from Sutcliffe, designed to complement British Airways' own extensive 'Fit for Business' philosophy. The Sutcliffe initiative was aimed at specific sections of the workforce who had not previously been reached by healthy eating schemes (e.g. maintenance engineers). The initiative also looked at ways of achieving measurable reductions in the fat content of served food. Sutcliffe was already serving plenty of healthy options such as salads and grilled fish, but they were only eaten by a small proportion of the workforce. There remained a group for whom pie and chips was always the most attractive option. Consequently, Sutcliffe took 12 popular dishes, such as shepherds' pie, and worked with nutritionists to reduce the fat content by 35 per cent. In other dishes they worked to increase fibre, and reduce added sugar and salt. Such has been the success of this approach that 40 per cent of the workforce at London Heathrow now choose the 'Fit for Business' option every day.

Simultaneously, Sutcliffe introduced healthy cooking methods - for example, grilling not frying – to the rest of the menu. They also led all their catering staff through a training session to aid their understanding of why this healthier approach to cooking was so essential. Without appreciating, and committing, to the more health conscious way of cooking food through 'The Golden Rules' seminar (see Appendix 5.1) the chefs would have easily returned to traditional habits. Graeme Thomas enthuses:

> *'Sutcliffe are so customer driven, and they faithfully and constantly keep any customer promise. Their first question is always, "What do you, the customer, want?" They are very flexible to both the client and the customers' demands. Another major factor is that Ian Mitchell himself can make major decisions on the spot.'*

This comment from Graeme Thomas could only be expressed about an organisation that had an entrepreneurial and enterprise culture; where local autonomy serves local customer relations. According to Frank Whittaker:

> *'This allows the customer to be a big fish in a small pool, and this is very much what we are trying to achieve. Our structure at Sutcliffe Catering is such that we are large enough to cope, but small enough to care. If our area managers lose a contract, every single person in that part of the organisation feels the pain of that customer loss.'*

Reviewing the customer service

Ian Mitchell spends the major part of his time 'walking' the job, staying close to his client, and his customers, and listening. He is able to monitor what his customers want through the catering committees that exist alongside every catering establishment within the London Heathrow environment.

The Sutcliffe manager responsible for each catering location will meet regularly with the customers who eat at that establishment to consider the service in that area, and the requirements they would like to achieve. It is the practice of these meetings to deal with matters of substance, as day to day concerns (such as 'dirty tables') are always dealt with on the spot by reference to the local catering managers. Major quality and service standards are monitored regularly through this consultative machinery and dealt with at the top. For example, all 'comment cards' completed in every catering establishment are returned to the top of the organisation; to both British Airways management, Graeme Thomas, and to Sutcliffe's Ian Mitchell. Again, this is a constant theme in excellence companies; customer feedback goes to the top of the management tree, and goes there for action.

As a corporate goal, British Airways have to be excellent employers and help their employees to do their job in such a way that British Airways, itself, achieves customer excellence. Looking after employees means that staff catering is not merely a welfare service but rather a major input to the quality of working life for all British Airways staff. Sutcliffe Catering, through Ian Mitchell, know that to succeed it must have a partnership with that philosophy. The restaurant business is all about peak and trough. For example, at 12 noon, staff enter the restaurant for their lunch and they must be back at their jobs within a limited period of time. However, the joint supplier/client philosophy is that quality and service must never be sacrificed for that 12 noon deadline. To ensure that this does not occur, quality assessment surveys are carried out on a frequent basis by Sutcliffe. These identify those areas of service where clients, customer, and indeed Sutcliffe staff themselves, consider what is important and in need of improvement. These surveys have proved invaluable in helping Sutcliffe to improve its service and performance. Always, but always, there is an action plan as a result of any service and quality assessment. (See Figure 5.2.)

Today, quality service managers are working throughout the Sutcliffe organisation to measure service from the customer's point of view, rather than by Sutcliffe's own standards. This has enabled Sutcliffe to evaluate its operating performance, and compare it to clients' expectations. In turn, this has allowed it to establish whether or not it is meeting its clients' requirements, and to continually promote quality and service awareness within all units.

Figure 5.2 Sutcliffe Catering: post-quality assessment survey action plan

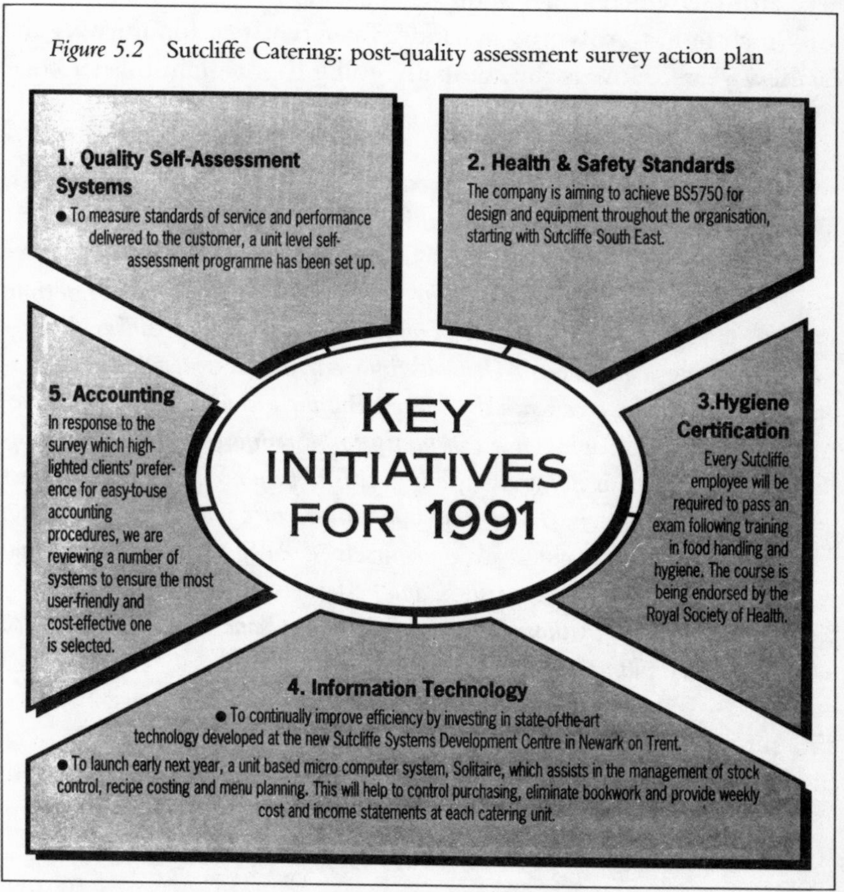

1. Quality Self-Assessment Systems
• To measure standards of service and performance delivered to the customer, a unit level self-assessment programme has been set up.
2. Health & Safety Standards
The company is aiming to achieve BS5750 for design and equipment throughout the organisation, starting with Sutcliffe South East.
KEY INITIATIVES FOR 1991
5. Accounting
In response to the survey which high-lighted clients' prefer-ence for easy-to-use accounting procedures, we are reviewing a number of systems to ensure the most user-friendly and cost-effective one is selected.
3.Hygiene Certification
Every Sutcliffe employee will be required to pass an exam following training in food handling and hygiene. The course is being endorsed by the Royal Society of Health.
4. Information Technology
• To continually improve efficiency by investing in state-of-the-art technology developed at the new Sutcliffe Systems Development Centre in Newark on Trent.
• To launch early next year, a unit based micro computer system, Solitaire, which assists in the management of stock control, recipe costing and menu planning. This will help to control purchasing, eliminate bookwork and provide weekly cost and income statements at each catering unit.

Don Davenport, however, remains as dictatorial as ever. He realises that there can only be one culture within Sutcliffe Catering, that of total customer service. It was Herman Hesse who said: 'When two cultures collide it is the only time when true suffering exists.' That, more than any other reason, is probably why Sutcliffe Catering devotes so much of its time, effort and revenue, to training in corporacy and consistency. Sutcliffe instills, in everyone, the customer service attitude which achieves quality behaviour.

Sutcliffe has grown by around 25 per cent per annum over the last few years. How is the company going to maintain this success? Don Davenport says:

> *'We will be striving to maintain our position as the best in the business, constantly sharpening our competitive edge. I believe that we can achieve it by improving every aspect of our business. From the service that we offer clients on a daily basis, to the way in which we look after and train our staff and, indeed, the way in which we develop the business. We are introducing a number of elements into our business development programme to help us to reach this target. But the visions, the mission statement, the philosophy, has constantly to be reinforced throughout Sutcliffe. Our goal is not growth, our goal is to be a high quality, customer service organisation. To do a high quality service job which means that we will be proud of our work, and ourselves. At Sutcliffe we believe that quality of total customer service, and performance, must be our motto for the next decade. Although the words "quality"and "service" are much abused, we plan to make them work for us.'*

I'm sure they will!

Appendix 5.1

British Airways' 'Fit for Business' programme

FIT FOR BUSINESS GOLDEN RULES

Everyone knows a balanced and varied diet is the key to healthy living. Medical research recommends a reduction in our fat intake in Britain as this is one of the major causes of heart disease and obesity.

All dishes which carry the "Fit For Business" symbol have been analysed by nutritionists to reduce the fat content in accordance with medical guidelines.

Every time you see the "Fit For Business" symbol on the menu this represents a dish that has been reduced in fat content to 35% or less of total kilocalories per average serving.

The reduction in fat content has been achieved by a change in food preparation and style of cooking.

- C.O.M.A. (Committee on Medical Aspects of Food) 1984 report
- NACNE (National Advisory Committee on Nutrition – Education) 1983 Discussion Document

Medical research has shown that a reduction in intake of fat from 42% to 35% of total kilocalories per day will assist in the prevention of heart disease.

All dishes which carry the "Fit for Business" symbol have been reduced in fat content without spoiling the taste. This has been achieved by changing the methods of preparation and style of cooking as laid down in the Golden Rules, some of which are:-

- Unsaturated fats are used at all times
- No added fats are used
- Meat – only trimmed meat is used
- Grilling and steaming are preferred methods of cooking

Recipes have been analysed and modified by Sutcliffe Catering Nutritional Services in conjunction with the Family Heart Association.

Appendix 5.2

British Airways: Healthy eating

SUMMARY OF THE GOLDEN RULES

Reducing fat

- Food will be grilled, baked, roasted, steamed, poached or boiled – *never* deep-fried.
- Lean meat will be used more often, further fat trimmed from all cuts and meat will be cooked without extra fat.
- Skin and underlying fat will be removed from poultry not being roasted. Duck and goose should not be used.
- Oily fish, especially trout, mackerel, herring and salmon will feature more often.
- Vegetable oil (sunflower, soya, corn, olive) or nut oil (peanut, walnut, hazelnut) is to be used for stir frying/salads.
- Semi-skimmed, skimmed or dried skimmed milk will be used in sauces, custards and milk puddings.
- Low fat dairy items (yoghurt, fromage frais, cheese) will take the place of high fat varieties.
- Thinly spread margarine rich in polyunsaturates or low fat spread will be used in sandwiches.
- Alternatives to high fat meat and pastry will be made available in salad bars.

Increasing fibre-rich starch

- Main dishes will include more starch-rich ingredients such as potatoes, pasta, rice and bread
- Wholegrain varieties (brown rice, wholewheat pasta, etc.) should feature more often than white varieties.
- Starch-rich toppings, such as bread, potato and oatmeal should take the place of pastry.
- More fresh, frozen and canned vegetables including pulses will be includes.
- Wider selection of desserts made from fruit will be available.

6. *Hyatt Carlton Tower – London*

Introduction

It was 30 years ago that the Carlton Tower first opened its doors to the public in the heart of London's Knightsbridge. In 1987, the five-star Hyatt Carlton Tower completed a £17 million refurbishment programme making the hotel one of the most luxurious in London. It is considered to be a smaller, personal type of hotel for the more discriminating traveller. It has some 225 rooms and suites, and approximately 340 employees.

It is operating within a highly competitive market-place where customers are spoilt for choice. Yet more than 40 per cent of the Hyatt Carlton Tower's guests are repeat business, and the maxim that the hotel tries to follow is that it must be more wary of internal inefficiency than any outside competition.

Its main objective, as indicated in its mission statement (see Figure 6.1), is to be one of the top three hotels in London, and one of the top ten hotels in Europe, by 1995. To achieve this, it places much emphasis on training and development. Today, Hyatt International has one of the most dynamic and respected customer service training programmes in its industry, with the training of all its personnel a top priority at boardroom level.

A key factor in achieving its mission statement objective is the performance of its employees. It agrees that competition is healthy, but for it to continue to achieve its goals, Hyatt Carlton Tower believes it is essential it meets, and exceeds, the expectations of its local and international guests. In this, the first of two case studies relating to the service industries, I discuss how Hyatt Carlton Tower nurtures excellence in every one of its employees in order to achieve total customer service.

HYATT CARLTON TOWER – TOTAL CUSTOMER SERVICE

> *'We try harder because we have not arrived yet. We feel that we can always do better – we are never complacent – we are only as good as the service experienced by the last customer. No one has ever complained to me that we do not have gold leaf on the ceiling, but they do complain if the service is not right!'*
>
> Michael Gray, *General Manager, Hyatt Carlton Tower, London.*

Towards the end of 1991, the Hyatt Hotels Corporation shut down its Chicago Headquarters for a day. All 550 executives and their support staff, from the president down, spent the day in their Hyatt hotels; carrying bags, making beds and waiting on tables for the customers in 95 Hyatt hotels and resorts throughout the USA.

This was known as Hyatt's 'In Touch Day' and was in response to a major customer service survey of some 700 frequent travellers. They had revealed to Hyatt their biggest fear for the 1990s was 'increasingly bad service from hotels, airlines and car rental companies'. The 'In Touch Day' experience gives senior management a first-hand opportunity to service the phalanx of businessmen who are Hyatt's customers. 'The only difference between competing hotels in the 1990s will be the quality of service,' says Darryl Hartley-Leonard, President of Hyatt Hotels Corporation who worked as a doorman, front desk clerk and bar tender. He says that the 'In Touch Day' gives corporate employers a chance to keep in touch with the customers and hotel employees:

> *'Most employees want to do a good job. How they perform is simply a reflection of whom they work for. I realised that out of more than 500 executives and employees in our corporate headquarters, almost 350 had never actually worked in a hotel. By doing service jobs for a day, maybe they will understand a bit more what service means.'*

Darryl Hartley-Leonard feels there is probably no issue more important to the hotel and travel industry in the next decade than service, especially considering the increasingly high level of expectations of both business and pleasure travellers. This is why there are other important initiatives coinciding with the Hyatt 'In Touch' programme. For example:

- Focus groups of hotel general managers who discuss service philosophy.
- An expansion of the Hyatt companies' Hyattalk programme, in which employees are encouraged to talk openly and frankly about their jobs, their hotels and their company with all levels of management.
- A customer rating system to reward individual hotels for the most favourable customer comment cards.
- A 'President's Service Council' to honour those Hyatt employees who have gone 'above and beyond' their jobs to provide service to the hotel guest.

Most people believe that the USA has moved from an industrial economy to a service economy and yet, more and more surveys indicate a continuing decline in USA service standards. Says Darryl Hartley-Leonard: 'The problem is not that people do not *want* to work any more. The problem is management. We have to remember that service demands constant attention, that service is something good managers must think about every day.'

As a seasoned business traveller, it is not the beautifully decorated hotels around the world that one remembers, but more the staff and the service. Darryl Hartley-Leonard agrees, and insists that the attentive, efficient service for which Hyatt Hotels has a reputation is a result of employee training and a participative management style. He believes that if a company's staff are having trouble delivering good service to a customer, management should look inward and not at the workforce, because: 'Service is a matter of attitude, and attitude is a product of management. 99 per cent of the people in this world want to do a good job; they want to feel good about their employer.'

Michael Gray, the General Manager of Hyatt's London Carlton Tower, believes that when employee satisfaction is high, customer service is high. Certainly, from my own experience, when service is poor there is simply no point in blaming staff. I recall being in a top hotel in Johannesburg, Southern Africa, where, upon complaining about poor banqueting service, I was told by the manager 'these people (employees) simply never listen'. I would say to that manager if they had got customer service right in the hotel boardroom they would get it right at the table. It is not that the staff did not listen, more that the boardroom did not commit. The executive management failed the organisation and hotel.

This belief is certainly endorsed in all of the case studies in this book. In all excellence companies it can be confirmed that manager/employee relationships are integral to the success of any service company. This was very much a point made in the opening Texaco case study when Glen Tilton, Texaco's UK Chairman, discussed the importance of bringing the boardroom to the customer, by opening up better channels of communication. The company should actively listen to the customers.

The 'In Touch Day' for Hyatt Hotels, in effect, brought the boardroom to the customer. Too often staff, and indeed some customers, feel that senior executives in the business are hidden in mahogany corridors and ivory towers and do not know what is actually going on at the frontier; that is the interface with the customer. This is a point made very strongly in the case study on Simon Access (chapter 10), where one of their major customers believed that Simon Access had 'lost contact' with them as a customer. Hyatt believes that a way to resolve this loss of contact is

Figure 6.1 Hyatt Carlton Tower mission statement

HOTEL MISSION STATEMENT

Objective:
By 1995 Hyatt Carlton Tower will, by consistency in its operation, be established as one of the top three hotels in London and one of the top ten hotels in Europe.

Our marketing objectives will position the hotel to achieve a performance that exceeds our natural market share, maximises room yield and creates a significant improvement in our market awareness.

Product:
A planned cycle of refurbishment and upgrading of guest rooms, public areas and food and beverage outlets will continue to ensure that, only within the limitations of the physical structure and of available funding, we will offer a product that reflects the luxury status of the hotel. The "consumable" Food and Beverage and Rooms products will be imaginative and reflective of all current trends and market demands.

Customer:
The success and acceptability of the physical product will be dependant on our guests experiencing – caring, efficient, personal and friendly service that will be achieved through a "back to basics" and "attention to detail" service philosophy and achieved by a total commitment to progressive and on-going training.

Employees:
We will continue to maximise employee productivity and contain payroll expenditure through the training and development of a flexible and adaptable work force whilst maintaining the service levels guests expect at a Park Hyatt Hotel.

We will maintain our image as a caring progressive and sought-after employer with the implementation of competitive and rewarding remuneration packages, a fair and consistent management offering career opportunities and on-going involvement with education institutions.

their 'In Touch' approach, which gives guests and employees the visible proof that senior management care about them and value their role. It also helps senior management in the company to feed a first hand viewpoint into the Hyatt system pin-pointing areas for service improvement.

REINFORCING THE CUSTOMER SERVICE MISSION

To drastically improve the quality of customer service is becoming a holy mission within the Hyatt Hotels organisation. Hyatt believes that spending two or three years systematically overhauling the way a company manages its employees, then imbuing them with a desire to make every customer's experience a pleasant one, pays off at the frontier. That is believed with feeling and fervour at the Hyatt Carlton Tower in London.

Vicky Brooke, Director of Human Resources, admits that a major part of her job is to remind all people of the Hyatt Carlton Tower's mission statement (see Figure 6.1). Also, to constantly emphasise to all staff at Hyatt that they have a major and original goal; to be the leading international hotel company. In reaching that goal, Vicky feels that one thing will never change:

> *'We are absolutely committed to developing excellence in our people and we do this through a progressive and committed approach to personnel development and training; constantly upgrading our programmes and customer service techniques to meet the changing needs of our industry.'*

Again, a consistent theme throughout all these studies is the major input to training in excellence companies. In every one of the case studies in this book, training has been a rigorous learning experience which reinforces the customer service mission. Hyatt is no exception. Cross-exposure training happens at every level of the Hyatt organisation and has immeasurable benefits. For the employees; it is their obtaining additional skills. For the guest; it is having a more knowledgeable member of staff looking after them.

For the hotel and organisation itself; it is a more flexible, multi-skilled workforce.

Hyatt believes that cross-exposing its employees to the job performed by employees in related departments – for example, kitchen employees working in a restaurant – not only fosters a better understanding and level of co-operation, but also helps to build a stronger more autonomous team. Cross-exposure can also happen between departments, hotels and even between countries.

The training function in every Hyatt hotel is supported by human resource specialists such as Vicky Brooke. Hyatt Hotels believes that the successful implementation of its service training relies on the skills and commitment of its training specialists. Perhaps the most important group of these are the departmental trainers at the front line of their operation. It is their training which ensures the implementation of consistent operating standards in the various areas of the hotel. They, therefore, have a great impact on the satisfaction of customers. These departmental trainers are recruited from the hotel's own management and supervisory personnel, and they are provided with the skills necessary to teach new employees, or re-train existing employees, in the various tasks which they are required to perform. In Hyatt this is not just job skills, and business appreciation, but also social skills where detailed input is given in areas ranging through attitude approach and positive behaviour.

This training is very similar to the intense role playing and face-to-face work problem briefings discussed in other studies in the book (such as Texaco, Dell and Portman Building Society). Again, this devolved training responsibility as far down the matrix as possible, and in a breadth of skills, is a constant theme throughout all the case studies. The training at line level in Hyatt is no less intense in its customer relations learning than in the earlier Texaco study or the Portman Building Society study which follows.

In a hotel such as the Hyatt Carlton Tower, the approach to training is also completely integrated with both the financial and business objectives of the hotel; as well as the development needs of the employees. In other words, this is not training for training's sake. Rather, it is training which has been developed from carefully researched and identified training needs, designed to support the overall objectives of the hotel. This is a major financial and time commitment. Within Hyatt, at least US $90 per employee, per annum, must go into the training budget; with a further US $16–20 per individual for training material alone.

Often, training programmes are launched like an advertising campaign. This allows employees to see the tangible importance being placed on it by the senior management, and also allows them to feel that education is entertaining.

As Vicky Brooke says: 'It is important that we have fun during our various training sessions.' For example, all staff attend a meeting

Figure 6.2 Hyatt Carlton Tower: staff invitation

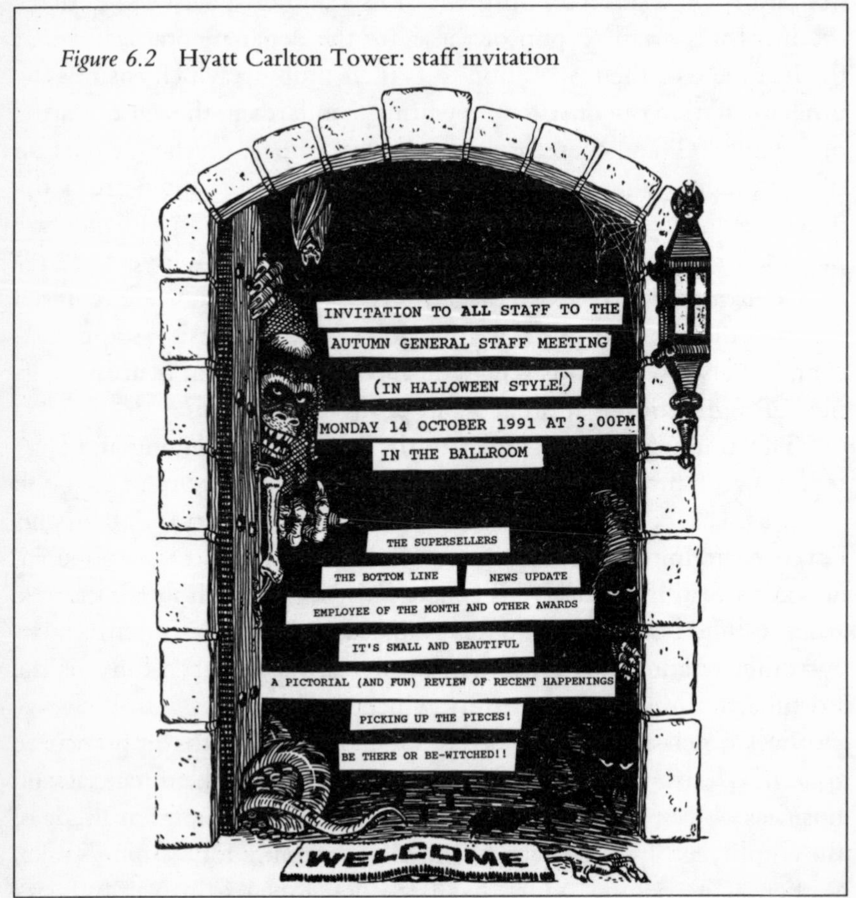

which combines learning with pleasure (see Figure 6.2). Such an event covers all aspects of the business from beating the drum of customer service values, to the reality of the economic environment within which the Hyatt Carlton Tower is having to operate. According to Michael Gray:

> *'It is an eye opener, when listening to the degree of interest and intensity of questions shown by staff, especially on the business issues. What we try to teach them is to think ahead for the guest, and that everyone in this hotel has a responsibility for sales, so they must have massive product knowledge and business awareness. Every member of staff has to remember that whilst a guest is staying in this hotel it is that guest's home; staff must be caring, as well as friendly and well informed.'*

Bernd Chorengel, President of Hyatt International Hotels, the company responsible for the Hyatt Carlton Tower, has initiated the hotel's own service awareness programme. Entitled 'Guest Expectations', it enhances Bernd Chorengel's 'back to basics' approach to managing his hotels:

> *'Following a world-wide audit amongst our frequent guests, we were able to identify (their) top expectations; to meet their real needs and not just our perception of their needs. To put it another way; do the ordinary things but do them extraordinarily well.'*

This is supported by Michael Gray's philosophy at the Hyatt Carlton Tower, where his main concern is to ensure that the basic elements of service the hotel guests require are provided absolutely correctly: 'Which means, the luggage arrives on time; the breakfast is as ordered, and on time; and, most important, that messages are properly delivered. As has been said, do the ordinary things extraordinarily well.' For myself, as a frequent business and pleasure traveller, I must acknowledge how right such a philosophy is. After all, it is usually the lack of these basic elements of service that are my most common complaints.

REVIEWING AND IMPROVING THE SERVICE STANDARD

There is a constant drive at the Hyatt Carlton Tower to monitor quality in order to maintain high standards of product and service. Audits are conducted on a regular basis by quality assurance teams comprising both rooms personnel, and food and beverage personnel. Their customer service audits are extensive, and it is this customer feedback which is considered to be the most vital part of monitoring customers' wants and expectations. All guests are encouraged to complete comment cards before departure, and these are returned to senior management to be dealt with promptly.

It has been another consistent theme throughout these case studies that, in excellence organisations, customer problems become opportunities for improvement; with all customer critiques and comments being given a major priority at boardroom level. The value of comment cards attached to products and services has never been underestimated, particularly by the Japanese (as indicated in the later Simon Access case study). I always complete them as I would like to see continual improvement in the areas that I, as a seasoned female traveller, wish to see as normal hotel standards. For example:

- An immediate warm and prompt welcome, someone who at least recognises me if I have been in the hotel a dozen times before.
- A comfortable room; preferably designed by a room user rather than an architect.
- A clean room that also recognises the fact that I am a business*woman* traveller, thereby ensuring that there may be a skirt press rather than a trouser press and padded coat hangers available.
- A restaurant and bar service where I can feel comfortable even if I am sitting on my own.

This may sound basic and simple, but it is seldom that many top class hotels seem to satisfy my basic expectations of hotel service, let alone exceed them.

As mentioned earlier, there are also focus groups. These are held quarterly, where regular guests are asked to give recommendations for improvements or changes to service and guest amenities. At the Hyatt Carlton Tower they have introduced 'Guest Encounter Groups'. Such an approach occurred with their fitness centre, where a group of members got together with hotel staff to discuss various aspects on guests' likes and dislikes and what they, the customer, wanted. According to Michael Gray:

> *'Guests have welcomed this opportunity to express their views on the hotel's services and product. I do feel that such an activity can only improve our ability to better care for our guests and – having the opportunity to let our hotel staff participate and receive direct feedback in respect of our guests' needs – will also ensure that the messages from our guests permeate the whole hotel.'*

This is another example consistent in excellence companies. It is the customers' feedback which is delivered to all staff; not boardroom indoctrination. This, again, has been well illustrated in the other case studies in this book.

The monitoring of guests' expectations is considered a vital part of Hyatt hotels achieving excellence. As Bernd Chorengel stresses: 'To maintain our competitive edge, the Guest Expectations programme must become the focus of all our employees and be implemented consistently in all our hotels.' For example, the customer audit for 'in room dining' (room service) identified the Hyatt Carlton Tower as needing to improve the telephone responding standard of some of their room service staff who were new to their positions.

This customer feedback was, again, married to staff development. A special course was therefore written, and tutored by the training and room service managers. Prior to this course, staff were recorded answering the telephones and the tapes were replayed during the subsequent training sessions, where role plays were also conducted. The learning environment is (see Figure 6.3) totally geared to actual job performance for customer service. These audits are an example of monitoring both the customer feedback to the

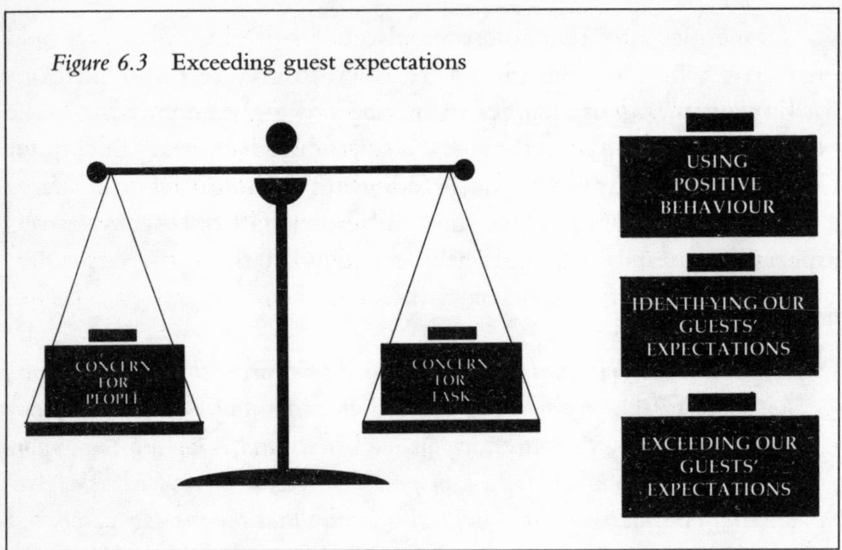

Figure 6.3 Exceeding guest expectations

hotel, as well as the hotel's own internal audit to monitor customer service and product quality. With this information, senior management are then able to go to the staff directly and let them understand where guests, themselves, feel service could be improved. This is another example of the boardroom coming to the customer. Rather than management impressing on all room service staff, for example, that they have not been doing the job right, the approach has been to say; this is what our information on customer feedback has revealed, now, how can we improve? Subsequent training is then built around exceeding guests' expectations.

By linking the customer service training programmes (e.g. the room service workshops) to the actual feedback of guests' expectations, staff are then able to be much more innovative and entrepreneurial. It is they who will highlight the ways that they, themselves, feel they can better contribute to improving service, productivity and reducing costs. At Hyatt Carlton Tower they do so regularly (see Figure 6.3).

Management allow practical risk-taking to occur very low down in the organisation, supporting good tries and, even, mistakes. Excellence companies treat all support staff as the root source of quality and service gain in their organisations. As Michael Gray puts it:

> *'We do not hire hands and feet. I am very proud of our team here, there are many examples of where they have gone beyond the call of duty to care for a guest in situations that cannot be legislated for in training manuals . . . (they) rely on their own reading of a situation and react accordingly. However, it has to be constantly reinforced, whether in the major training effort, or at our quarterly staff meetings for all the employees. My philosophy on our hotel is that; although we are 30 years old now and, therefore, could be considered to have "arrived", and be well established and have everything in place, we cannot in any way risk falling into a complacent mode of attitude.'*

Service, as we have seen, is about 'people'. All the excellence companies realise that it is the human assets which are as vital within an organisation as the material and capital investment. Treating employees well, in order that they want to give good service, is a fundamental part of service excellence. In the Hyatt hotels it is quite simply making every employee want to talk about 'my hotel'. Management have to be taught how to manage attitude in just the same way that they have to be taught about finance or distribution. As Darryl Hartley-Leonard says:

> *'To manage attitude, we need to realise that there is a big difference between service and servitude; servitude went out with the last century. Today, we operate in a society of equals, where everyone truly believes that they are the same. An autocratic style just will not work. You cannot legislate attitude like you can production quotas. We must take out the intimidation in management; and build in the partnership.'*

In service excellent companies management consistently encourages its employees to be entrepreneurs, and lets them know that good ideas can come from both bottom-up as well as top-down. The variety of ways for improvement that emanated from the Hyatt Carlton Tower with the 'Let Us' campaign provide a good example of this in action. (See Figure 6.4.) At Hyatt Carlton Tower they are

Figure 6.4 'Let Us' campaign

WINNING IDEAS

- Send bulk of hotel mail by 2nd Class postage.
- No international phone calls before 1.00pm.
- All international faxes to be sent after 8.00pm.
- All internal memos/correspondence to be doubled sided and use smaller paper for smaller memos.
- Promote "bin end" wines in restaurants at special rates.
- Only use fax *cover* sheets when absolutely necessary and begin message on the fax cover sheet wherever possible.
- Turn off all gas rings and other appliances when not in use.
- Take care in keeping fridge/freezer doors closed at all times to save energy.
- Maintain stocks at lowest levels.
- Make all staff aware of the need to economise and be proud of it.
- Do our own departmental cleaning.
- Ensure good day to day maintenance of machines and electrical equipment and report any faults to maintenance immediately so equipment does not deteriorate.

already acting on many of the recommendations which have been raised by employees at all levels. Some of these can easily be seen by the guests, whilst others exert their influence behind the scenes and help the Hyatt Carlton Tower do its business. What better way, according to Michael Gray, to 'convince your employees that how they do their jobs really does make a difference, and, as a result, motivates them to want to give the customer better service.' Service begins at the top in any organisation. According to Darryl Hartley-Leonard:

> *'Whether you are a retail manager, an architect or a company president, if what your staff is doing is not getting you more and more satisfied customers, and more and more business, then you need to look at yourself. Not to the staff.'*

Excellence companies never stop thinking about customers. Customer service is not on any balance sheet but it does make the difference in an organisation's bottom line every day of the year, every hour of the day. As Michael Gray said: 'Service demands constant attention, and constant example from all management. In the Hyatt Carlton Tower, senior management are simply not allowed to be miserable!'

Appendix 6.1

Room service telephone selling skills

Cue	**Content**
Introduction	Welcome to the 'Room Service Telephone Selling Skills' Course – 3 hrs approx. in duration with tea break to introduce you all to: New HCT Room Service standards (effective from now) Result of Guest Expectations audit and the HI identified standards.
Course Content	Subject as follows: Telephone Handling • Standard of answering/telephone behaviour • Fun Quiz for you to complete! Selling Techniques • Product Knowledge • Upselling methods
Course objectives	By the end of the course, you will be able to:- 1. Answer the telephone politely and correctly, using the HCT standard of answering. 2. Recognise the importance of having accurate knowledge of the Room Service Menu and hotel's products and services in order to maximise customer satisfaction and sales. 3. Use effective telephone-upselling skills to maximise sales within Room Service. ANY QUESTIONS?
Hyatt International qualities Sales Agents in Room Service	This information extract from Guest Expectations Manual. The employee should be highly professional with the following qualities. 1. Excellent communication skills 2. Good telephone voice 3. Ability to speak different languages. 4. Excellent product knowledge. 5. Good Sales Techniques. Do you have these qualities ????
Telephone Techniques – Guest Expectations Procedure	So, lets start by looking at our Telephone Manner and identify the HI procedures, Clear Procedure should be implemented with regards to telephone answering standards, covering the following:- • Greeting • Use of guest's name • General Courtesy • Upselling techniques • Repetition of order • Estimation of delivery time

Appendix 6.1 (cont)

Cue	Content
Greeting First impression	Q. What impression should we convey initially to the caller? A. Friendly Interested Polite Clear Enthusiastic Professional
Tape Recording	How do you come across? You are about to find out!! We have taken the liberty of recording you in action over the past few days and here are the results! What is your opinion? Individual Feedback on each person's recording.
Tone of voice	Q. What is it about their communication which gives this impression? A. Tone/Pitch of voice Emphasis of words Intonation (Music) Speed of Speech It's not *what* you say, it is the *way* in which you say it! Your tone of voice has a great deal of power. Use this feedback in assisting you in improving your own weaknesses. Remember! How you feel when other depts. or companies speak to you in an unfriendly, unhelpful manner.
HCT standard of Answering	It is also essential that we use the hotel's standard of answering correctly. Q. Why is it important to have a standard? A. Consistency – Prevents employees improvising and using inappropriate vocabulary.
Use of Guest Name	Q. Why is it important to use guest name? A. Personalised service. The new telephone system with digital display will assist you in using guest name. • Try to use it during 2nd sentence you say. • Q. What do you do if Mr Bloggs has a female on other end? • A. Use "Mrs" version. • Q. What action would you take if name is completely wrong? • A. Notify reception.
General Courtesy	Q. What words do we use to display general courtesy? A. Thank you/Yes, Please etc. N.B. Selling Skills will be covered during second section.

7. *Portman Building Society*

Introduction

This second case study from the service sector relates to the financial services industry and Portman Building Society. Portman Building Society is the strongest UK regional building society. The family tree (see Figure 7.1), is a guide to the mergers and changes of name of the building societies that have combined to create Portman.

Portman Building Society employs a total of almost 1,000 full-time staff, 459 of whom work in administration-related activities, with their branch network absorbing approximately 520 staff. Within the branch network they have 32 branch managers, and another 19 area managers. In October 1990 the Regency and West of England Building Society and the Portman Wessex Building Society merged to form Portman Building Society. This is the largest merger in the UK successfully accomplished between two major regional building societies. The Society is firmly established among the top 20 building societies in the UK.

The early 1990s were not easy years for building societies and other financial institutions. Difficulties were experienced in the housing market, with a depressed state caused through a worsening economic situation and high interest rates. The market-place also experienced intense competition. Against that background of considerable strain it was essential that Portman Building Society maintained a competitive edge for its investment and mortgage business.

The Portman Building Society is committed to a policy of training

Figure 7.1 Portman Building Society family tree

The Family Tree of the Portman Building Society shows that the history of the Society goes back to 1846 and is very firmly rooted in the South of England. Since that time, there have been a number of mergers and name changes but one thing which hasn't changed is the Society's belief in the importance of customer service and traditional values.

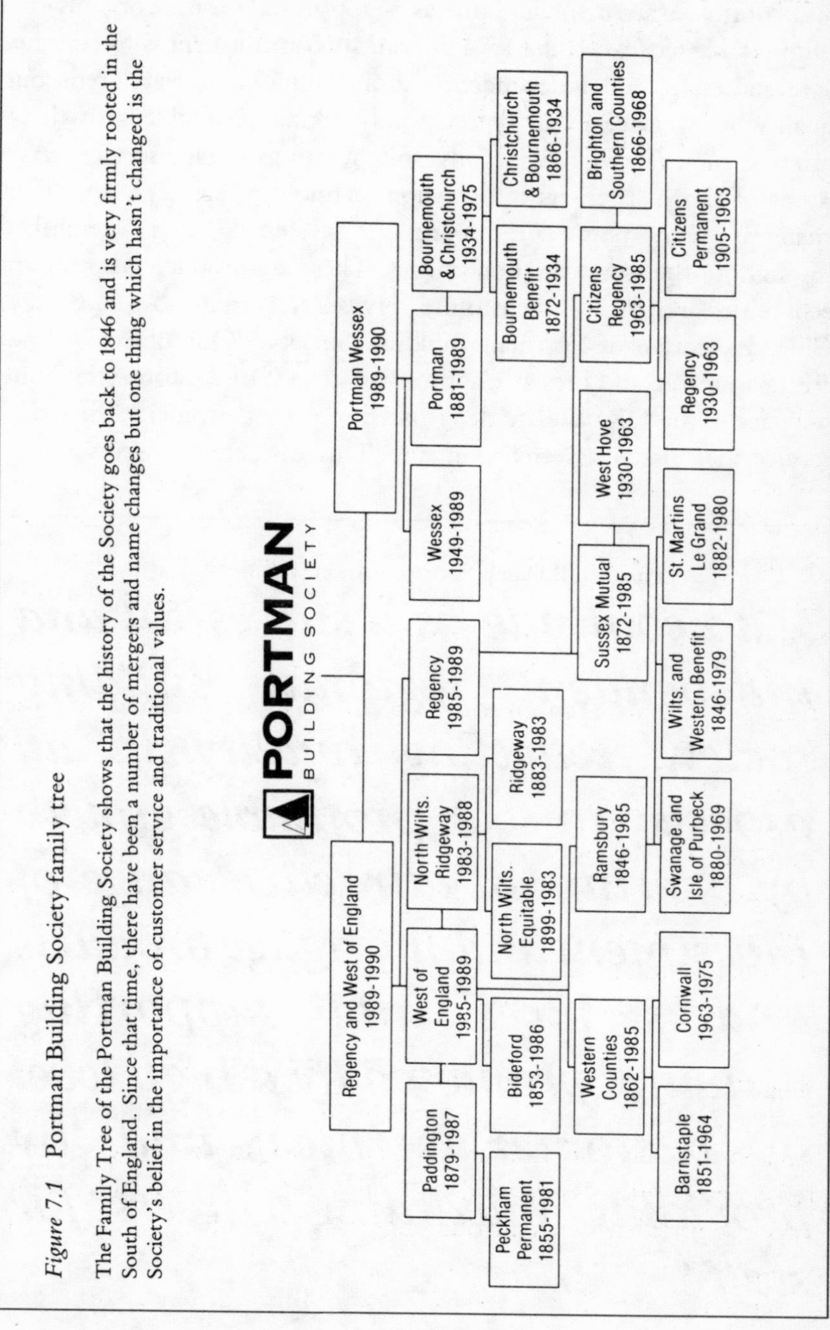

and communication for its staff, as is appropriate for an organisation with total assets exceeding £2.4 billion. Its commitment is to continue as a successful and independent regional building society; reflecting quality and service in all aspects, and seeking profitable growth by offering an attractive range of investment and mortgage services. As a result of the merger, its information technology has seen important changes; with new communications systems being established throughout the administration centres. These are producing significant economies and enhanced customer service. According to Ken Culley, Chief Executive of Portman Building Society. 'Our objective is to create an image and presence appropriate to one of the top 20 building societies in the UK. We are determined to offer customers a first class service in a first class environment.' This case study discusses how

Figure 7.2 Portman Building Society mission statement

"....to continue as a successful and independent regional building society, reflecting quality in all aspects; to seek profitable growth by offering an attractive range of investment and mortgage products and services and supporting activities promoted by a high level of customer service; and by providing rewarding careers for staff ".

Portman Building Society has journeyed from being a society driven by account numbers to a 'customer driven' society, as epitomised in its mission statement (see Figure 7.2).

PORTMAN BUILDING SOCIETY – TOTAL CUSTOMER SERVICE

> *'We believe that quality and customer service underlies every sales transaction put through one of our branches. It is therefore essential that we recruit people who believe in service excellence and quality and who will want to care for our customers.'*
>
> Pauline Clenshaw, *Head of Training and Development, Portman Building Society, Bournemouth.*

In Portman Building Society, staff talk about 'QUEST'; Quality Underlies Every Sales and Service Transaction. QUEST has been a major training initiative undertaken to improve the service that the Society gives to its customers, but also to improve the service which staff give to each other within the organisation. Portman Building Society is most insistent that customer service means internal as well as external customers.

Given the family tree of the Society and the most recent merger, it was important that the senior management of the newly-formed Society were aware of any cultural differences between the staff. Also, where all employees felt there could be improvement, to build on the foundations outlined in the Society's mission statement and establish objectives in order to achieve quality customer service throughout the organisation. What is attractive about the Portman Building Society mission statement is the way it subsequently spells out what the Statement of Objectives actually means at the workplace. (See Figure 7.3.)

As mentioned earlier, everyone at Portman Building Society is somebody else's customer. Whether they are external customers (the people who buy the products and services that the Society offers), or internal customers (the colleagues who work together on a day-to-

Figure 7.3 What the mission statement actually means at the work place

Our Mission Statement

"To continue as a successful independent regional Building Society reflecting quality in all aspects and to seek profitable growth by offering an attractive range of investment and mortgage products and services and supporting activities provided by a high level of customer service and providing rewarding careers for its staff."

What does this mean?

1. Our "success" will be measured against the average of the top 20 Building Societies.

2. Remaining "independent" is reliant upon both natural growth and complementary mergers i.e. mergers which increase our geographical spread but are not significant enough for us to change our name, image or corporate objectives.

3. We intend to remain a "regional Building Society" based in the South.

4. "Quality and Service in all aspects" is the responsibility of each and every one of us in everything we do. It is what will make the difference between us and the rest.

5. We will achieve "profitable growth" by developing our products, increasing our size and attracting more customers whilst controlling our costs for the benefit of everyone.

6. We will offer "an attractive range" by developing and selling products which satisfy market needs and which are leaders in their field.

7. Our main emphasis is to concentrate on our "investment and mortgage products and services" as they are the core of our business.

8. Subsidiaries and agencies will be integrated and used as "supporting activities" in order to help achieve the Society's aims.

9. Providing a "high level of customer service" is the responsibility of all of us. We all have customers – be they the public or other members of staff. We must always look for ways to improve service.

10. The Portman will offer "rewarding careers for its staff" in order to attract, motivate and retain suitably skilled people by creating an environment in which they are able and encouraged to succeed.

11. Through what we **do** we need to **show** our customers that we mean it when we say:

"What's important to you, is important to us"

day basis). With this in mind, it was important that the Portman Building Society discovered exactly what all of its various customers wanted and needed. This was the reason for the Portman Building Society to undertake two major surveys.

One was addressed to all staff, whilst the second was distributed to customers prior to the last merger. Over 80,000 customers completed and returned the customer survey (see Appendix). The Society had been prepared to listen to its customers, but they were unprepared for such a magnificent response! One thousand questionnaires were then sent out to staff, and around 65 per cent were returned with remarkably similar opinions; even from those staff emanating from different building society backgrounds. The survey to staff comprised some 70 questions and, given that number of issues to answer, the response rate is remarkably good. Staff were asked for their views on a whole range of business management issues, plus their job role. How they felt about existing customer service, and where improvements could be made, was a major part of the survey. The results were fed back to the staff and major positive and negative responses discussed (see Figure 7.4). Proposals on how the Society would take the negative staff statements on board were all addressed in a statement to all staff from Ken Culley (see Figure 7.5).

According to John Clarke, General Manager Marketing and Corporate Affairs, it was important that the Portman Building Society discovered how service-orientated its staff were:

> *'Are they historically customer or volume orientated? This is important, as there has to be a marriage between staff relations – how the staff feel they themselves are treated by us, the management – and customer relations – how staff, in turn, service the customer. Staff must want to have a good day and give good customer service. They will not do that if the internal climate is not conducive to treating people as individuals within a service excellence and quality culture.'*

As part of the questionnaire, staff were therefore asked to expand on how they felt about their job and what they believed customer service was all about. The important point here is that this was not seen

Figure 7.4 Results of customer survey 1990

The Top Six Positively Agreed Statements

Statement	Percentage			
	1	2	3	4*
I know what is expected of me	44	47	6	2
I can approach my Manager/Supervisor	44	40	11	5
People are encouraged to attend courses	33	42	18	6
New work methods are often being introduced	29	41	24	5
I am very settled in my job	23	43	18	14
My Manager always tells me about changes	22	40	24	13

The Top Six Negative Responses

Statement	Percentage			
	1	2	3	4*
People do not know organisational plans	50	41	7	2
The systems we use could be greatly improved	54	35	10	1
Skills and knowledge are picked up, not learned	39	50	10	1
People get feedback on unsatisfactory work	30	46	20	3
People feel insecure in current positions	40	33	23	4
Good performance is always rewarded	2	19	43	35

***Key 1.** Strongly agree **2.** Tend to agree **3.** Tend to disagree **4.** Strongly disagree
In every case the total may not equal 100, as 'unsatisfactory' answers arose on a few responses.

Figure 7.5 Response to staff negative statements

People do not know Organisational Plans
(91% Strongly Agreed or Tended to Agree)

- The previous Bulletin set out the Society's Mission Statement and some key corporate objectives, and a detailed strategic plan is now being evolved to cover the Society's longer term strategies.
- Once this strategic plan has been approved by the Society's Board and Senior Management, it will be published and operational plans down to departmental level will be devised and implemented.
- The key objective will be to ensure fulfilment of the operational efforts towards the Society's major goals.

The Systems we use could be Greatly Improved
(89% Strongly Agreed or Tended to Agree)

- The consultants Touche Ross have completed a comprehensive review of the Society's Information Technology and made certain recommendations which are now being addressed. Branches will have recently received details of the new branch terminal system, the installation of which commences this month with a target to complete installation at all of the Society's branches by the end of the year.
- The installation of this new branch terminal system will ensure that the Society can meet the needs of the organisation and the building of a coherent information system will also ensure the ability to meet the needs of the Society's business in the longer term.

Skills and Knowledge are Picked Up not Learned
(89% Strongly Agreed or Tended to Agree)

- Following the merger last year the principal thrust of the Society's training effort has been geared to fulfil the immediate needs of staff following that merger. Training in the future will be more geared to the needs of the individual and a training plan for 1992 is already being written.
- As part of the personal objective setting and personal development plans, which form a part of the current exercise in relation to job evaluation and the introduction of performance-related pay, training will become more directed to help the individual fulfil their personal development needs and their personal objectives.

People get Feedback on Unsatisfactory Work
(76% Strongly Agreed or Tended to Agree)

People Feel Insecure in Current Positions
(73% Strongly Agreed or Tended to Agree)

Good Performance is Always Rewarded
(78% Strongly Disagreed or Tended to Disagree)

- I recognise that these three responses reflect matters of great personal importance to staff members. The redundancies recently announced by the Society were unavoidable. It is vital that the Society addresses key areas such as its management expenses to ensure that we can remain profitable. Additionally, the elimination of unprofitable activities is essential to preserve the security of the majority of staff, and to create a strong foundation for the Society's long term future.
- The job evaluation exercise which has already been commenced, coupled with the eventual introduction of performance appraisal and performance related pay, will ensure that those staff who work hard to make a personal contribution to the well being of the Society as a whole, can feel secure in achieving defined standards as well as receiving just reward for the efforts which they are making.

as a talk shop. In keeping with other case studies in this book, it was imperative that management were seen to act on the negative responses highlighted by staff. This had been done, in part, by Ken Culley's response (see Figure 7.5) and continues through workplace discussions, training environments and the 'Targeting Quality and Service' panel mentioned later.

Committing to Customer Care

It has been emphasised in all of these case studies how much training intensity goes on in truly service excellent companies. However, this fanaticism and fervour for training must be coupled with a deeply ingrained corporate philosophy that says 'make people winners' and 'treat people as adults'. John Clarke goes further. He firmly believes that, for an organisation to survive and achieve excellence, its beliefs and values must be set in concrete and all its policies and actions built upon that foundation. The training programmes instill in everyone in the organisation a faithful following of the value system. In fact, more than that, 'all staff must be advocates and devotees of the company's value system'.

This is a vital point. For example, when Digital Ayr attempted, in the 1980s, to launch a PC in the market-place at the wrong time it had to abandon the idea, change its structure and redirect its technological direction. It was able to change everything about itself except those beliefs ingrained in its basic philosophy and team approach as outlined in Digital's case study (see chapter 2). In fact, every organisation in this book is clear on what it stands for; requiring a strong set of shared values, and coherent beliefs and objectives, understood by all in the organisation.

Nevertheless, it is unlikely that any of these excellence companies would be here if their organisation leader were not the strongest sectary and supporter of the values system and mission statement. Both John Clarke and John Gully (Head of Corporate Affairs) strongly believe that Portman Building Society could never have changed direction, to being a more customer-focused organisation, without the staunch support of their Chief Executive and main board. This, too, is endorsed in other studies. In British Gas – South Eastern (see chapter 3) the Regional Management Committee were in parley for a considerable time appreciating that their major function as senior executives would be to get people further down the line; from where they were, to where they had never been. Their job, as leaders of the reorganised British Gas Region, was not just to adjure an alchemy of advancement of the corporate vision, but also to set targets and actions which would give a distinctive identity to their 'Striving for Excellence' philosophy. Similarly, Ken Culley, Portman Building Society's Chief Executive, states: 'We must be committed to quality and excellence in all things; people, products and system. We must also be committed to being successful; to creating an environment in which the staff are able and encouraged to succeed.'

Having identified staff needs (through the internal survey) and external customer needs and requirements (from the 80,000 response, to the customer survey), Portman Building Society was then in a position to implement all of the information into the variety of training programmes needed. In this way it could engender the mission statement and service excellence philosophy. Quality, service, and the corporate objectives are all interlinked, and are constantly reinforced. (See Figure 7.6.)

Portman Building Society has taken all of its managers through extensive training, and this initiative is being increased. Regional Managers attend the training programmes, which are particularly linked to targeting quality, the mission statement, customer service excellence and QUEST. Pauline Clenshaw explains the importance of such training:

> *'It is vital that they "buy into" the ethos of something like QUEST. It must be their commitment too. This is paramount, as it is they who must carry QUEST beliefs through the organisation structure to all those in their teams who interface with the customer.'*

The entire learning environment becomes focused on the customer environment, as can be seen from much of their training programme content. (See Figure 7.7.)

Figure 7.6 Reinforcing quality, service and the corporate objectives

- **corporate objective:**
  To achieve profitable growth in both assets and liabilities; this is to be achieved by both organic growth and complementary mergers.

  THIS MEANS –
  Growing together by product; by outlet; by customer.

- **corporate objective:**
  To maintain Capital Ratios and Cost Income Ratios which are better than the average of the largest 20 Building Societies.

  THIS MEANS –
  Controlling our costs for the benefits of everyone.

- **corporate objectives**
  To provide service excellence, targeting customers with appropriate products and services and providing them in a quality way.

  THIS MEANS –
  Providing service beyond the customers' expectations.

- **corporate objectives**
  To develop and sell products which satisfy markets needs, and which are leaders in their field, focusing on core mortgage and investment products.

  THIS MEANS –
  Maintaining our reputation for high standard products and services.

- **corporate objectives**
  To ensure that the Society attracts, motivates and retains suitably skilled staff.

  THIS MEANS –
  Creating an environment in which staff are able and encouraged to succeed.

- **corporate objectives**
  To integrate and fully use subsidiaries and agencies to support the Society's aims.

  THIS MEANS –
  Working together, delivering quality products and services in a quality way.

QUALITY IS . . . not just attending a course, or smiling more, or wearing a badge.
QUALITY IS . . . all about THE WAY WE DO THINGS AROUND HERE.

Figure 7.7 Portman Building Society training material

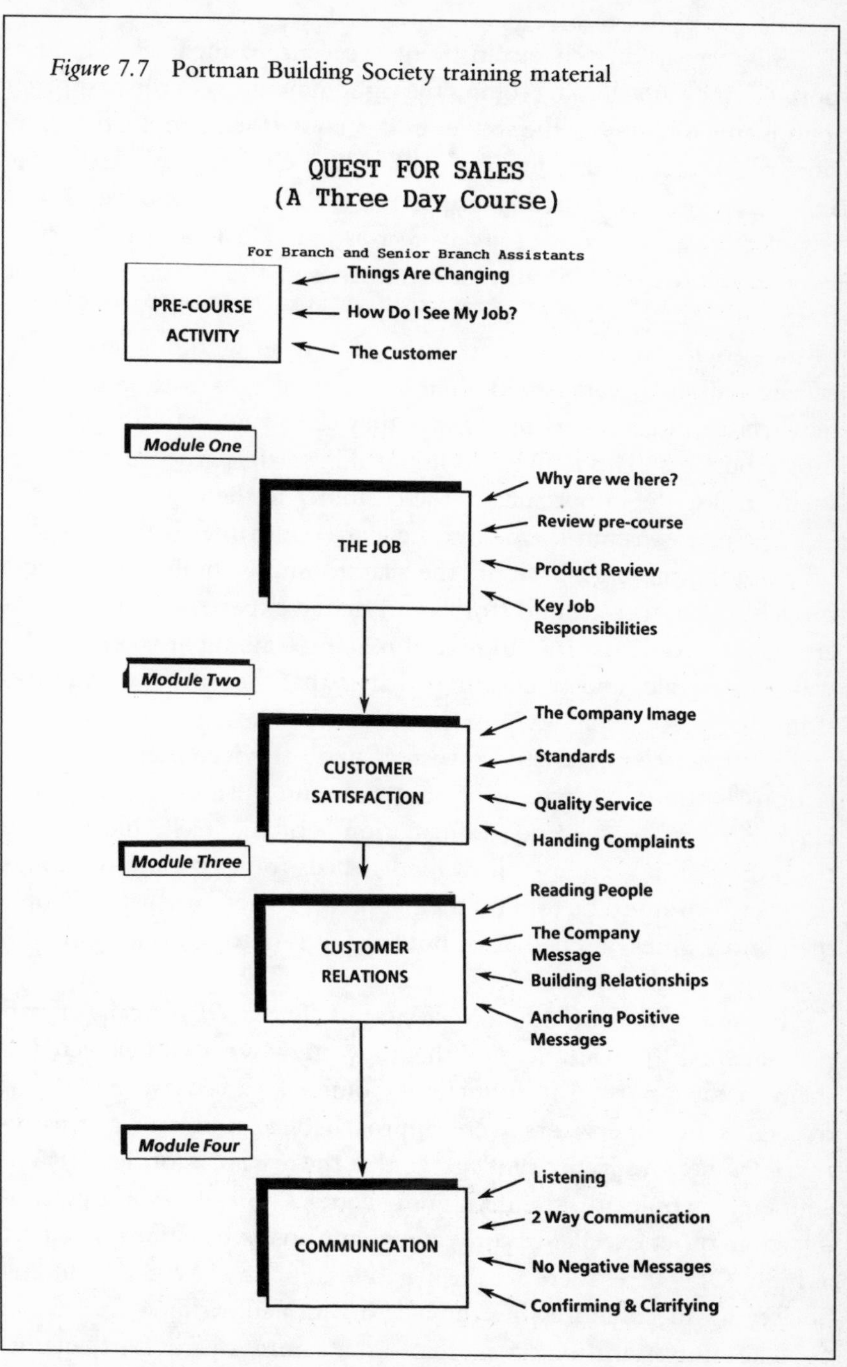

Another striking characteristic of excellence companies is the importance they attach to recruiting the right individuals in the first place. This is true of many of the studies in this book (for example, the selection, recruitment and training of staff at Dell Computers in chapter 9. In a way, this is currently happening in the Metropolitan Police (chapter 4), as they now actively recruit individuals into the Service who have their 'PLUS' attitude to work and the organisation. The Portman is similar as Pauline Clenshaw explains: 'We want to be sure of the people we recruit, and that they can fit in with our service excellence culture.' Portman Building Society also likes to ensure that new recruits enter a work area where they can get a feel for the job, and for the business. This is all cardinal to making staff, particularly new recruits, realise the importance of the customer to the organisation.

Again, a constant theme in excellence companies is the way that off-the-job training, back in the classroom, is built around role models; invariably around stories and shared experiences on customers' actual problems. It is all part of making training at work as relevant as possible, and reinforcing to staff that they must see matters from the customer's viewpoint, not just their own.

A further characteristic consistent to all service excellent organisations is the wide sharing of company and business information. Having access to so much information – often, itself, blossoming from the training input – allows individuals to get on and do things without waiting to be told by their superior to get on with it. People then know quickly whether or not the job is getting done, and who is doing well or poorly.

In the Portman Building Society staff survey, 91 per cent of staff respondents, for example, said that they knew what was expected of them in their normal job function. Some 84 percent believed their managers or supervisors were approachable about any company-related issue, and 75 per cent agreed that the organisation actively encouraged people to attend training courses. Similar surveys conducted in other excellence companies have positive responses that are as high. Of course, there are the negatives, and the Portman Building Society has been addressing these as mentioned earlier.

The important point is that in a more open, participative

management style, staff and management are more able to share these concerns than if they were in a paramilitary (chain of command) type of organisation. If I have a major concern about being a customer-focused type of organisation, it is the time that managers have to give to passing information down the system. When staff do not know what is going on with the business, psychological warfare occurs. This is much worse for morale than any other management action or, rather, lack of. It is difficult to imagine how an organisation can be listening to its customers when it is not communicating or hearing its staff. Many companies will spend thousands of pounds on product launches and sales pitches, in order to win customers, but will spend no time at all on giving feedback to their staff on how they are actually doing at the workplace. Work-life without feedback is a killing activity. How can companies honestly hope to give living customer service from dying servers?

REINFORCING CUSTOMER CARE

If we take listening a stage further, we can witness how seriously they monitor customer complaints at the Portman Building Society. They realise that, to develop a programme of constant review and improvement of customer service, the monitoring of customer complaints must be managed at the most senior level in the organisation. Any complaint to the Portman Building Society is immediately forwarded to John Gully for action. 'This customer monitoring can provide invaluable information,' says John Gully, 'our Targeting Quality and Service Panel, which reviews major areas for improving customer service (both internally and externally) needs to have all of this information. It's our bias for action.' The make-up of the Panel is interesting in that it consists of senior management and a skills technician:

- General Manager (Marketing and Corporate Affairs).
- General Manager (Personnel and Training).
- Head of Corporate Affairs.
- Head of Training.
- A project analyst.

The composition of the panel is expanded or contracted periodically, as appropriate; if, and when, specific skills from other areas are required. This is done in order to address issues raised, such as those relating to the more serious negative responses from the staff survey. John Clarke also sees part of the remit for the panel as helping people throughout the organisation to understand the mutual benefits of achieving service excellence. John feels that this is particularly important at supervisory level:

> *'Where once their attitude was account-driven it now has to be service-orientated. This means that where once their supervisory role was controlling, checking and policing, it has now become one of selling the benefits of service excellence down the line; praising, motivating and leading the staff to achieve a total quality and customer service attitude.'*

This is always a difficult area in any organisation striving towards excellence. There will always be some managers who you simply cannot turn around. This was very much the case in the Metropolitan Police study (chapter 4). This is why the heavy investment in training is essential, as is the need for 'champions'. It seems easy to say that if you treat people as adults and as partners, with dignity and respect, they in turn will donate that through the organisation; to the customers they work alongside and to those that that they serve. However, although this may sound like common sense management, common sense is not so common. There will always be managers where 'all looks yellow to the jaundiced eye'. This is why it is so vital, in an excellence company, to have a variety of systems, styles, beliefs and intrinsic values, all reinforcing each other. It soon becomes clear in a company who is paying lip-service to the value system, and some companies simply will not tolerate this. In those companies the strengths of all the internal systems supporting customer excellence often serve to ostracise the lip-servers.

Consistency of management practice is often a major problem. That is why the training input, for example, for all the managers in the Portman Building Society is so critical. One simply cannot afford to have the message of customer service excellence being undermined by managers who do not reflect, or reinforce, the core values to their staff and teams. In significant service excellent companies, managers realise that they must be role models; they must be conscious of the messages that their behaviour sends out to others.

Some of the companies in this book have, in fact, got this right. A major part of the learning process in the management training sessions has been for managers to receive detailed feedback on their strengths and weaknesses; not only from their peer groups, but also from subordinates. In other case studies there have been management appraisal systems which have reinforced good management practice. Annual pay awards are not solely linked to financial or operational results, but also to the whole ethos of what the company is trying to achieve and how that manager is practicing what the mission statement is preaching.

If one is going to have a partnership between the organisation and its customers, then this partnership must also occur within the organisation itself. That is why cross-functional training, and integration, is pre-eminent in progressive companies. In some organisations you would almost think that departments were in competition with one another; the 'not invented here' syndrome. This is why the role models set by the top management in an organisation, like the Portman Building Society, is critical. They are conscious that their customer focus is being watched closely by managers further down the organisation. They appreciate that internal customers often get much worse treatment than the external ones. This is why I think QUEST has made an important contribution to a noticeable change in attitude at Portman Building Society. Portman appreciates that a customer-driven culture is as much about marketing as delivery.

The Portman Building Society is now investing in further technology which will enable it to start developing the same type of individual relationship with its customers as the corner shop. The close one-to-one relationships often experienced between two individuals doing business together. Knowing the other's needs, tracking what they want and recommending products and services to them. In essence, linking the customer service loop by thinking of the customer at the point of sale, as well as at the point of delivery. The

Portman Building Society is achieving this by furnishing its database extensively from the surveys of customers and staff alike.

At a time when financial institutions, at least in the UK, have come in for much criticism – banks, in particular, having become so distrusted by their customers – it is interesting to note what the Portman Building Society does that many of its competitors do not do. It attempts to focus continually on customers and be driven by customer needs, not the rules, procedures and account numbers. Some of the banks, for instance, insist on autocratic, centralised decision-making. Their head offices have demanded rules on lending, charges and the treatment of customers, to the point where the local manager has lost most of his or her discretion, and all of his or her entrepreneurialism. Many of the major clearing banks' customers would say that the managers they deal with have become too calculating, callous and clenched in their approach and attitude towards customers. Perhaps the customers of the 1990s want the traditional bank manager back – that kindly figure in the community who used to serve small businesses and private customers with care and courtesy.

This probably all sounds very simple, but then excellence companies are built on very simplisitic values. They focus on what the customer wants; on service, on quality, on being flexible, informal and innovative. Essentially, they focus on people. I spoke to one lady in a Portman Building Society branch who could simply not believe that every product she sold would not be of the highest quality, or that every service would not be maintained at the highest standard for virtually every customer. That may sound simplistic, but it is possibly the main reason why a building society like the Portman may well be gaining the customer edge over its competitors through total customer service.

Appendix 7.1A

Portman Building Society customer survey 1990

Your Society is determined to provide members with the best possible service. You can help us achieve this by taking just a few minutes to complete the following survey. We believe we can use the information you supply to ensure that our range of services fully meet the needs of our customers.
No name or identifiable personal details are requested and the survey form is completely anonymous and confidential.
We hope you will help us, and a pre-paid envelope is provided for you to return the survey.

Please tick where appropriate

1 With which of the Societies that now make up the Portman Building Society did you first open your account?

- ☐ Bideford
- ☐ Citizens Regency
- ☐ North Wilts Ridgeway
- ☐ Paddington
- ☐ Portman
- ☐ Portman Wessex
- ☐ Ramsbury
- ☐ Regency
- ☐ Regency & West of England
- ☐ Sussex Mutual
- ☐ Wessex
- ☐ West of England
- ☐ Western Counties
- ☐ Other

2 How long have you held an account with the Society?

- ☐ 1 year or less
- ☐ Over 1 year up to 5 years
- ☐ Over 5 years up to 10 years
- ☐ Over 10 years

3 Do you live near a branch office?

☐ Yes ☐ No

If so, please indicate which branch office

Town ________________

4 Generally how do you feel about the service you receive when you visit or telephone your local branch office?

- ☐ Very satisfied
- ☐ Satisfied
- ☐ Not very satisfied
- ☐ Dissatisfied

5 Do you ever telephone or write to the Society's Head Office or Administration Centre?

☐ Yes ☐ No

If yes please indicate how you feel about the service you receive.

- ☐ Very satisfied
- ☐ Satisfied
- ☐ Not very satisfied
- ☐ Dissatisfied

6 Which of the following accounts do you hold with this Society or other financial institution?

Account Type	This Society	Another building society	A bank or other institution
Instant Access Savings	☐	☐	☐
Investment Account requiring notice for withdrawals	☐	☐	☐
Monthly Interest Account	☐	☐	☐
Fixed Interest Bond	☐	☐	☐
Cheque Book Account	☐	☐	☐
Mortgage Loan	☐	☐	☐
Personal Loan	☐	☐	☐
Personal Equity Plan (PEPs)		☐	☐

7 If you do not hold a cheque book account with a building society would you be interested in this service?

☐ Yes ☐ No ☐ Not certain

8 Would you be interested in being able to make withdrawals from your savings account using a plastic card in a cash dispenser?

☐ Yes ☐ No ☐ Not certain

Appendix 7.1B

Portman Building Society customer survey 1990

9 Please indicate which new accounts or services you would like to see the Society offer in the future.

- ☐ TESSA (Tax exempt savings)
- ☐ Fixed Rate Mortgages
- ☐ Estate Agency
- ☐ Motor Insurance
- ☐ Pension Advice
- ☐ Holiday Insurance
- ☐ First Time Buyers Mortgage
- ☐ Charity donations deducted from investment interest

Any other new account or service you would like considered.

10 How interested would you be if the Society published a Customer Newsletter?

- ☐ Very interested
- ☐ Interested
- ☐ Not very interested
- ☐ Not at all interested

The following information will be treated in the strictest confidence and used for analysis purposes only. Your reply is completely anonymous.

11 Please indicate whether you or your spouse is a non-taxpayer.

- ☐ Yes
- ☐ No

Do either you or your spouse hold an account on which interest is paid without deduction of Tax (gross interest)?

- ☐ Yes
- ☐ No

12 Are you:

- ☐ Male
- ☐ Female

13 Are you:

- ☐ Employed: Full time
- ☐ Employed: Part-time
- ☐ Housewife
- ☐ Self Employed
- ☐ Retired
- ☐ Student
- ☐ Other

14 Please indicate your age group.

- ☐ under 18
- ☐ 18 to 24
- ☐ 25 to 34
- ☐ 35 to 44
- ☐ 45 to 54
- ☐ 55 to 64
- ☐ 65 to 74
- ☐ 75 plus

15 Please indicate your type of housing.

- ☐ Own home with a mortgage
- ☐ Own home – no mortgage
- ☐ Council – rented
- ☐ Private – rented
- ☐ Living with parents
- ☐ Service quarters
- ☐ Other

Thank you for your help.

PORTMAN
BUILDING SOCIETY

8. National Health Service – Hastings

Introduction

At some stage in our life, many of us will be customers of the National Health Service (NHS). The task of achieving total customer service in the NHS is formidable, and this case study reviews how a part of the NHS is attempting to improve greater excellence through its customer service approach.

First, a background to the current situation within the NHS. In early 1992, *The Patient's Charter* came into effect. It is a central part of the Government's programme to improve and modernise the delivery of the NHS service to the public; whilst continuing to reaffirm the fundamental principles of the NHS. *The Patient's Charter* sets out, for the first time, customers' rights to service and care within the NHS. There are National and Local Charter Standards, which the Government intends to see achieved.

Customers of the NHS already have seven existing rights (see Figure 8.1) and in 1992 these were increased by a further three. Charter rights are guaranteed, and if a customer believes they are being denied one of these National Charter Rights they can write to the Chief Executive of the NHS who is empowered to investigate the matter. If a customer has been denied a particular right the Chief Executive will take action to ensure that this is corrected.

The National Charter Standards are not legal rights, but major and specific standards which the Government looks to the NHS to achieve. The Government is ensuring the collection and publication

Figure 8.1 The Patient's Charter Rights

Every citizen has the following established National Health Service rights:

- to receive healthcare on the basis of clinical need, regardless of ability to pay;
- to be registered with a GP;
- to receive emergency medical care at any time, through your GP or the emergency ambulance service and hospital accident and emergency departments;
- to be referred to a consultant, acceptable to you, when your GP thinks it necessary, and to be referred for a second opinion if you and your GP agree this is desirable;
- to be given a clear explanation of any treatment proposed, including any risks and any alternatives, before you decide whether you will agree to the treatment;
- to have access to your health records, and to know that those working for the NHS are under a legal duty to keep their contents confidential;
- to choose whether or not you wish to take part in medical research or medical student training.

On 1 April 1992, the Government introduced three important new rights:

- To be given detailed information on local health services, including quality standards and maximum waiting times.
- To be guaranteed admission for treatment by a specific date no later than two years from the day when your consultant places you on a waiting list.
- To have any complaint about NHS services – whoever provides them – investigated and to receive a full and prompt written reply from the chief executive or general manager.

of information on the achievement of these standards at national and local level. Where performance is unsatisfactory, the Secretary of State requires the Chief Executive of the NHS to take action to put things right. In addition to the National Charter Standards, the Government believes that other standards are better set at local levels; where they can more accurately reflect differing local circumstances. During 1992 the Government has required health authorities

Figure 8.2 Local Charter Standards

- In addition to the National Charter Standards, there are many other aspects of service which are important to you and which your health authority therefore needs to consider.

- From 1 April 1992, authorities will increasingly set and publicise clear Local Charter Standards on these matters, including:
  - waiting time for first outpatient appointments;
  - waiting times in accident and emergency departments, after your need for treatment has been assessed;
  - waiting times for taking you home after you have been treated, where your doctor says you have a medical need for NHS transport;
  - enabling you and your visitors to find your way around hospitals, through enquiry points and better signposting;
  - ensuring that the staff you meet face to face wear name badges.

- Your health authority will also publicise the name of the person you should contact if you want more information about the Local Charter Standards they have set.

to develop and publish their own Local Charter Standards. (See Figure 8.2.)

All of these rights are monitored and published. With the National Charter Standards, a health authority must publish information about its performance against these standards annually, together with the name of the person to whom any customer should write with any comments or complaints. Every year the Secretary of State will discuss these performance measurements with the Chief Executive who, again, will take action where this has been unsatisfactory. The Department of Health will publish details of this action. This will allow any member of a community to know how well, or indeed how badly, their local hospital and health authority are doing.

The District Health Authority will also publish an annual report of achievement against its Local Standards and, in the following year's report, that authority will have to say what action has been taken where necessary to improve its performance and customer service. The requirement on Regional and District Health Authorities to publish information about the services they provide, and their performance in relation to Local and National Charter Standards, is intended to help customers make informed choices about care and treatment in their area. From 1992, any individual should be able to get information on such items as:

- Local Charter Standards.
- The services that their health authority has purchased.
- How waiting times for out-patient, day case and in-patient by hospital, speciality, and individual consultant are set out in a standard and easily digestible way.
- How to complain about NHS services.
- How to maintain and improve their own health.

During 1993 every individual will be able to find out how successful their health authority has been in relation to the National and Local Charter Standards. This, of course, is already happening. For example, a survey by *The Sunday Times* was the most comprehensive of its kind when it was published in early 1992 as a consumer guide to drive the market reforms deeper into the NHS.

As mentioned earlier, this means an onus on the NHS to be just that; a service. One that always puts the customer (the patient) first, providing services that meet clearly defined national and local standards, and in ways responsive to people's views and needs. *The Patient's Charter* is a central part of achieving this objective, by seeking to ensure consistent high customer standards. It is hoped that this will make health authorities more efficient, representing good value for money, achieved through better management of their resources. This will also mean change. Health authorities and hospitals know that, in order to achieve these objectives, their organisation must adapt to become more patient-led; i.e. customer-driven. Service excellence and quality have got to become a way of life as the NHS environment becomes more competitive.

The NHS underwent several reforms introduced in the NHS and Community Care Act of 1990. At the heart of these NHS reforms is the principle of separate responsibilities for the following areas.

Purchasing healthcare

This is mainly the work of the newly-formed health authorities who now have a strategic role to improve the health of their residents by:

- Assessing need.
- Identifying service requirements.
- Purchasing services through contracts with providers.

Providing healthcare

This is the work of units who give care and treatment. From 1991 this has been carried out according to contracts agreed with 'purchasers' specifying:

- Work to be done.
- Standards to be met.
- Money to be allocated.

In their new role, District Health Authorities therefore now have no involvement with the day-to-day running of services. They can purchase services from a wide range of providers and, because of their more specialised function, are likely to merge in the future combining responsibilities for a wider geographical area. It is the purchasing of services from a wide range of providers that has put the onus on the units to provide high customer service and satisfaction; to standards which may even exceed those outlined earlier. The actual delivery of healthcare services remains a large and important task. I have selected a microcosm of the NHS where I believe they are taking on the challenge of the demands for the new NHS.

The hospitals within the Hastings Health Service deliver care locally to around 170,000 people, (what it calls its 'customer base') and employs nearly 3,000 staff. Such a complex organisation needs clear leadership and accountable management if it is to perform effectively. An essential focus for their management is needed in the following areas:

- A focus of responsibility to the local community for maintaining and improving the standard of local healthcare delivery.
- A focus of leadership for staff, guiding and motivating their work with patients.

During the last year Hastings Health Authority have provided care and treatment in hospitals, clinics and people's homes. This treatment involves a wide range of skilled staff who last year worked to provide:

- 25,000 hospital admissions.
- 115,000 out-patient consultations.
- 45,000 accident and emergency treatments.
- 18,000 therapy sessions
- 1,800 babies delivered.
- 80,000 radiology examinations.
- 250,000 pathology requests.
- 220,000 home visits.
- 21,000 community clinic consultations and treatments.

They have a right to be proud of such a record of service, but they openly admit that they must improve it, and want to improve it. This case study will discuss the foundations that they have laid for improving their customer service to their community in the Hastings and Rother areas of South East England.

Aims of the Hastings Health Unit

STATEMENT OF PURPOSE

The Hastings Health Unit's primary aims are:

(i) To offer an integrated and comprehensive range of hospital and community services, responsive to local needs and aspirations.

(ii) To provide a high quality service at all times, combining clinical excellence with patient satisfaction, recognising the contribution of all staff to the quality of patient care.

(iii) To minimise patient dependency on hospital-based services through an increasing focus on community care and health promotion.

HASTINGS HEALTHCARE

Principles, Purposes and Values

Our aim is to provide healthcare to people living in and around Hastings and Rother. Our guiding principles will be to:

- Offer an integrated and comprehensive range of hospital and community services, responsive to local needs and aspirations.
- Provide a high quality service at all times, combining clinical excellence with patient satisfaction.
- Value our staff, implementing policies that attract, retain, develop and motivate each individual employee.
- Develop a culture which thrives on independence, rewards individual achievement and encourages innovation in all its activities.

HASTINGS HEALTHCARE – TOTAL CUSTOMER SERVICE

'The history of the NHS has always been about valuing the patient; our customer. It has been less successful in generating such valued messages to its staff. Yet this is where it has to start. The best marketing tool that any organisation has is its staff. If you do not involve, motivate and commit them to your value system then you will never get total quality and customer service. Customer service is all about people values, which means also having to value oneself. This is reflected in the culture of an organisation and ultimately upon all those we work alongside, and serve. I doubt whether we can ever have a "fine feel" for others, if we do not have it for ourselves.'

Dilly Millward, *Director of Nursing and Quality Assurance, Hastings Health Service.*

During the summer of 1991 one of the most comprehensive and powerful market research studies ever carried out for the National Health Service (NHS) was conducted across East Sussex. The results of the study, undertaken by the British Market Research Bureau for Brighton, Eastbourne and Hastings Health Authorities, provided specific information about local hospitals and how they were viewed by their customers; the patients. Some 4,267 questionnaires were completed by people who had been patients in nine of the county's hospitals and the results have been used to help set future quality standards of patient care and service. The data provided information on how the patients viewed the service they received in a number of areas, including:

- Waiting times.
- Admission procedures and information.
- Wards; including decor, noise and comfort.
- Nursing and medical care.
- Hospital food.

- Pain control.
- Arrangements for going home.
- Assessment of treatment.
- Overall perception of stay in hospital.

According to Colin Tarry, Acting District General Manager at the Hastings Health Service:

> *'This imposing investigation into customer satisfaction was designed to pick up what was important to the patient, rather than to ourselves. There was a 70 per cent return rate to the survey and it gave us some hard core information which we are now building into our values and principles of service.'*

For so much of the NHS it is usually the other way round. Systems and structures are built precisely on employee perceptions of the way customer service should be undertaken and maintained. This survey has allowed Hastings Health Service to work on a whole range of issues relating to the reforms within the NHS, as well as towards the standards of service it feels it must achieve in order to gain the competitive edge. David Townsley, Acting Chief Executive explains:

> *'We want to put ourselves in a position where none of our community go, or want to go, elsewhere. We want people to come to us both from within our area and from outside. That's why it was important that we knew what our public thought about us. Now we have to listen and take it on board.'*

As vital as it is to know what existing patients felt about the hospitals they had been treated within, the next stage of the extensive market research is to gain the perceptions of the cold public, that is the potential customer. Knowing the general public's perception of health service care will help Hastings Health Service build an allegiance to its residents and community. There is another pay-off with this type of information, that we will soon discover.

PLANNING FOR CUSTOMER SERVICE

In excellence organisations there is a lot of time spent on finding out a particular plus point that the organisation can offer its customer; where you are better at something than anybody else. Many of the organisations in this book have worked very hard at dividing their customer base into strict segments in order that they can provide niche or tailored products and services. Colin Tarry believes that extending the customer-based market research will help Hastings Health Service to know what business it is in; whether it is the business of health or the business of healthcare. Again, this debating point of the 'business mission' has been an integral part of boardroom discussions when journeying towards service excellence. It formed a principal component in the British Gas – South Eastern Regional Management Committee forums (chapter 3). It has also been an important consideration at Dell Computers (chapter 9), who have a major objective of always having a steady flow of new products. Often this is done before their customers actually realise they need something new, but it does allow the company to dominate its niche.

The important consideration, certainly at Hasting Health Service, is to build your existing customer's needs, and potential customers' requirements, into the organisation's business plan. Within the Hastings Health Service there has been a significant change in the planning process arising directly from the implementation of the NHS and Community Care Act. Health providers now have to secure their income through contracts with healthcare purchasers such as health authorities and GP fundholders.

A more structured approach to planning service provision is essential in order to establish that the provider can meet the terms of contract agreed with the purchaser. This is vital because, as we mentioned earlier, providers will be in competition with each other, and price and quality will clearly be major determinants in whether contracts are secured or not. For many hospitals and units, business planning, and indeed having a business at all, is alien to their culture. Even more so, when such a plan is dominated by what the customers actually want.

At Hastings, the business planning process is seen as providing a vital communications exercise between the corporate centre and all the support services. According to Charles Ellis, the Business Development Director:

> *'You cannot achieve excellence, service, quality at line level unless those people understand the objectives of the business plan. It is not sufficient to just know about your own job, it is vital to appreciate the environment within which Hastings has to vie for customers.'*

Charles Ellis insists there must be business planning, and this in consultation with all the various units. A business plan, linked to the mission statement, is important in order to:

- Set corporate direction and establish corporate priorities.
- Support these priorities with definitive action plans, with emphasis on 'action'.
- Ensure clarity for all staff of the organisation direction, and individual aims and objectives.
- Be specific about what can be provided in terms of quality, volume and price.
- Establish and demonstrate economic viability.
- Provide a means for monitoring Hastings' progress against established priorities.
- Encourage flexibility and innovation within a well-established corporate framework.

This business planning process provides, according to Charles Ellis: 'An essential bond between the Centre and the various directorates, units and support services which all help to achieve corporacy. The entire business plan is then linked to unit and individual objectives.' What is interesting at Hastings is how they have taken the statement of purpose and translated that into an action plan for the future, while setting it in the context of an assessment of the current status of a unit.

Figure 8.3 Hastings Health Service business planning process

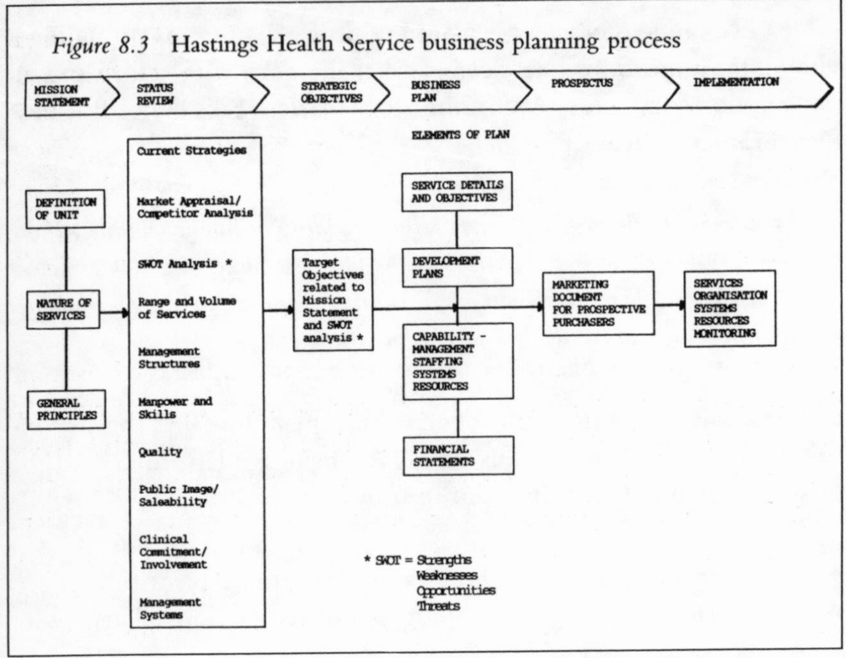

CHANGING THE CULTURE FOR CUSTOMER SERVICE

The important process that would lead to the achieving of such a unit action objective is a constant review of internal strengths and weaknesses of that department or unit; its opportunities and threats. In the Hastings Health Unit, I was impressed by the fact that it would publicly highlight its strengths but also would discuss its weaknesses, and in a very honest fashion. Actually, the Hastings Health Unit does not think it does this very well, but I disagree. It is no easy matter to sit down and be truly honest. David Townsley explains the approach:

> *'This is a whole new way of thinking and a major attitude change. It is a new culture. There are many people within the health service who are very cynical . . . they are suspicious of their peers, sometimes of specific groups, and often of those at the most senior level in the organisation.*

> *We are asking people down the line to take "ownership" of the Hastings Health Authority, and show how their Unit can do better to allow us to not only retain our existing business, but also to attract new business. I am not saying that people do not do their jobs well. What I am saying is that in order for all people, at all levels, to feel proud, and to be "ambassadors" for the service, they have to be much more involved. That is where the combination of the business plan and team briefing occurs!' (See Figure 8.3.)*

Allow me to give an example of how this occurs within the Hastings Health Service (see Figure 8.4). The hotel services department is a vital part of any healthcare facility (see Figure 8.5). The objectives and targets for improving hotel services would be mentioned in the overall corporate business plan. The hotel services group would then meet at line level to discuss the implications. They would discuss how they could meet the objectives in the business plan, and where they themselves could improve their service to the customers.

These group meetings discuss problems that affect people and their performance at work. The reader will see how similar this approach is to that in other studies, particularly the Paddington Green Division team meetings (chapter 4). However, the important point is that people are talking about how objectives are going to be achieved, and where service can be improved. It is a discussion that is directly linked to the overall corporate plan and its mission statements, also examining how these actively apply at the interface with the customers. It requires staff looking at themselves, and asking: What are we doing now? What have we got to achieve? How are we going to get there? What have we got to do better in order to reach that objective? Their own 'value system' as indicated in Dilly Millward's opening quote.

In a lot of organisations I have been involved with, there has been much talk about involving the staff in 'corporacy'. In reality, however, there have been an awful lot of words and waffle, and very little work action plan. If there is no action plan built into the quality and service framework – with senior management commitment to that plan – you can be assured that only one thing will happen; nothing.

Figure 8.4 The hotel services department's service aims

HOTEL SERVICES

Service Objectives	Process to achieve Objective	Target/Action
To multi-skill all Departments within Hotel Services to become more efficient and more cost effective.	Reprofiling of Hotel Services staff where appropriate.	Evaluation process has commenced to identify groups to be reprofiled. New pay structure being drawn up. Complete reprofiling by March 1992.
To encompass a corporate image within the Hotel Services Department.	Provision of a new staff uniform.	A feasibility study has been undertaken of purposely designed uniforms being purchased. A suitable alternative from a ready to wear catalogue is being assessed. Complete objective by March 1992.

Aim of Service

- To provide a safe, clean environment for staff and patients.
- To provide a 24-hour portering service to support clinical activities.
- To provide healthy and appetising food to staff and patients and where appropriate to meet special dietary requirements.
- To provide accommodation for appropriate grades of staff.
- To provide an efficient and courteous reception and switchboard service.
- To provide an efficient transport service which enhances the medical care provided.
- To provide uniforms to all grades of staff and where appropriate soft furnishings to enhance the environment for staff and parties.

Figure 8.5 Unit objectives for 1991/92

1. To achieve a reduction in the overall length of waiting times, with a specific reduction in the numbers of long-waiters by:
   i) the successful application of waiting list funds
   ii) effective internal management of lists
2. To increase the proportion of in-patient procedures carried out as day cases; in particular, through the successful development of the day surgery unit at Bexhill; but also looking towards maximising the use of the future medical investigations suite in Phase 1 of the Conquest Hospital.
3. To reach a long-term solution to the future of ENT and Ophthalmology services.
4. To progress the joint Adult Mental Health Strategy.
5. To progress the joint Learning Disabilities Strategy.
6. To develop a strategy for child health services which provides a basis for decisions on short-term service issues.
7. To develop a strategy for elderly services, taking into account the requirements of the Community Care Act.
8. To improve the current quality of service by the implementation of a variety of unit-wide and directorate-led quality initiatives.
9. To ensure the successful commissioning of Phase 1 of the Conquest Hospital.
10. To progress the planning of Phase 2 through the preparation of a detailed design brief.
11. To achieve contracted activity levels within the available resources.
12. To continue the implementation of the Resource Management programme.
13. To develop a marketing strategy for the Hastings Health Unit.
14. To increase staff satisfaction and motivation through the implementation of communication and training policies.
15. To continue to review skill-mix through reprofiling exercises and competency analysis.
16. To raise staff awareness of the importance of health promotion as a benefit to patients.
17. To strengthen the links between community services and Primary Health Care Teams.

British Gas – South Eastern, in their case study (chapter 3), are a good case in point. Specific objectives agreed at regional level became relevant action targets to improve customer service at the district interface level. It seems to be an indispensable facet of service excellent organisations. However, achieving this in highly cynical organisations is difficult.

INNOVATING AND MANAGING CUSTOMER SERVICE CHANGE

Sue Webb is the Senior Nurse in Quality and Practice Development within Hastings. She has been a facilitator or, more realistically, a change-agent and it has been her job to help people work through a new culture and to take ownership of improving their own, and their unit's objectives:

> *'Working as a change-agent within the rapidly changing health services does present many challenges. However, whilst the process of translating vision into reality, and theory into practice, may be satisfying, it is often very frustrating. In a climate of major change, for example, coming into line with the new standards for quality and service, people need an identified individual to whom they can refer and seek support – their "champion". The change-agent must be viewed as objective, a link between all levels of the organisation. Remember, ownership of change is with those implementing the change and not with the change-agent. The role of the change-agent will depend upon the context of the change which is being managed.'*

All effective change requires the agent to act as a catalyst, whether that change is strategic, incremental or operational. This is very much a challenge for a person like Sue Webb. She has to identify whose hearts she has won, and who are just playing lip-service to the whole new value system of a changing culture in order to stay ahead. However, one person with courage can make a majority and this is where the 'champions' come to the fore in any organisational change. I referred to them in the British Gas – South Eastern study;

those who believe in the specific targets, objectives and service that the organisation has in mind. Those who steer parts of the organisation away from negation to nourishment of the goals at various levels within the organisation.

In other studies it has been discussed how innovation has been a consistent theme in excellence organisations. This does not just mean innovation in the sense of creative people developing new ideas, products and services. It has been used much more in the context of innovative companies responding swiftly to change of any type in their organisations. At Digital (chapter 2), for example, as the needs of their customers moved so did Digital. At British Gas – South Eastern Region (chapter 3), as the skills of their competitors began to emerge so they had to realign. With the Metropolitan Police Service (chapter 4), as the mood of the public they served had dramatically changed so the policing organisation has also had to change, and quickly.

Innovation in many of the organisations in this book has meant adjusting, transforming, adapting; not just their skills, nor simply their structure, but also their culture. Excellence companies have achieved that kind of innovative talent and this is what change-agents like Sue Webb have to try to create in an organisation that has been very process or systems led, rather than consumer or market-place driven. A major problem, highlighted by Sue Webb, concerns change taking time:

> *'Where change is imposed too quickly, or where change is considered to be irrelevant, there will be resistance and any change may only be short term. All those change-agents must continually assess and measure the process and outcome of change. Effective lasting change is the result of well-planned, manageable, bite-sized chunks that create interest and motivation, a sense of achievement and pride; thus creating relationships and a climate conducive to ongoing service progress and development.'*

To be a change-agent is a challenging role, and the person must be appropriately qualified and trained. I have seen many organisational change programmes fail simply because of the incompetence of the trainers or facilitators involved in the change process. Sue Webb has been working as a change-agent for ten years. Her observations and experience have led her to a number of conclusions concerning the requirements which must be met by anyone being utilised in an organisation to help implement the change and steer the organisation from its traditions to its future. Some of the skills and qualities that should be evident in a change-agent include:

- Enjoying working with people.
- Believing in what you are doing, being able to motivate others and remain positive in difficult times.
- Good interpersonal communication skills, written and in public presentation.
- Assessing the progress of change, determining the pace at which change is introduced.
- Patience and, some would say, stamina.
- Recognising where there is no commitment and mere lip-service to change.
- Understanding, and being able to manage, team and group dynamics.
- Teaching skills, such as the ability to use appropriate methods of information-giving and identifying training needs.

There is, of course, a long way to go at Hastings Health Service. As indicated earlier, it is going to have a much closer relationship with its customers' needs and requirements through the survey approach and also from the way that it handles patient enquiries and complaints. Dolly Daniel is the Consumer Relations Officer at Hastings, and her post is accountable to the Director of Nursing and Quality Assurance. Again, as has been the case in many other studies in this book, the role of co-ordinating and handling customer complaints is seen as a senior task in the management structure. According to Dolly Daniel, the handling of complaints:

'Is being firmly integrated with key quality and customer satisfaction work. This integration is, I believe, crucial to bring all staff on board in adopting an innovative team approach through customer relations, complaints and improved service. Visits to customers who complain have become a fundamental part of our striving to become more "customer friendly", and this has met with a very positive response from those customers.'

Hastings Health Service is now in the throes of a 'roadshow' which will take to all staff the importance of the new environment within which the Health Service in Hastings has to operate. It will also demonstrate the implications of initiatives such as *The Patient's Charter*. According to Dilly Millward: 'This will help raise the awareness of all of our staff to the major challenges being presented in general, and to our staff in particular.' The roadshow forms part of the customer relations strategy now being developed at Hastings.

Figure 8.6 Unit philosophy

IRVINE UNIT PHILOSOPHY

The IRVINE UNIT creates a safe friendly environment for patients, their carers and the staff.

All are treated with dignity, respect and honesty.

Rehabilitation is provided by a team of professionals to the highest standard using the available resources.

This gives the patient the opportunity to improve their quality of life and plan their future, their rights and wishes being of paramount importance.

Some directorates and units are already there. Appreciating that the customers (the patients) effectively pay everyone's wages, they are already developing philosophies for improved patient care and customer service. Sister Liz Pearce of the Irvine Unit – a rehabilitation unit for elderly patients – recently met with all of the team working on her ward, to discuss the business plan and how its objectives could be translated at line level. Their philosophy (see Figure 8.6) is simple, clear cut, understood and agreed by all. Sister Liz Pearce is to be congratulated on having produced a philosophy of care, free from any of the jargon one sees so often on mission and value statements.

There is no doubt the above has resulted, as Dilly Millward said in her opening quote, from people feeling good about themselves first. It then follows that they will feel good about others. I feel confident Hastings can ride out the cynicism. They deserve success.

9. Dell Computer Corporation UK

INTRODUCTION

Dell Computer Corporation was founded in 1984 by Michael Dell, then aged 19. Because of Dell Computer Corporation's phenomenal growth and modest entrepreneurial beginnings, it has been called an American success story. When *Fortune*, the USA's prestigious business magazine, commissioned a survey in late 1991 to find the country's 100 fastest growing entrepreneurial companies, it was Michael Dell whose face appeared on the magazine's front cover heading the $679 million-a-year computer firm.

Dell is a company recognised for its dedication to customer care. Its business is selling personal computers directly to end users. It has been operating in the UK since 1987, and in that time its world-wide revenues have grown. In its last reported quarter, revenues were 65 per cent up on the previous year. It is a young, innovative, dynamic organisation, currently employing some 250 staff at Bracknell in Berkshire, England.

Customer service has always been Dell's mission. It is constantly voted at the top of computer press lists for overall customer satisfaction. It also comes top of the polls in the computer user stakes. Dell is extraordinarily successful because it designs, develops, manufactures, sells, services and supports high performance, customised, configured personal computers of unusually high quality and value. The users of Dell products include individuals, small to medium sized businesses, major international corporations, government agencies and educational institutions. Its commitment to innovation and technological leadership, at affordable prices, has earned it a place amongst top ranked computer manufacturers in the world.

Dell maintains, as a top priority, a strong research and development programme whose primary responsibility is to anticipate its customers' needs with leading technology. This case study discusses how Dell UK has evolved an organisational structure and performance management philosophy which enables it to be the premier personal computer company in the UK. Its major goal is to be the UK business community's third largest supplier of personal computers. In order to support this long-term goal, the objective of its organisation structure is to secure competitive advantage by organising to respond to customer needs.

Simply, Dell's story is one of business profitability and success through more attentive and controlled customer care. Customer service has been its key competitive advantage.

Essentially, its major long-term aggressive growth demands that Dell must satisfy customer needs more effectively than its competitors. The company is therefore organised behind its customers. This requires great collaboration between support functions. Less of taking the parochial view of the function, and more focus on the customer. The management style at Dell is one of leadership which energises and empowers teamwork. Its training is geared to having all staff appreciate what happens from a customer point of view. The case study also highlights Dell's performance management approach which is intrinsic to the motivation and development of all its staff. It also builds the foundation for staff wanting to give their best to Dell and their customers.

DELL COMPUTER CORPORATION UK – TOTAL CUSTOMER SERVICE

'Only by listening to customers and responding quickly and professionally to their needs, will Dell continue to be successful. Customer care and service is our number one priority and any customer with an issue to resolve is only ever one step away from myself.'

Martin Slagter, *Managing Director, Dell Computer Corporation, UK.*

Dell UK's business commitment is to focus on customer needs. Its continuing success story is primarily due to meeting those needs by providing value-for-money systems with the performance, support and service its customers require. Dell is a company based on a philosophy that has totally redefined the way people buy computers. At Dell, a supportive and continual relationship between the customer and the supplier is fundamental to its approach to business. Dell calls is 'direct relationship marketing'. (See Figure 9.1.)

Figure 9.1 How direct relationship marketing works

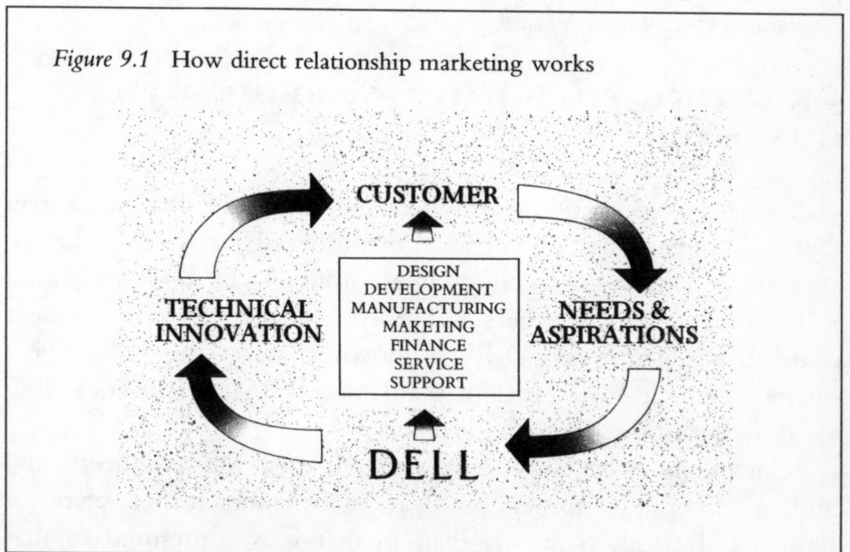

Direct relationship marketing is a philosophy that involves holding regular dialogue with customers that goes far beyond the simple sales transaction of buying a personal computer. According to Martin Slagter, Managing Director of Dell UK:

> *'This means that, as a manufacturer, we listen to our customers. They tell us the products and services that they need, both today and in the future, and with our in-house research and development (R&D) resources we can respond quickly; designing and building systems for our customers' specification, and taking full responsibility for providing an unparalleled package of service and support.'*

Dell believes that by taking direct responsibility for every aspect of its business, it can guarantee to give complete satisfaction in every aspect of its customers' business. According to Ray Ursell, head of Dell's UK Customer Service:

> *'That is, satisfaction with the quality of every Dell product and the service we provide; satisfaction with the price and with the extensive maintenance and support package. It is this direct relationship marketing that has placed Dell at the top of every leading customer satisfaction poll on both sides of the Atlantic.'*

Creating the company behind the customer

Dell's strategy is unique to the personal computer (PC) market in that the company has always seen customer satisfaction as its key to success, and has structured itself accordingly. Its direct working relationship with customers not only cuts out the costly dealer channel, but also makes Dell's production, marketing and support operation much more efficient than those of manufacturers selling via dealers and distributors.

Customers select a system to match their business needs and budget. Every computer built at the manufacturing plant in Limerick, Ireland, is an original, in that it is configured to that customer's specification. Design, development, manufacturing, sales, marketing, servicing and support all remains under Dell's control. As the designer and developer of its own products, Dell is in a position to offer comprehensive support and service for them. Dell also offers the customer – the end user – access to that process. Michael Dell, the company's founder and Chairman explains:

> *'It is really quite simple, we interact directly with our customers; our end users. We have freephone technical support lines set up to support the customer over the phone, we provide an on-site service at the customer's location, and our products change and evolve as the customer's needs evolve . . . we are always responding to those needs. The PC is an integral part of operating our customer's business and when that PC goes down their whole business goes down. You have got to have the solution to their problem quickly, and Dell has been able to provide that much more effectively than our competitors. What's more, we intend to continue to do that because we believe that is the right way to do business.'*

As Ray Ursell also says:

> *'We have great, award-winning personal computers and this, coupled with our customer involvements, means we are able to offer our customers – who we call our business partners – a total solution. No other PC manufacturer services and supports its products as completely, or as well, as we do here at Dell!'*

The customer support organisation actually begins before Dell even ships the order. After personally configuring the customer's system to their exact needs, it is run through a battery of diagnostic tests. The customer receives an animated tutorial disk which is interactive and easy to follow. It teaches the customer everything that they need to know about using their Dell system. As Michael Dell indicated earlier, when the customer's computing needs change and grow, Dell's sales and technical support staff help suggest and recommend new solutions. Technicians include product designers and engineers who work closely with Dell's R&D department, allowing Dell to stay current on the latest advances in PC technology. News of these advances is available to customers every business day through dedicated freephone lines. Dell also warrants each system it manufactures to be free of defects in both material and workmanship, and all of this for one full year at no extra cost.

As a computer user myself, my frequent concern is the long time I have often had to wait for a service technician or engineer to deal with my problems. Dell appreciates this and that is why its direct channel for end users – to talk for free to the technical support lines – is such a fundamental part of its customer service. The customer has access to this free technical helpline whether they are a big corporation or a single user who is working from home.

As soon as someone buys or leases a Dell PC, Dell will create a personalised record which keeps track of what the customer bought, when it was bought and what particular customer configuration was included. In fact, Dell keeps a file concerning everything connected with the purchase, and this is information that is available the moment the customer calls the technical support or advice helplines. The development of such a customer database – and direct marketing that can be run on the back of it – is proving to be a major driving innovation of marketing and customer service in excellence companies.

Creating customer compassion

As the PC evolves and becomes a strategic tool, the end user relationship with the supplier becomes increasingly important. Dell foresaw this change of emphasis, and has linked all of its departments with internal telecommunications and information systems. This means that each department has all the relevant customer information immediately to hand. Dell believes that you cannot do a good job of responding to your customer's needs unless you have instant access to this information. By structuring its organisation around the customer it feels it can provide the highest level of customer satisfaction. A satisfaction that was confirmed by *Computer Weekly*, an industry publication which measures performance reliability, value, compatibility, documentation, service and support. Dell has been in the top two in all of their surveys held over the last three years. As Michael Dell puts it:

> *'Naturally we are pleased with this attention and recognition, but what is more important to us at Dell is our passion to establish and maintain a long-term one-to-one relationship with each of our customers. A relationship that is based on our passion for total and complete customer satisfaction.'*

A major way of providing this customer satisfaction is, as mentioned earlier, the free telephone technical support lines. Unlimited telephone support is available for the lifetime of the product to customers via a freephone service (0800 414 575: Monday to Friday from 9.00 a.m. to 5.30 p.m.). Dell's experience has shown that 90 per cent of enquiries can be solved over the telephone. It is backed up by 12 months' on-site maintenance which guarantees that, if needed, a qualified engineer will visit the customer by the end of the next working day. As with the Texaco case study, great emphasis is placed on answering the phone quickly; or rather, urgently. At Texaco it was within eight seconds, and in my customer survey undertaken for this study, telephone calls were answered consistently within a couple of rings at Dell.

Dell also have a customer care department which is the place for customers to call regarding any non-technical problem. This could be a misunderstanding, general enquiry or complaint relating to their products, shipment or service. Again, customers come through on a dedicated line and Dell pays for their call.

The total weekly incoming calls to Dell are approximately 13,000. It deals with technical support calls of some 3,000 per week and more than 5,000 calls a week relating to sales and shipments. Dell is constantly monitoring the customers' satisfaction with its technical and support hotlines. It appreciates that no matter how good it is there is a constant need to improve. (See Figure 9.2.)

The customer care department co-ordinates all the necessary people and/or departments and follows through any problem. As one user said to me, 'Dell do not rest with your problem until they are satisfied that you are satisfied'. Another Dell user told me, 'the thing with Dell is the feeling you get that they will never compromise on service'.

Of course, this creates a difficulty in that, as number one, they have to stay there. It is a bit like Marks and Spencer. They consistently give high quality of product and service; so much so, that customers have grown to expect it. There is bitter disappointment when there is a lowering of standard. Recently, a colleague bought some peaches at Marks and Spencer, and they were not very good. On complaining to them their response was immediate to the customer, coming within 48 hours, in the form of an apology and a credit voucher, usually for more than the cost of the faulty product.

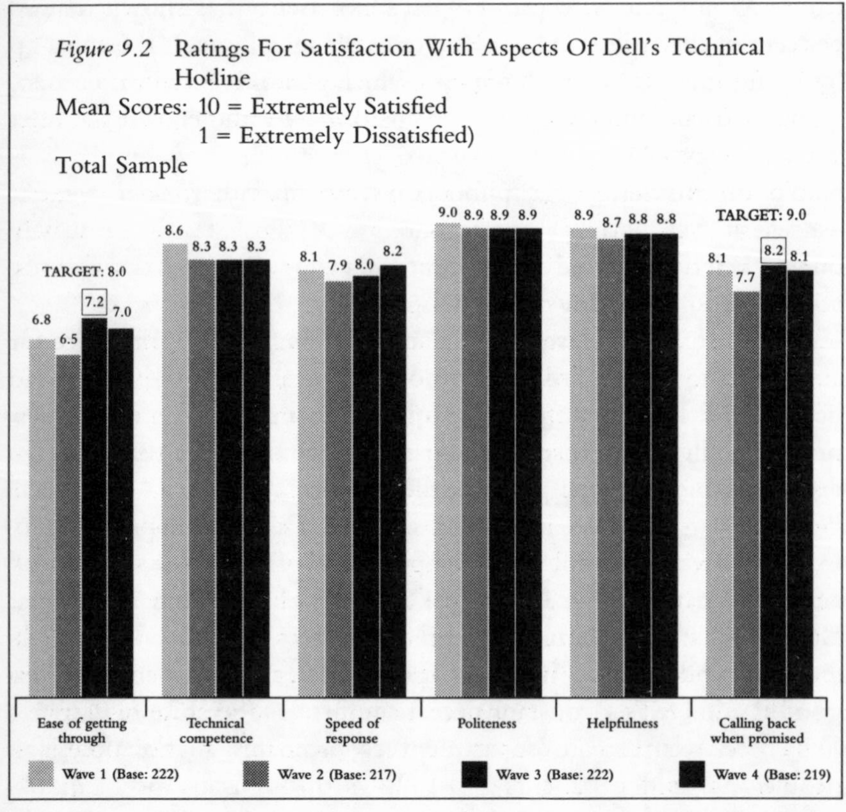

Figure 9.2 Ratings For Satisfaction With Aspects Of Dell's Technical Hotline
Mean Scores: 10 = Extremely Satisfied
1 = Extremely Dissatisfied)
Total Sample

However, I was told that it does not end at that. A manager is then dispatched to Italy to find out why the peaches were not as good as they should have been. This is an example of where Marks and Spencer imposes its very high standard of customer satisfaction requirement upon its suppliers and, indeed, upon anyone it chooses to do business with.

DEVELOPING STAFF FOR CUSTOMER SERVICE

Organisations in this book, like Dell, view customer care and service, not as an option, but as the ultimate competitive advantage. The managers I have talked to throughout all the case study companies do not put customer care in the hands of their human resources department, PR department, or training department. It is not that glib. It is more a total transformation of the company, with everyone in the organisation realising that failure to give customer service is terminal.

To achieve this requires all employees to have a strong business awareness, particularly at line level and at those functions which directly interface with the customer. In fact, two consistent themes arise in all service excellent companies. First, there is the cross-function training and integration that evolves within the companies to enable attitudes to be changed. Second, there is the increasing devolution to line level. For this to occur in a responsible manner requires much training in interpersonal and team-based skills as well as business skills development. To assess the skills required, excellence companies are very keen on appraisal at regular intervals. Dell is no exception, with all employees going through what is known as 'performance management'. Interestingly enough, even the customer comes into the six-monthly appraisal system. Details of the Dell appraisal system are given in Appendix 9.1 (at the end of this chapter). As Dell's performance management rating scale for appraisal has been structured to reflect 'success' more information on this is given in Appendix 9.2.

Lip-service is often paid to appraisals, but not so in excellence companies. Here, there is always an immediate action plan after the appraisal, linked to both development and earnings reviews (as in Appendix 9.3 and 9.4). According to Claire Allen, Human Resources Director:

> *'The performance management document, which every employee in Dell receives, is the most important booklet any employee has within Dell. It demonstrates how every individual can achieve:*
>
> - *Job satisfaction.*
> - *Personal development.*
> - *Increased earnings.*
>
> *The performance management document shows how the above goals, and those of Dell UK, can be achieved through the performance management process. An individual's growth development exists hand-in-hand with Dell's growth.'*

The 'performance management' document contains a job description (every Dell employee has a detailed job description) and a performance plan, which is a summary of objectives for each individual to focus upon during a six-month time frame (see Appendix 9.5 and 9.6). These are agreed between an individual and their manager and can include:

- Specific projects.
- Current priorities within the job description.
- Personal objectives in order for an individual to develop within their job.

These objectives are, by their nature, individual. Performance plans will therefore vary between employees, even within the same job role. The objectives within the performance plan are time-based in order to help individuals identify their own priorities over a period of six months. The performance action plan, in effect, helps individuals focus on their priorities and ensures there is no lip-service paid to the entire process.

Performance management, as practised at Dell, is another consistent theme within excellence companies. All individuals throughout the company are treated well so that they want to give their best to one another, to their company, and ultimately to the customer. The individuals are then used to the maximum of their ability in order to give high service performance. As with all development processes the effectiveness of performance management is influenced by the commitment shown by those involved. Both the individual and their manager have a responsibility to make the performance management process work. It is a binding company commitment that an individual schedules time in their own, and their manager/supervisor's, dairy for their monthly review.

In excellence companies it strikes me that there is always major emphasis placed on linking an individual's job objectives and attitudes to those of the company. This is certainly true in Dell where every individual's performance management is directly linked to the Dell UK goals. (See Figure 9.3.)

Customer-focused behaviour

Some would say that in order to achieve high standards of customer satisfaction you have to change people's attitudes. According to Claire Allen it is more than that. You have to keep employees focused on the Dell goals, reinforce the mission, and keep them motivated to respond to customer needs. As Claire puts it: 'Having the right attitude and the right mission is only part of the answer to giving constant customer satisfaction. People must be trained in the right behaviours and we need to give them the abilities to make things happen.'

At Dell, a way of achieving this has been the implementation of a behavioural skills programme which has involved four major elements.

- Leadership skills for all management.
- Personnel feedback.
- Team building.
- Influencing skills.

As Martin Slagter commented:

'In a constantly changing environment, we have needed to ensure that our people are empowered to respond to our customers. Coping with the sort of growth which Dell has been experiencing brings many strains. For example, over the last year we have seen our employee base increase by some 22 per cent and we have launched a new product every month

Figure 9.3 Dell UK Goals

- **To be the UK business community's third largest supplier of personal computers within two years.**
- **Generate more revenue through the sales of Personal Computers, and their associated products and services, than the UK's largest dealer.**
- **Establish "Direct Relationship Marketing" as the BEST way for businesses to fulfill their personal computing needs.**
- **Establish recognition of Dell by employees, competitors and society as a whole, as a credible, recognised "Major Player" in the UK providing our employees with challenging work, potential for career development, and the salary and benefits for a good standard of living.**
- **We are committed to the basic philosophy of creating the highest levels of customer satisfaction in our industry through the effective management and development of our people, our products, and our operational and strategic methods.**
- **In addition, we intend to produce (as a minimum) the best operational and financial performance of any Dell IBU while striving to achieve the goals set out above.**

for the last 12 months. All against the back-drop of increasing competition and very demanding customers.

'The leadership programme, delivered to every people manager in Dell, gives them the ability to identify the motivations of their individual team members and have the capability to respond to these. How many managers get honest feedback on their performance appraisal from their teams, and their customers? Not many. If we are to motivate our managers to reinforce and refine their newly acquired behaviours, we need to give them this. We have used a feedback programme to speed up their individual learning.'

At Dell, in keeping with other studies in this book, attitude questions to staff and to customers are frequent. Staff have to complete an attitude survey, covering such issues as:

- Understanding Dell's main goals and objectives.
- Understanding how to contribute to customer service.
- How effective is your manager at providing clear measures of what you need to do well?
- Are lines of communication at Dell clear?

Answers to issues such as those posed above are fed back into the learning development programmes, such as the leadership skills course mentioned by Martin Slagter.

Management cannot learn in isolation. It is vital that all the training is geared towards changing attitudes to an approach to work in order that they are totally customer-focused. Says Claire Allen:

'Keeping our people here at Dell focused on the customer is more than just attitude. It is about skill and the behavioural approach, and training is vital to ensuring people are focused on our mission – our dedication to customer care – and to keeping all staff motivated to customer needs.'

This 'people skills' approach in training is fundamental to every organisation in this book. Such training gives staff insight into how their actions and behaviour effects results. It does so by providing them with two kinds of skill; 'diagnostic skills' and 'prescriptive skills'. Diagnostic skills are those skills that recognise that people are different, and identify those differences. Prescriptive skills are the active skills for dealing with people as unique human beings. In the training sessions, managers are taught to understand the different patterns of behaviour. Through models, the manager's observations are organised into categories of behaviour, not people. Having gained insight into behaviour, people are then ready to learn the different prescriptive skills. These are the actions managers can take now they have recognised that people behave in different ways.

Managers also learn comprehensive problem-solving approaches. This teaches managers how to work with their peers and subordinates in order that they, together, can solve problems. These problems are related to areas such as poor quality, conflict, poor customer service attitudes; all the problems that, in fact, arise among people at work. According to Claire Allen:

> *'Skills such as motivating, communicating, coaching, influencing and dealing with all kinds of subordinates are vital for customer-driven organisations. For example, managing someone who likes to show off is very different from managing someone who hates the limelight; or managing a friendly outgoing character compared with a person who does not want to be pals. The training programmes do not just focus on handling subordinates; any dealings with people, at any level, affect results one way or another. Managers can deal with people better if they first understand their own behaviour as well as that of their subordinates, peers and superiors.'*

In essence, excellence companies put a greal deal of effort into management training as well as training for those members of staff actually interfacing with the customers. They realise that a manager needs people skills as well as administrative and technical ones. It is this type of leadership training that the Metropolitan Police (chapter 4), for example, are putting much effort into as part of their 'making PLUS stick' initiative. Without training in people and interpersonal skills a manager will have trouble leading an individual or team.

Teamwork at Dell is vital. For example, whenever it has product launches it involves every area of the company. Much emphasis is placed, therefore, on making sure that team behaviours are collaborative, productive, and customer-focused. Group activities are audited and, again, training sessions teach people how to be team members. The core of all the training at Dell is quite simply to share common business objectives and be trained in the right behaviour and skills to keep the company's competitive edge. According to Martin Slagter.

> *'It has been important at Dell to also have the right business management process to link every individual into our corporate service objectives. The performance management process describes, and defines, for each individual what they need to do to help the organisation meet its service goals. It therefore focuses the individual, through their job role, on satisfying customer needs, so that when we conduct a performance assessment we can feed back to them their achievement in these areas. It becomes a constant process for improvement. Because an individual's performance is directly linked to compensation there is also a direct link between their earnings and customer satisfaction.'*

Dell believes that it is a long way ahead of the competition because of is strength in people. It appreciates that is has no perfect processes or systems, particularly as it is a developing company and coping with growth. It knows, too, that although it has an illustrious product, well accoladed, it is by no means perfect. It believes that it is good because it has won people's hearts and minds towards a culture which is dedicated to customer service. This also stems from the way that it chooses new recruits, who are selected on their adaptability to be customer-focused. During the interview a great many questions are asked, and various areas explored. For example:

- To what extent does the individual being interviewed demonstrate empathy to work colleagues in terms of their ideas and feelings. For instance, do I involve others in discussions?

- Does the individual prefer to work in team-based work environments. For instance, do I gain pleasure from people's company?
- How does the individual respond under stress; what level of emotional control do they exhibit. For instance, do I refuse to let people upset me?

Customer service must be seen to have the highest priority in the firm. In Dell there is a weekly 'customer satisfaction' meeting which the Managing Director himself attends, or chairs. In his diary it is given supreme status. It must not be missed. It is cross-functional with representations from all sides of the business.

Given Dell's achievements in customer service many readers will believe that they do not seem to have a problem. But as they grow and expand they know that it will take more than the right attitude and the right mission statement to give them a long-term competitive edge. They insist that their people need to be trained in the right behaviours for effective customer service. They are under no illusion. As Martin Slagter says:

> *'In an increasingly competitive market, where product differentiation is harder to achieve, it will be our people who will make Dell's difference. By investing in their abilities, we can ensure that we will continue to be a leader in customer satisfaction. It is simply no good understanding the mission if you do not know how to make it happen.'*

Dell does.

Appendix 9.1

PERFORMANCE MANAGEMENT

The Appraisal

The appraisal is a formal review of your performance over the last 6 months, and a time to discuss how to continue your development over the next 6.

The appraisal meeting should be a two-way discussion during which all elements of your job description and performance plan are reviewed. You will be asked for your views on your performance and your manager will give you his/hers. You should already have a good idea of how you have performed, if you have had regular review/feedback meetings with your manager.

What will my manager do?
You will probably find that your manager has spoken to your 'customers' (either colleagues with whom you liaise on a regular basis, or external customers), in order to gain balance feedback on your performance. He/she will also have reviewed your appraisal with you Senior Manager prior to the meeting.

What should I do?
You should prepare for the appraiesal meeting. The more you prepare for it the more productive you will find it.

Areas which you may want to consider are:

- Review you own job description and performance plan; how have you performed against these?
- What do you enjoy in your role, what motivates you?
- What are you strengths/improvement areas?
- How would you like to develop?

You should receive a full appraisal every 6 months

Appendix 9.2

PERFORMANCE MANAGEMENT

Performance rating descriptions

1. Can define, then exceed all objectives. Always exceeds the necessary skills and abilities required of the job. Possesses exceptional knowledge of all the major aspects of the total job and has had broad experience in each of these areas.
2. Consistently exceeds the established objectives and the necessary skills and abilities required of the job. Possesses a high level of knowledge of the major aspect of the total job and has had experience in each of these areas.
3. Achieves and frequently exceeds the established objectives. Demonstrates the necessary skills and abilities required of the job and frequently exceeds job requirements. Possesses knowledge of the major aspects of the total job and has had experience in each of these areas.
4. Achieves the established objectives. Demonstrates the necessary skills and abilities required of the job. Possesses knowledge of the major aspects of the total job and has had experience in most of these areas.
5. Achieves some of the established objectives, although requires some improvement in certain areas. Possesses the necessary skills and abilities required of the job. Possesses knowledge of the major aspects of the total job and has had experience in most of these areas.
6. Does not meet established objectives. Does not demostrate the necessary knowledge, skills, and abilities required of the total job. Counselling and improvement must take place.

Appendix 9.2A

PERFORMANCE MANAGEMENT

The rating scale

Your individual responsibilities and your overall performance will be assigned a rating from a 6 point scale (shown below).

Unlike many scales where an 'average' score is 3, the Dell scale has been structured differently. We have designed it to reflect 'success' at a number of levels, rather than several levels of 'failure'. This allows us to truly recognise those who make significant achievements.

As you will see, Ratings 1 to 5 are all positive reflecting 'exceptional performance' through to 'needing some improvement'. Each rating in this group therefore confirms that the individual has the appropriate skills to undertake the job, but is applying these to varying degrees.

Only rating 6 is negative, and reflects that the individual does not have the necessary skills for their job role.

You may wish to read these ratings before you have your appraisal meeting to confirm your own understanding.

Appendix 9.3

PERFORMANCE MANAGEMENT

The development plan

Out of your appraisal discussion, you are likely to have identified areas for development. These might include:

- specific skills which will enhance your job performance
- specific job areas which will add breadth to your job knowledge

Whatever the nature of the area, you will need to take action to achieve the plan. Action areas can cover a number of tasks for example:

- experience of different work processes
- extending personal knowledge through self teaching
- extending personal skills by working alongside a suitably skilled colleague attending an appraisal meeting
- undertaking a specific project.

Formal training might also be a recommendation, however most development activity can and should occur in the workplace where it is most relevant.

Development plans define the 'What?' and 'How?'

Appendix 9.4A

PERFORMANCE MANAGEMENT

The earnings review

The earnings review is Dell's way of rewarding you for the development which you have shown in your job.

By linking your overall appraisal rating to the increase which you receive, you are clearly able to see how to influence your earnings.

Your earnings review will occur after 12 months in your job role (see Example 1 overleaf).

However it is worth noting that you can be promoted at any time during the year, and your earnings will be reviewed at the time of your promotion. The next page demonstrates this in Example 2.

In reviewing your earnings, Dell will also reference what the external market is paying. This is reflected in your earnings range which your manager can explain to you in more detail.

Your earnings will be reviewed every 12 months.

Appendix 9.4B

PERFORMANCE MANAGEMENT

How will my earnings be reviewed?

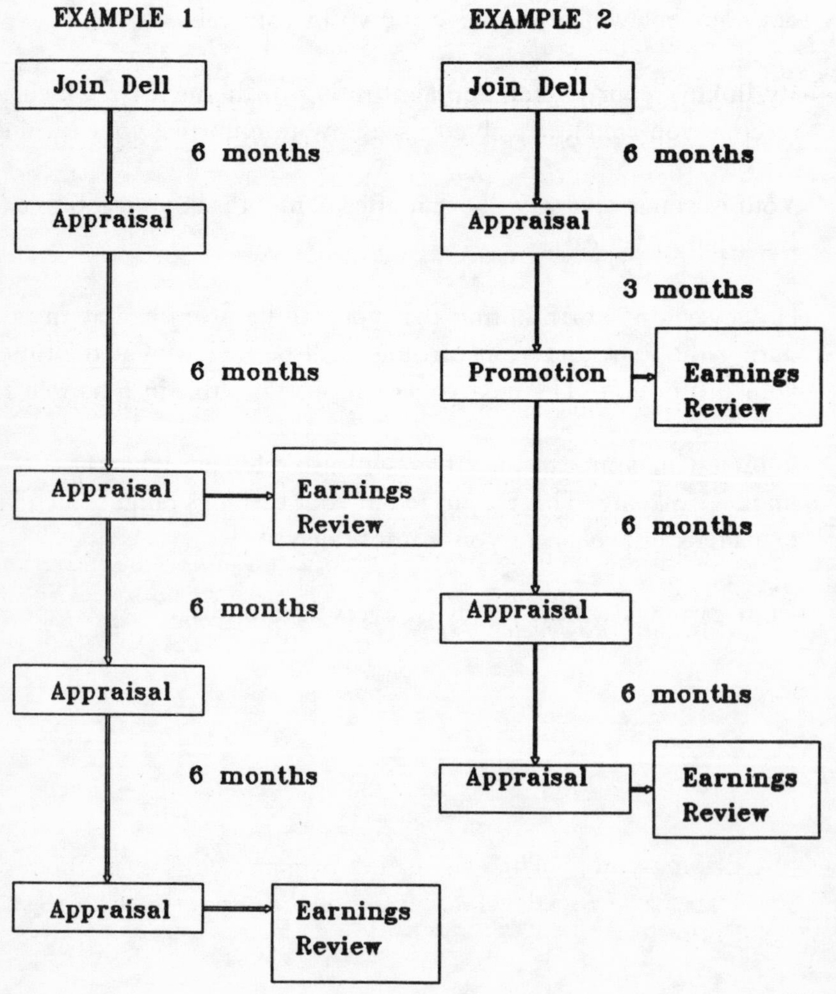

Appendix 9.5

PERFORMANCE MANAGEMENT

How does it work?

Dell UK has a plan for developing our business which is agreed with our US Corporate body.

Out of this plan, every function (from Finance to Manufacturing) can establish its own goals and objectives and it is from these that your job requirements are identified.

The performance management process supports this by:

- helping you to identify these job requirements, (through you *job description*)
- assisting you in prioritising them, (through your *performance plan*)
- giving you guidance and help to achieve these objectives (through the *monthly review*)
- recognising your achievements (through the *appraisal*)
- identifying specific activities to enhance your capabilities (through the *development plan*)

and finally

- rewarding you for this achievement (through the *earnings review*)

By helping you to achieve your performance objectives, the process ensures that your development directly supports the growth of Dell UK.

Appendix 9.6

PERFORMANCE MANAGEMENT

The monthly review

As you are now aware, the performance management process at Del is designed to help you agree your personal objectives and obtain guidance and help to achieve these.

The monthly review is an important means for you to obtain guidance and it is intended to:

- let you and your manager review your current work priorities, and re-evaluate these if new business demands are in conflict.
- give you an opportunity to discuss any current problems you are experiencing, and get help from your manager to resolve these.
- give your manager a chance to feedback and discuss with you, your current performance.
- provide an opportunity to add/change the objectives within your performance plan, to reflect changing business priorities.

Your performance plan should be reviewed once a month.

PERFORMANCE MANAGEMENT

The process

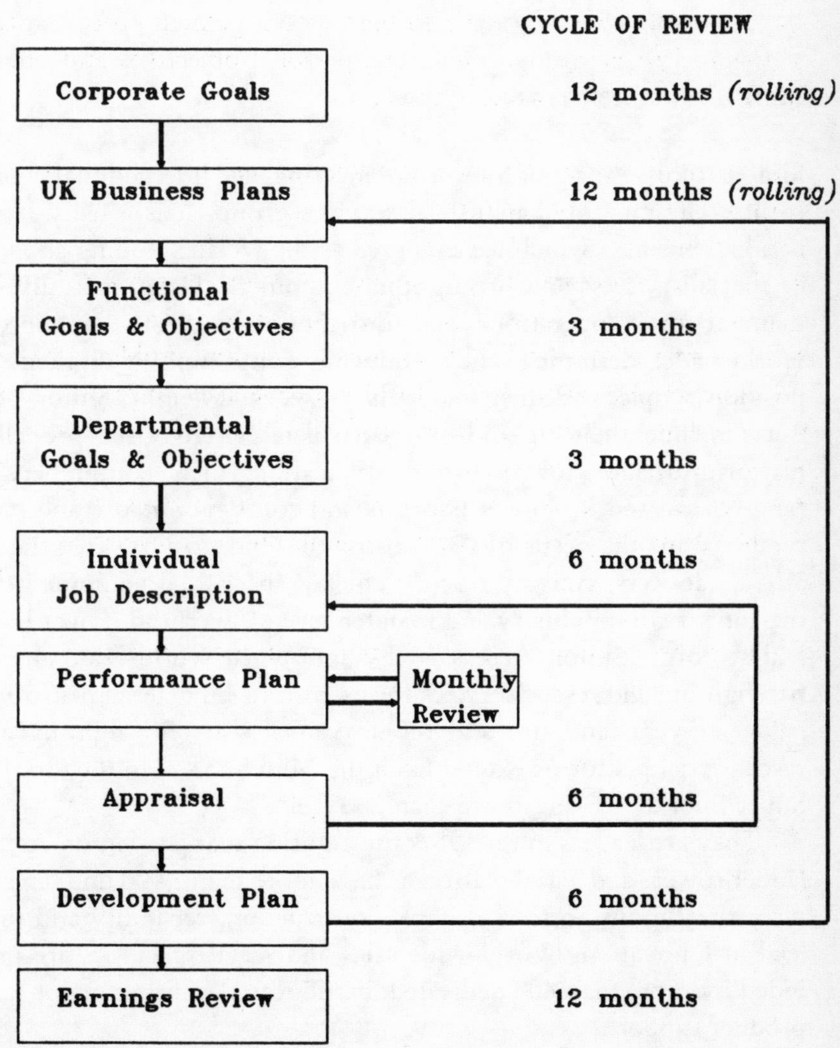

10. Simon Access

Introduction

Simon Access is part of Simon Engineering, the international equipment contracting and industrial services group. It is a truly international business which has emerged as the world's leading supplier of specialist access and fire-fighting equipment. Geographically, its manufacturing operations and distribution network are spread world-wide; designing and producing supporting equipment to position people, and their materials, to work at height. Simon products include: their 'up-and-over' articulated range of self-propelled platform designs for industrial application; their comprehensive range of rugged booms, scissorlifts and truck mounted cranes tailored to meet the needs of the construction industry; state of the art aircraft de-icers, runway rescue vehicles; specialised equipment for the construction industry and maintenance of overhead power lines, and so forth. Simon Access is also renowned world-wide among fire-fighting and rescue services for its custom-built aerial platforms, ladder towers, and fire and rescue vehicles. Its fire-fighting and rescue aerial platforms extend from the Mini Snorkel to the ultimate Super Snorkel soaring more than 200 feet.

They are leaders in the USA fire-fighting market. Simon Access ladder towers and aerial platforms have more than 1,000 units in service; a testimony to their durable construction, reliability and their lead in innovation. World-wide sales and service facilities are provided by more than 400 dedicated distributors, ensuring major local product support.

Not long ago, Simon Engineering was a widely diversified group with a spread of disparate businesses. Today, four divisions bring together closely related businesses, and the synergy between them is exploited in large scale co-operative projects. This much more focused group has a quarter of its sales, and rather more of its profits, coming from Simon Access Division. Globally it is well balanced, with one third of its business derived from the UK, one third from the USA, and one third from the rest of the world.

Simon-Dudley Limited

Simon-Dudley Limited is a member of the Simon Access Division. It is based in Dudley, in the West Midlands of England, and designs and manufacturers the range of Simon Snorkel fire-fighting equipment, rescue platforms and access equipment. The essence of its customer service reputation is its proactive design approach, particularly its detailed dialogue with distributors and customers, together with innovative engineering. The result is a range of products that lead their field by fully meeting both market and customer needs.

Simon-Dudley has been in business for some 40 years, and employs approximately 260 people. Its annual turnover exceeds £15 million. There is no doubt that Simon-Dudley has been successful and profitable. Perhaps that was part of its problem; self-satisfaction and complacency helping to lose customer contact. It operates in a rapidly changing market where close market contact is essential. It operates mainly in the fire-fighting sector, and its 30-acre manufacturing plant at Dudley, near Birmingham, is considered to be the home of the world famous Simon Snorkel, the aerial fire-fighter. Its greatest achievement came in 1984, when it produced the Simon Super Snorkel which broke the height barrier with a low profile, high performance appliance giving 62 metres (202 ft) upreach, 23 metres outreach and only 12 metres long on the road; shorter than most hydraulic platforms having only half its upreach. More than 10,000 Snorkel units have been sold world-wide to 142 countries. The 1990s have seen Simon-Dudley develop their telescopic Snorkels, bringing Simon Access into new areas of aerial manoeuvrability through a machine designed specifically to meet the requirements of fire services world-wide.

Simon Access needs the best of both worlds. It wants the close contact between manufacturer and customer at the market-place. Simultaneously, Simon Access needs to be a global business presenting itself world-wide as a single company, whilst still achieving the entrepreneurial enterprise of the individual companies within the Group. This case study discusses the cultural changes which have been demanded within the Simon Access Division, and at Simon-Dudley, to retrieve and achieve customer service excellence.

Figure 10.1 Simon Access organisation

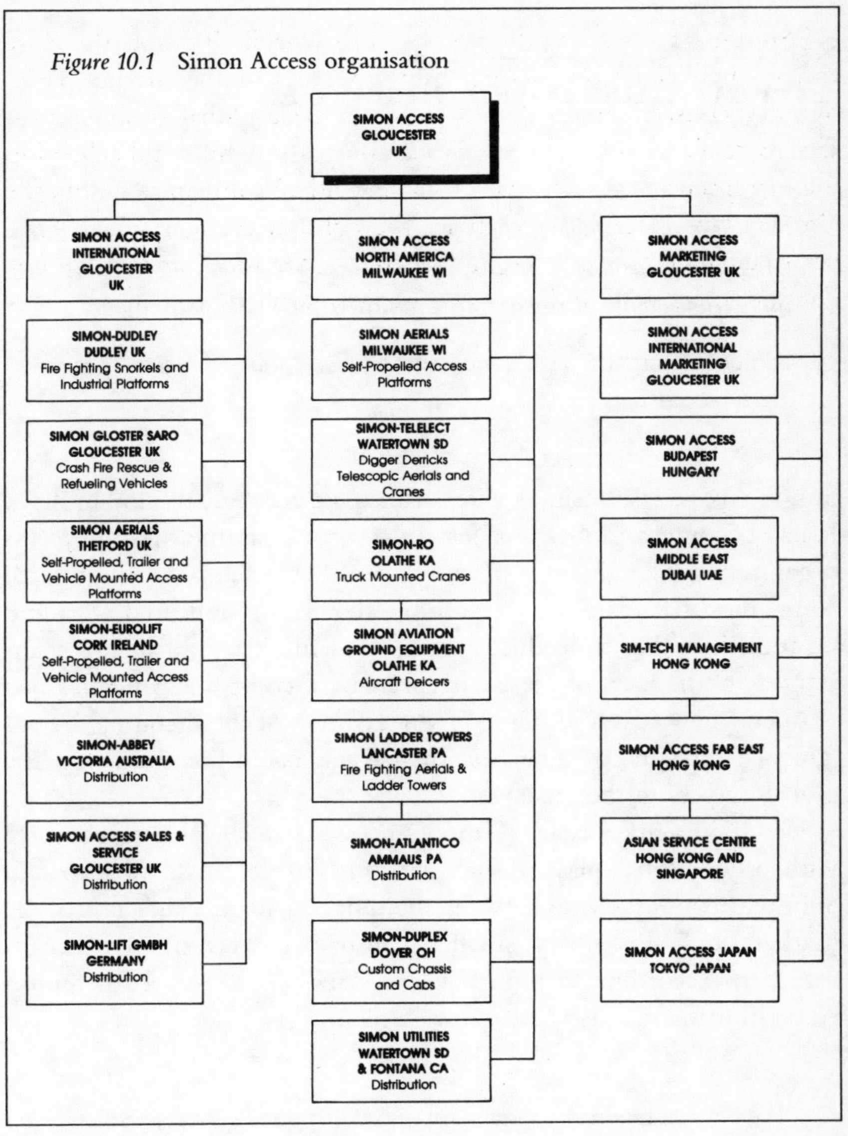

Simon Access – Total Customer Service

'Making the change to being a customer-led company is one thing. Making the ideal stick is another, and requires a continuous effort. It is this second wave of commitment which is the really telling one.'

Malcolm Parkinson, *Managing Director, Simon-Dudley, Simon Access Division.*

Simon Access is a business with a turnover in excess of £150 million. It has become a global business by takeover as the Simon Access organisation chart indicates (see Figure 10.1). Each of the individual companies that make up the Simon Access Division hold a leading position in either a product sector, or a market, and in many instances, both. Each of these entrepreneurial companies operates in a market where it is a leader. However, none of these companies are 'global' and none of them, on their own, could compete with the global players in the business.

To gain market share, Simon Access has to be able to compete with other global players such as JLG, Grove, Aichi Sharyo and Snorkel Economy, who between them have a 40 per cent share of the market, and also many smaller companies who supply the remainder. According to John Barker, Managing Director for Simon Access Division, this means:

'We have to retain small company flexibility, and speed of response, but think on a world-class scale and behave like a large company. We have plenty of room in the market to expand; it is growing at anywhere between 5 per cent and 15 per cent per annum, and in a few exceptional areas even faster. What we have to do to be successful is to build a global, coherent, dominant access business, yet maintain the individuality of each business.'

Simon Access has to be innovative in its capacity to react quickly, operate independently, and keep close to its market. At the same time it must be perceived as a single, major international business, with a consistent global presence and image.

It may well be that Simon Access will have to trade off some of the autonomy associated with its individual privately owned companies in exchange for the advantage in being a strong, global, public company. Its immediate objective is to double present turnover by 1994. There are various ways to achieve this. For example, there is the synergy aspect. This would include endeavours such as the use of shared sales/service facilities and the sale of one company's products by another. It may also include sharing market research and market information, engineering ideas and resources, making use of combined purchasing power and 'piggy-backing' products of one company on the reputation of others.

However, Simon Access believes that a major way to grow is through organic development of its companies, to increase market share of existing markets and to improve its company performance. It believes that this is largely up to company management to achieve and would include; improved quality, after-sales care and maintenance, world-class performance, and achieving greater excellence in customer relations and service.

Basically, Simon Access has the best individually, and now it has to create the best corporately. In essence it must make the whole greater than the sum of the parts. It will necessitate some co-ordination from the Simon Access Group – for example, in key areas such as marketing and product development – but without losing the individual enterprise and initiative at individual company level. In order to be perceived as a single company, Simon Access must have a consistent cult, and an identity as a single unit with a common commitment to its market and reputation.

This process began in 1991, with an easily identifiable business definition and mission statement which takes the Simon Access global vision throughout all of its companies and their 2,500 employees (see Figure 10.2). A mission statement or boardroom vision, however, is simply not enough on its own. To achieve the objectives mentioned earlier, and to grow through organic development, requires a change of attitude, and behaviour at all levels in the organisation. In other words a total change in corporate culture.

This sets an enormous task not only at Simon Access divisional level but also at the boardroom level within each of the individual companies throughout the group. As many of the studies in this book have illustrated, changing any corporate culture is not simply a matter of setting new objectives or redirecting goals. Neither is it about what people say and what they think. It is much more to do with people's beliefs, their shared values, the way they feel and actually behave. A culture cannot arrive over a weekend, and it must grow from within; driven, steered and monitored by strong (some

Figure 10.2 Simon Access business definition and mission statement

. . . business definition

Simon Access is the world's leading supplier of specialist access equipment that provides a safe and cost-effective method of positioning people and materials to work at height.

. . . mission statement

Simon Access is committed to world leadership in access markets by providing its customers with fully-supported, cost-effective and innovative access solutions, with special emphasis on quality and performance.

Through an aggressive policy of new product development, selective acquisition and distributor development, Simon Access will exploit the benefits of group synergy in design, engineering, manufacturing and marketing worldwide, while retaining flexibility for quick response to customer needs.

would say tough) visible, effective, efficient and consistent leadership. How has this been achieved within the Simon Access Division, and one of its major companies in the organisation Simon-Dudley?

KNOW YOUR OWN BUSINESS – KNOW YOUR OWN COMPETITION

First of all, it has been vital that every one of the employees worldwide understands the market-place within which Simon Access has to succeed. Some of this has already been discussed, and Simon Access knows that perhaps its toughest competition will come from the Japanese. During the past two decades, Japan has conquered vast sectors of global manufacturing. More recently, almost unnoticed by its competitors, Japan is transforming itself from a nation which manufactures to one which also provides services. Buried in alarming statistics one can discover that between 1986 and 1990 Japan's service sector grew by more than 30 per cent, compared to slightly more than a 20 per cent increase in manufacturing. Japan's services now account for some 65 per cent of that nation's GNP; overtaking Germany, pulling level with the UK and now ranking second only to the USA. Japan is determined to become the leading global service provider; with launches of products in finance, transport and travel, retailing, healthcare, and innovative communications into Western countries.

Simon Access is aware that the major Japanese competitors in its industry are much more dedicated to satisfying customer needs and expectations than Simon Access has ever been. One thing that has always impressed me when working within Japanese organisations, such as Nissan, is the way they constantly measure customer satisfaction. This process is at the heart of their corporate strategy. Japanese companies concentrate on customer service, quality, product reliability, guarantees, and improving customer relations through information technology. When I was working in Nissan they had innumerable ways for monitoring customer satisfaction. In fact, many of these measurements have been adopted by the excellence organisations in this book. For example, the following:

- Regular meetings between customers and senior management.
- Detailed market research of existing customers' expectations and needs, and those of potential customers.
- Surveys and questionnaires yielding information from both internal and external customers regarding what can be done to improve both products and service.
- Customer clinics and quality and service forums which listen and act on areas for service excellence improvement.
- Comment cards attached to products, or delivered with the service, which are encouraged to be completed by the user. On their return to the organisation they are always seen and acted upon by a senior management member.
- Comprehensive analysis of customer complaints which are always seen as an opportunity for improvement.
- Support helplines and free telephone numbers; such as those in the Texaco (chapter 1) and Dell (chapter 9) studies.

What singles out the companies in this book from many others in the UK is the overwhelming number of managers who stress the importance of customer satisfaction, and having a customer care programme (the *Sunday Times*/MORI Poll on customer service indicated at the beginning of this book, is an illustration of this). These managers and their organisations are, however, comfortably complacent when it comes to creating the climate and environment which monitors customers' needs and expectations. In contrast, the majority of Japanese leaders that I have met are committed to using whatever resource it will take to anticipate what the customer wants. It is against this background of Japanese dedication to 'being the best' in product reliability and customer service that Simon Access began to change their culture; defined as a 'Best of Both Worlds' approach.

In principal, the 'Best of Both Worlds' is the need to have close contact with manufacturer and market-place, and be seen as a local supplier by the local market. At the same time, a need to be able to present itself world-wide as a single company and be seen as a global supplier by its major customers. Managing Director John Barker explains:

> *'Our continued success in a highly competitive world market-place depends on establishing a clear understanding throughout our 2,500 employees world-wide of the implications of the Simon Access culture. In essence, this culture is defined by the "Best of Both Worlds" approach, which signifies a consistent and coherent culture which values the customers, fosters quality, and exploits the full potential for synergy in a global engineering organisation.'*

The Simon Access culture programme is a long, demanding and expensive task. It is nevertheless seen as an essential element in making every employee aware of the need for change, and the goals to be achieved. This understanding will far exceed the effect of any instruction from corporate headquarters. It is important that everyone understands the business Simon Access is in, and is committed to the future direction of that business. In service excellent companies everyone has detailed knowledge on what the competition does as well! The reader may have got an impression from the introduction to this case study that Simon Access's business mission, and product, is to lift people up in the air to do a job. John Barker's task has been to make everyone realise that they do not make lifting equipment, but rather they 'create access solutions'. This is essential, for the former implies a product-driven organisation, and the latter a customer-led company. Senior managers from each of the individual companies which form the Simon Access organisation have been brought together to understand the 'Best of Both Worlds' approach and to become committed to it. The training programme involves small group sessions in the UK and preparation includes pre-course reading on such key elements as:

- An examination of the global competition within the Simon Access industry.
- The essentials of a customer-focused organisation and becoming a customer-led company.

- Building world-class quality and service through world-class performance.
- Achieving excellence from shared experience.

These intensive work groups include the identification of actions which can be implemented at individual work unit and company level in support of the corporate objective. Again, the translation of a boardroom vision through 'ownership' by senior management towards active workplace improvements has been a consistent theme in all of the studies in this book. For example, British Gas (chapter 3) realised there was no point in the regional headquarters board vanishing for five days merely to return with visions, philosophies, missions, concepts and talk. Each member of the management team had to return, and put into action what had been agreed as the business mission and value statement. Major initiatives were actually taken on board at district level which ultimately paid off, as new management behaviour involved staff right down the organisation, where it then interfaced with the customer. So it was to be in Simon Access Division.

Simon Access's cultural change has focused on the customer. We will see later in this study that this was important as, in many parts of the organisation, Simon Access had lost touch with the customer despite having a successful and profitable product. Building a profitable and close relationship with the customer was therefore a common theme which pulled Simon Access management together. The working sessions and seminars for all management throughout the organisation has developed the customer-led focus. It has made management realise that not only can customer service excellence be a real competitive advantage, but also the partnership between the customer and the manufacturer can make for improved profitability.

This is a recurring theme throughout service excellent organisations. Introducing a new product, which Simon Access successfully did in the 1980s with its Simon Super Snorkel, can allow the organisation to gain competitive advantage, but usually for only a limited period of time. It may give a few months, or perhaps a few years lead time, but it will not keep an organisation ahead; competitors soon catch up (as was very much the case in the early 1980s with IBM). Two problems emerge, and one is the size of the organisation itself. Smaller competitors and companies are usually able to move much more quickly than larger, more inflexible, organisations. This is especially true where the smaller competitors have, of necessity, to be in closer touch with the customer. The second problem arises when you have a successful and profitable business where complacency becomes the norm. In this instance too many managers believe that success is a destination and not a journey. They do not always anticipate their customers' needs and requirements ahead of their competition. A point well recognised by Japanese business.

It is perhaps unfair to single out IBM as an instance of the above a decade ago. Other world-wide conglomerates have fallen into a similar trap. General Motors in the USA would be another example, as would some of the famous UK corporate names of the 1980s who no longer survive in the 1990s.

Simon Access was aware of this dilemma. Malcolm Parkinson, Managing Director of Simon-Dudley (who manufactures the Simon Snorkel series) openly admits that, whilst it had a highly successful and profitable business, it lost customer contact. It did not listen to what its customers actually wanted, nor their perceptions. He says:

> *'We had an amazing product lead; but we were not a customer-led organisation at that time. You must create customer loyalty in order that the customer will stay with you, even if your competitors catch up on your product lead and (themselves) take a short-term lead.'*

This was the major message that had to be conveyed throughout Simon Access and to all of its employees. Quite simply, a customer-led culture and organisation within Simon Access would create real competitive advantage within a global market-place.

Directing the customer focus

Simon-Dudley had an interesting way of introducing the message of customer service giving the legitimate competitive edge to their labour force. As Malcolm Parkinson explains:

> *'One of our first moves was to take everyone in the company to a major international exhibition on fire-fighting equipment held at the National Exhibition Centre (NEC) in Birmingham. Unbelievably, the majority of people working at Simon-Dudley thought we had a free field, with no competitors to be concerned about. The exhibition gave them a very different view. They were able to see other machines, to judge our quality against others from around the world and, crucially, to see for themselves that to survive, we must constantly strive to be better.'*

If these employees had been working in a hotel, or at a Texaco service station, in a building society such as the Portman or a computer company, they would probably have realised that they have major competitors within their industry. Traditionally, however, in the English Midlands workers tend to be rather insular. It is probably easy to assume, when you see all the fire engines in your neighbourhood using Simon Access equipment, that the customers have no choice other than to buy your engineering.

At the NEC exhibition there were also many customers of Simon Access equipment type. For many of the workers in Simon-Dudley it was the first time that they had actually come face to face with a customer. This is possibly when the first basic understanding of the Simon Access mission statement occurred. Direct contact with the customer allowed employees to have a better understanding of those customers' needs. Perhaps it also created a better understanding of the real, and vital, consequences of complacency in quality and service. Says Malcolm Parkinson: 'Without this realisation and basic understanding, it would not have been possible to create a work culture at Simon-Dudley in which continuous service improvement became, not an objective, but a way of life.'

The value of customer satisfaction

An important element in making the cultural change which was demanded at Simon Access – in order to achieve customer service excellence at Simon-Dudley – was a policy of actively involving staff at all levels in the customer relationship. There had to be a lot of effort put into this as there was a need to break down the traditionally insular attitudes of engineering workers in the West Midlands, and to engender a real feeling of involvement and satisfaction in service and quality. Going to the exhibition, and meeting customers, gave much impetus to launching the 'Best of Both Worlds' approach. But, who was the customer? What many employees did not realise was Simon-Dudley's major customers were the 300 plus world-wide distributors who then sold into different markets. However, their customers were also the operators and users of the equipment, and they were the customers that Simon-Dudley had tended to forget about.

The reasons that the employees at Simon-Dudley had not realised the importance of this extended customer base, through to the actual user of the access and fire-fighting equipment, was simply due to this not being appreciated anywhere within the Simon Access organisation. Says John Barker:

> *'The primary lesson we have learnt is that there are important differences around the world in customer expectations. This is due more to deep-set local preferences than to differing perceptions of what constitutes service and quality. An example of this would be the construction industry culture in the USA which takes a rugged approach to equipment, therefore our attitude to customer service has to be tailored for those type of needs. In Europe and Japan, by contrast, construction is undertaken in a different way; machines are expected to be more highly finished, and built to higher ergonomic standards.'*

It was vitally important, therefore, that Simon Access, and Simon-Dudley, were much more responsive to the local customer's needs, in particular the users of their equipment. A fireman in Los Angeles, for example, wants different fire-fighting equipment than a fireman in Edinburgh. Adapting to market preferences, and identifying customer needs, has been a solid foundation for the 'Best of Both Worlds' approach.

John Barker and his senior management team are now turning

their attention to the potential customers in Japan. As I indicated earlier, the Japanese are very used to having their customer expectations anticipated as well as met. With a domestic market estimated at £240 million, and growing at a rate in excess of 20 per cent per annum, Japan is considered to be one of the world's largest markets for access equipment. In the arena of customer service and quality the Japanese market is a mature and sophisticated one, and one of Simon Access's major competitors is a Japanese manufacturer. John Barker explains:

> *'It was clear that if Simon Access was to establish a true world-leader status we needed to be able to take on that competition and at all levels. In customer service terms, our competitor has a well established network of local service centres and agents, and they were advertising a 30-minute response to any customer call-out within Japan. This is an enormous challenge for us to meet – we think we are doing well with two hours! But we have decided to meet it head-on. We are currently working on this project, and our own response time is improving rapidly. I am very confident that we will eventually match our competition.'*

This 'listening' to the customer in a more global sense is being re-inforced during 1992 when the Simon Access 'synergy' meeting for the management team – to discuss current and future business and customer service 'Best of Both Worlds' philosophy – is held in Japan. This is taking place in order that they can have closer contact with the market-place, and listen to their potential customers' wants and needs. Closer to home, this already takes place with their UK customers.

DEVELOPING A POLICY OF CONSTANT CUSTOMER REVIEW

The West Midlands Fire Brigade is one of the UK's largest fire services, with its control room handling over 80,000 calls every year. Major incidents such as motorway multiple crashes and high-rise fires are all routed through the Brigade's efficient computerised central control. It is from this room that the Brigade's resources of men and machines are directed into action in a manner reminiscent of a battle headquarters.

West Midlands Fire Brigade is a major Simon-Dudley customer. It uses several Simon Snorkels for rescue and fire-fighting at incidents involving high-level buildings. The Brigade's close proximity to Simon-Dudley's manufacturing plant at Dudley made it an ideal choice for me to see how the customer service programme – implemented from the highest levels of a global Simon Access organisation – was manifesting itself at the sharp end.

Until stranded in mid-air at the top of one of their Simon Snorkels (as I was!) one has little appreciation of how essential it is for the customer, the fire-fighter, to have total confidence in the product. Also, to know that their views have been represented at the design stage, and their requirements taken on board during production. As one fireman explained 'this equipment is one of our team, part of the watch'. The Assistant Chief Fire Officer at West Midlands Fire Brigade is John Palmer. He has seen Simon Access's philosophy towards improved customer service pay off in the Brigade's relationship with the supplier of the equipment, Simon-Dudley:

> *'It's fair to say that a few years ago Simon-Dudley had much ground to make up in its contact with its customers. It had a superb quality product, but it simply was not listening to the customer. Like many other UK manufacturers, it seemed to work on the basis that it knew what was good for the customer, and that we should be grateful for what we received.'*

John Palmer admits that Simon-Dudley had forgotten that its customer did have choice. As firemen, charged with the responsibility of rescue and saving life and protecting property, they often risk their own safety. It is therefore vital that they feel confident with the equipment which is their major tool of the trade. 'It is,' says John Palmer, 'reassuring to know that a manufacturer of essential equipment does listen carefully to our needs, and responds to them.'

One of the ways in which this vital customer communication is achieved is through a user group. This is very much along the lines of the Japanese approach mentioned earlier and more commonly known as a 'customer clinic'. The important point about the Simon-Dudley user group is, in keeping with similar forums mentioned in other studies in this book, a listening brief for the supplier of the product or service. It provides an opportunity not to be defensive when criticisms are raised, but rather to maximise the opportunity of being able to supply what the customer actually wants. The Simon Snorkel, for example, is very much part of the fire crew team; their confidence, or lack of it, in the equipment can have a sensitising effect upon morale. The user group meeting is much aware of this and therefore takes the meeting very seriously. The user group meets on a regular basis, and involves brigade engineers and senior officers in frank and open discussion with technical and management staff from Simon-Dudley and Simon Access. The user group are viewed as a key element in a concerted effort to improve multilateral communications between manufacturers, customers and users. The meetings include representatives of fire brigades from all over the UK, and are chaired by one of the users; a significant factor in all excellence companies which sets the context and importance of the customer's importance and involvement. A forum is created in which discussion can range widely from design policy to technical details affecting the use of the machines in live service conditions.

The exercise has proved so effective that moves are now being made to extend the idea to Simon-Dudley customers outside the UK. Sometimes, this overall umbrella group may form sub-groups to look at particular technical problems, or perhaps review the training that will be required to support different operational circumstances. John Palmer feels that:

> *'The user group is an extremely useful element from our point of view. Essentially it is a two-way communication. The meetings are frank, but by no means simply a case of us complaining to Simon-Dudley. There have been many occasions where Simon Access and Simon-Dudley's technicians have been able to point out particular maintenance procedures which will pre-empt a problem. There is no doubt there has been a radical change since those days when Simon-Dudley lost its customers through not listening.'*

There are longer-term benefits of good customer communications. For example, Simon-Dudley has recently launched a hydraulic fire-fighting platform which includes a number of special design features. These have been identified during discussions with the fire professionals in the user group. According to John Palmer, this marks 'a further milestone in Simon-Dudley's impressive progress towards being a truly customer-led manufacturer'.

CONTINUED IMPROVEMENT OF CUSTOMER SERVICE AT THE WORKPLACE

At the beginning of this case study, Malcolm Parkinson said that making the change to being a customer-led company was one thing, making it stick was another. Two major ways have occurred throughout Simon-Dudley to reinforce the customer-led image, and make it stick.

First, there is the major training effort right across Simon Access. It commenced, as I said earlier, with all the senior management throughout the group. This then cascaded down the organisation to enable all employees to understand the 'Best of Both Worlds' approach. Customer service training, and interpersonal skills, are being developed across the board in Simon-Dudley as part of its commitment to what is known as World Class Performance (WCP). On the shop floor at Simon-Dudley I was impressed by the progress being made.

The customer services department was right next door to the production plant. Working from there is Nigel Burton, Simon-Dudley's Customer Services Manager. Burton was brought in from a service environment, British Airways, to help develop the 'Best of Both Worlds' approach and to steer the support and training required in a customer-led environment. He views the approach thus:

'The job of achieving customer service excellence depends on involving every single person within Simon-Dudley, and constantly working towards stronger team spirit. We have to get through to everyone the fact that a sale is not the end, but rather the beginning of a customer -

relationship. Customer relations are here on the shop floor and that is where the department that serves them best is placed.'

Again, this is a consistent theme in all of the excellence companies. Training for customer service is devolved down to the workface and the point closest to the interaction with the customer. Nigel Burton walks out of his office door straight onto the production plant, and that is how it should be.

There are also visible targets and achievements displayed in colourful detail around the plant. This enables all of the workforce to be constantly reminded that they are a customer-led organisation. This visible information, about the company's products and its competitiveness, developed from the visits to the international fire-fighting exhibition. It has been part of the philosophy of ensuring that continual service improvement becomes a way of life. Visiting customers to Simon-Dudley are brought to the production floor and encouraged to talk with the people actually building the machines. This is all part of the World Class Performance (WCP) approach throughout Simon Access.

It is worth, at this stage in the study, discussing further the concept of WCP and how it relates to customer service. WCP is a combination of best business practices throughout the business cycle; from product conception, design, manufacturing, planning, production, sales and customer service. The goal is to produce high quality products at low cost, and with a quick response to customer needs. Simon Access defines the product not just as the hardware but the 'total' product, including customer care and service.

To achieve class A in WCP, which is what Simon-Dudley is actively putting forward, each company must attain a 90 per cent rating following assessment of 78 key business procedures. WCP incorporates the principles of total quality management, manufacturing resource planning, and just-in-time inventory management. It is a total corporate philosophy that brings into the business process customers, suppliers and employees. Customers are involved in the business both in the product planning stage, and in the assessment of quality and levels of customer service. Suppliers are involved in component quality and on-time delivery. Employee involvement is critical to ensure that the commitment to WCP is understood throughout the company from the top down.

When Simon-Dudley launched WCP, the whole company was taken off-site for an afternoon and presentations made by directors and senior managers. This has been followed by internal and external training meetings. The project is run internally by a core team leader reporting to the Managing Director, but each department, down to the shop floor level, participates. Feedback is continuous through regular communication and discussion sessions, coupled with the prominent display boards showing progress on the factory floor. The performance measures are actively perused in team briefings. Again, this is a constant theme in excellence companies; talking at the workplace about their job, their customer and how product, service, performance and profitability can all be improved. Nigel Burton, Customer Service Manager, says:

> *'This customer service and care aspect is important and customer care training sessions are a major feature in the WCP process. After almost two years' hard work, Simon-Dudley are at class B level and we are aiming to achieve A status in the coming year. Accreditation is not, of course, a once and for all step. There has to be regular updating process. Monitoring and maintaining the standards, once achieved, is vital.'*

Accreditation is by outside specialists and Simon-Dudley has worked progressively with an accreditation specialist throughout the process.

One management tool in assessing the continuing effectiveness of the programme is the regular reporting of 'non financial performance measures' (NFPMs). Simon-Dudley has identified some ten key NFPMs covering issues including:

- Accuracy of the engineering specifications to customer requirements.
- Accuracy of bills of materials.
- Performance of vendors.
- Factory adherence to production schedules.

- Delivery performance.
- Customer service response.

Nigel Burton stresses that the constant monitoring of these NFPMs (see Figure 10.2) to Class A standards is a key management responsibility: 'It is taken very seriously, and fundamental to the continued commitment to customer care.'

Figure 10.3 WCP Performance Measures

	Actual		Forecast			
	Dec 90	Sept 91	Dec 91	June 92	Dec 92	Target
⋆Bom accuracy	50	96	98	98	98	99
Routing accuracy	n/m	n/m	98	98	98	99
⋆Master schedule	n/m	76	80	90	95	95
⋆Vendor on-time	76	51	60	80	95	95
Output control	n/m	90	94	95	95	98
Works productivity	n/m	71	82	83	85	90
Kits no shortages	28	59	60	80	95	95
⋆Spares delivery (24 hrs)						
Warranty	83	90	90	92	92	92
Retail	67	44	85	85	85	85
⋆Machine delivery (within week)	30	67	60	65	70	95
⋆Inventory accuracy	n/m	74	95	95	95	97

⋆ = mandatory measures

n/m = not measured

☐ = Class 'A' quality level

Another way the message can be reinforced is to actually take members of the production plant out into the field to meet the customers, as well as the customers coming into the manufacturing facility. A large percentage of the workforce will have been out in the field working with their customer counterparts. In 1992, 90 per cent of Simon-Dudley's output was for export markets. For some employees this has meant travelling to locations such as Korea and South America, a broadening of horizons which will have immeasurable benefits for the workforce.

MAKING IT STICK

It is the second wave of commitment which is, as Malcolm Parkinson put it 'the really telling one'. The easy parts are overcoming the initial inertia, and achieving the first stage targets. The really difficult step in becoming a customer-led company is moving on from those initial targets and making the customer service principle the basis of the Simon-Dudley way of life.

The way Simon-Dudley is approaching this difficult stage is to constantly question all of its actions. Malcolm Parkinson says:

> *'Our methods of operating – the relationships between ourselves, our customers, and our suppliers – must become open to criticism rather than be defensive. We must encourage everyone at all levels to listen to our customers, to compare our performance with competitors, and to constantly ask the question, Why? and, more important, Why not?'*

Simon-Dudley has had a history of transient senior management. It has therefore been important for the workforce to witness the visibility, and the strong team effort, of the Simon Access boardroom philosophy right the way down through the system. One way this was illustrated was the decision to achieve maximum impact for the 'Best of Both Worlds' approach. The importance of the WCP programme and the customer service principle was demonstrated by closing the entire factory for half a day, leaving only a temporary switchboard operator on-site. This showed a visible commitment to

WCP and customer service from the highest level in the company. Everyone was taken by coach to a local centre, where the entire company was, according to Michael Parkinson:

> *'Introduced to what we were trying to achieve together. It was important that everyone took ownership of our problems and customer service. The launch presentations and the training programmes throughout Simon-Dudley, have all been carried out by the management because we believe that this is an important starting point in creating the team approach which is so central to any customer service programme's ultimate success.'*

This constant reinforcement of the customer service message through cultural change is essential, as deep set cultures cannot be changed overnight and there will always be the cynics. That is why visible leadership is so vital, at all levels. The amount of management effort and time it takes to run a genuine customer-led organisation should never be underestimated. Simon Access management are very conscious that their teamwork, and the customer-focus, are being watched closely down the organisation. 'It is a long-term process,' says Malcolm Parkinson, 'requiring a great deal of management commitment and investment, but the task of achieving customer service excellence depends on involving all our people, and constantly working towards a stronger team spirit'.

Throughout this book it can be seen that the service excellent companies treat their rank and file employees as the major source of quality and service gain. John Barker sees it as the shop floor being the major resource of ideas, not just a pair of hands making a Snorkel. Another consistent factor throughout service excellent companies is their sheer ability to 'get on with it'. When they have a problem, they put a group of people together for a period of time and tell them to solve it. They then implement the solution. This needs an organisation that is not stultified by bureaucracy; one that is entrepreneurial, and always learning.

There is a long way to go at Simon Access, and in Simon-Dudley. You get a feeling of urgency around the place, but it is coming from the leadership rather than from events. The place appears to be invaded by 'management through expectation'. Everyone is expecting the workforce to do well, and to catch them doing it right. It is an energetic approach to customer service and you get the feeling that if you do not agree with, or believe in, the new customer-led philosophy throughout Simon Access then there is no place for you in that organisation.

This is, in fact, another theme consistent throughout all service excellent companies; the strong, domineering leadership that is essential to drive change through the organisation, and to constantly reinforce the business mission of service excellence. Perhaps the last word should be left to a fireman from Greater Manchester who, when asked by me what he thought of the Simon Snorkel said: 'It's great; well it's made by a great company, isn't it.'

That's the type of feedback one has come to expect from the customers of service excellence organisations. It is a fitting tribute to conclude this book.

INDEX

OF
THE LEARNING CURVE